DOWNSTREAM DORSET
RIVER TALES AND LOCAL HISTORY

by
Mary van Coller

'The beautiful in nature is the unmarred result of God's first creative or forming work, and … the beautiful in art is the result of an unmistaken working of men in accordance with the beautiful in nature.'

Thoughts on Beauty and Art by Rev. William Barnes (Dorset dialect poet)

Downstream Dorset – River Tales and Local History

Published by Country Books/Spiral Publishing Ltd

Country Books
38 Pulla Hill Drive,
Storrington, West Sussex, RH20 3LS

Tel: 07889 234 964
email: jonathan@spiralpublishing.com
paul@spiralpublishing.com

www.countrybooks.biz

Paperback ISBN-978-1-7395824-0-1

© 2022 Mary van Coller

The rights of Mary van Coller for this edition have been asserted in accordance with the Copyright, Designs and Patents Act 1993.

All rights reserved. No part of this publication may be reproduced, stored in a retrieval system, or transmitted, in any way or form, or by any means, electronic, mechanical, photocopying, or otherwise, without the prior permission of the author and publisher.

British Library Cataloguing in Publication Data.
A catalogue record for this book is available from the British Library.

Printed and bound in England by Scantech Lithographic Ltd,
17 Burgess Road, Ivyhouse Lane, Hastings, East Sussex TN35 4NR

To order copies of *Downstream Dorset – River Tales and Local History* go to:
www.downstreamdorset.co.uk

Front cover picture of Sturminster Newton Mill ©Shutterstock/Adrian Baker

Acknowledgements

Thank you

My heartfelt thanks to so many of my family and friends who have shared in the adventures of researching *Downstream Dorset*, especially my ever-supportive husband Ryan, my son Ian and his lovely wife Pam and my mum-in-law Margaret. They have given me their wisdom, knowledge, encouragement and love during this whole project, along with a lot of fun!

Thank you to the wonderful people of Dorset who have been happy to share their time and their stories – and even willing to have their photos included.

My thanks to Lady Fellowes for her infectious enthusiasm and encouragements.

On behalf of all Dorset residents and visitors, my profound gratitude to the Dorset and Somerset Air Ambulance for their vitally important service to us all. Thank you for purchasing *Downstream Dorset* and supporting their work.

Writing this book has been like hunting for treasure trove. I hope that you too will be inspired to visit places and make your own discoveries about this beautiful county of Dorset.

What a joy it has been!

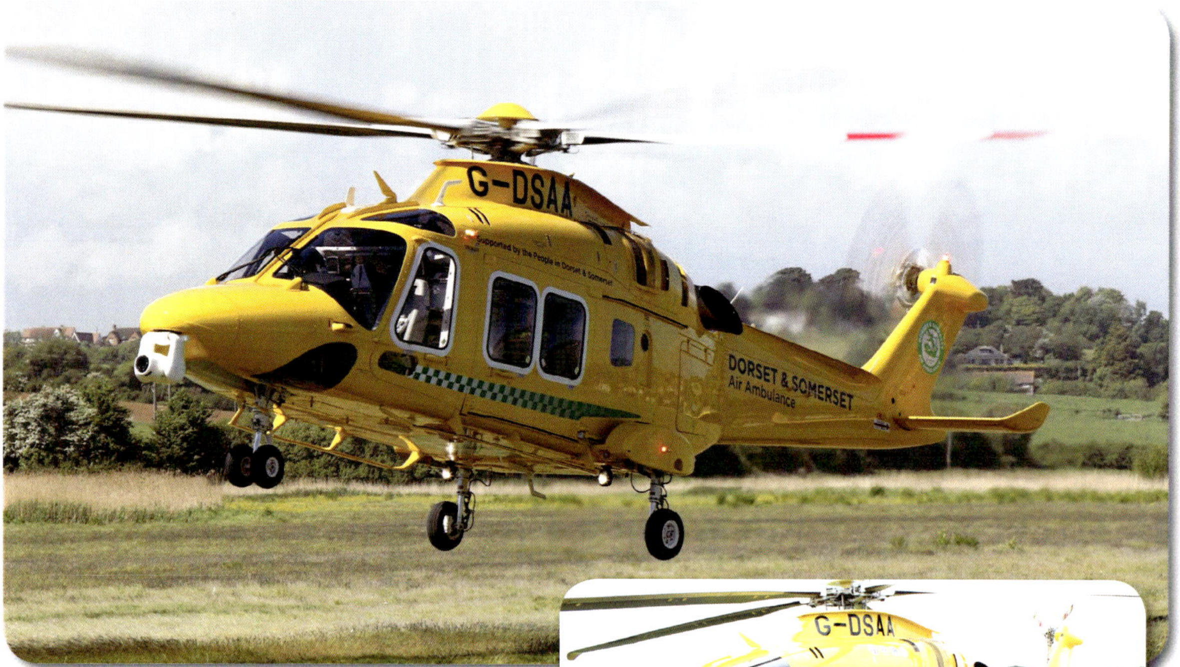
G-DSAA
DORSET & SOMERSET
Air Ambulance

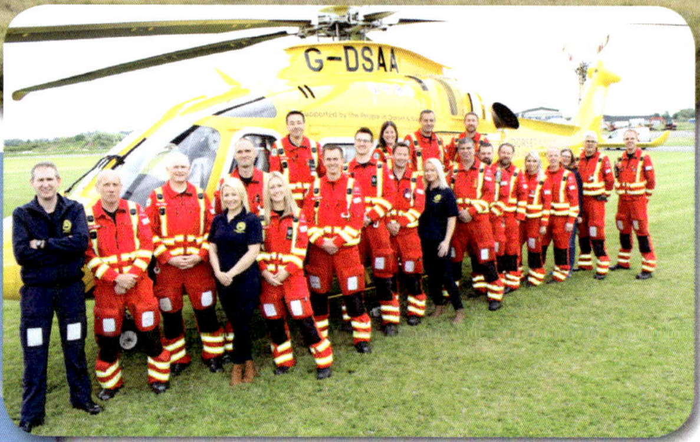
G-DSAA

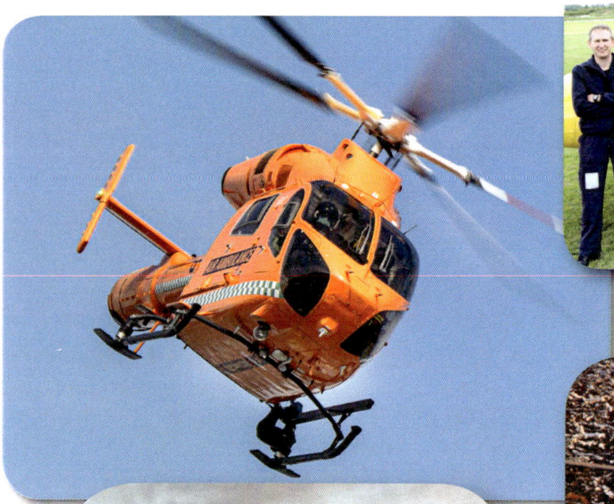

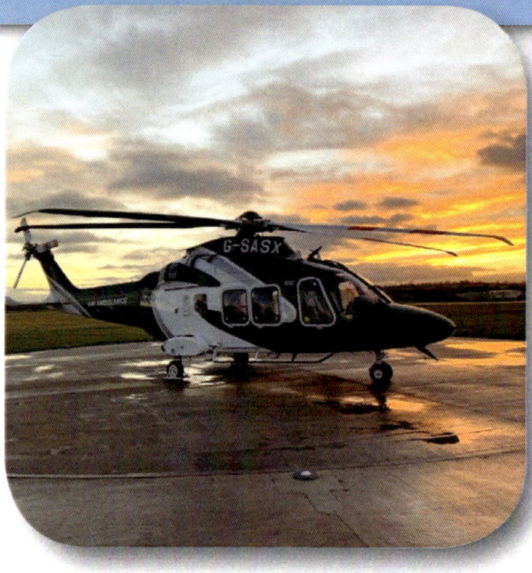
G-SASX

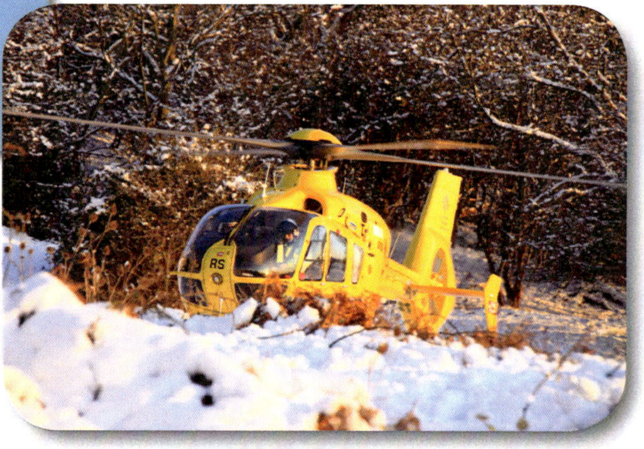
RS

Air Ambulance

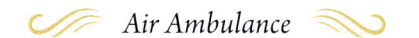

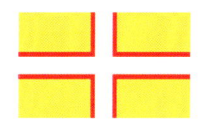

Dorset and Somerset Air Ambulance Service

Dorset and Somerset Air Ambulance is a registered charity, established to provide relief from sickness and injury for the people of Dorset and Somerset, by the provision of an air ambulance, with air and road-delivered critical care capability. The charity receives no direct funding from the Government or the National Lottery and relies on the generosity of the public for support. Operational costs are over £5 million a year and the approximate cost per mission is £3,000.

The charity's airbase is situated at Henstridge Airfield on the Dorset/Somerset border. From there, they can be at any point in the two counties in less than 20 minutes. More importantly, the helicopter can, if required, then take a patient to the nearest Major Trauma Centre in the South West within a further 20 minutes.

By purchasing Downstream Dorset you are supporting the Dorset and Somerset Air Ambulance Service as 20% of profits will be donated to the vital work they do.

If you would like to find out more about the Dorset and Somerset Air Ambulance their website is:

www.dsairambulance.org.uk

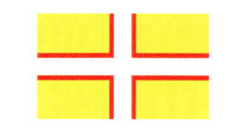

Contents

Dorset and Somerset Air Ambulance	vi
Dorset Rivers Map	xii
Introduction	1

Section 1 — 3
North Dorset, excluding R. Stour and its tributaries

Chapter 1	4
River Yeo	
Chapter 2	8
Wriggle River	
Chapter 3	14
River Parrett	

Section 2 — 17
West Dorset from the Dorset-Devon border traveling eastwards

Chapter 4	18
River Axe	
Chapter 5	22
River Lim	
Chapter 6	24
River Char	
Chapter 7	30
River Winniford	
Chapter 8	32
River Brit	
Chapter 9	38
River Simene	
Chapter 10	40
River Asker	
Chapter 11	44
River Bride	
Chapter 12	48
Fleet Lagoon	
Chapter 13	54
Culverwell Stream	
Chapter 14	58
River Wey	
Chapter 15	62
River Jordan	
Chapter 16	66
Smaller West Dorset Rivers and Streams	

p43

Section 3 71
*The Isle of Purbeck from
St Oswald's Bay to Poole Harbour*
Chapter 17 72
Purbeck Streams
Chapter 18 82
Corfe River
Chapter 19 90
Swanbrook River

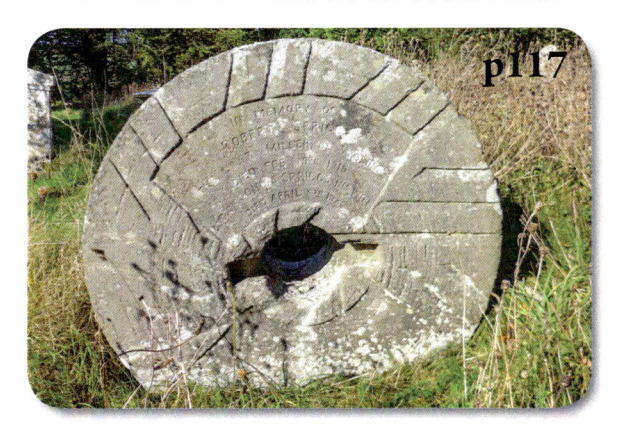

Section 4 95
*Poole Harbour's Rivers
and their tributaries*
Chapter 20 96
River Frome
Chapter 21 110
Wraxall Brook
Chapter 22 112
River Hooke
Chapter 23 116
Sydling Water
Chapter 24 118
River Cerne
Chapter 25 122
South Winterborne River
Chapter 26 126
Tadnoll Brook
Chapter 27 130
River Win
Chapter 28 132
River Piddle
Chapter 29 140
Devils Brook
Chapter 30 144
Bere Stream
Chapter 31 148
Sherford River
Chapter 32 152
Luscombe Valley Stream

ix

Section 5 155
River Stour and its tributaries
Chapter 33 156
River Stour
Chapter 34 176
River Cale, Filley Brook and Bow Brook
Chapter 35 178
Bibbern Brook
Chapter 36 180
River Lydden
Chapter 37 184
Caundle Brook with River Cam
Chapter 38 190
River Divelish
Chapter 39 192
Key, Stirchell, Twyford and Manston Brooks
Chapter 40 198
Fontmell Brook
Chapter 41 200
River Iwerne
Chapter 42 204
River Tarrant
Chapter 43 210
River Winterborne
Chapter 44 216
River Allen
with Gussage Brook and Crichel Stream
Chapter 45 224
Uddens Water
Chapter 46 230
River Crane – Moors River
Chapter 47 234
River Avon
Chapter 48 238
Smaller Tributaries of the River Stour

p161

p202

p226

Contents

Section 6 247
East Dorset from Poole Harbour to the Dorset- Hampshire border

Chapter 49 248
Branksome Chine Stream

Chapter 50 252
Alum Chine Stream

Chapter 51 254
River Bourne

Chapter 52 260
River Mude

Chapter 53 262
Bure Brook

Chapter 54 264
Walkford Brook

Bibliography 266

Index 267

p257

p252

p258

p263

xi

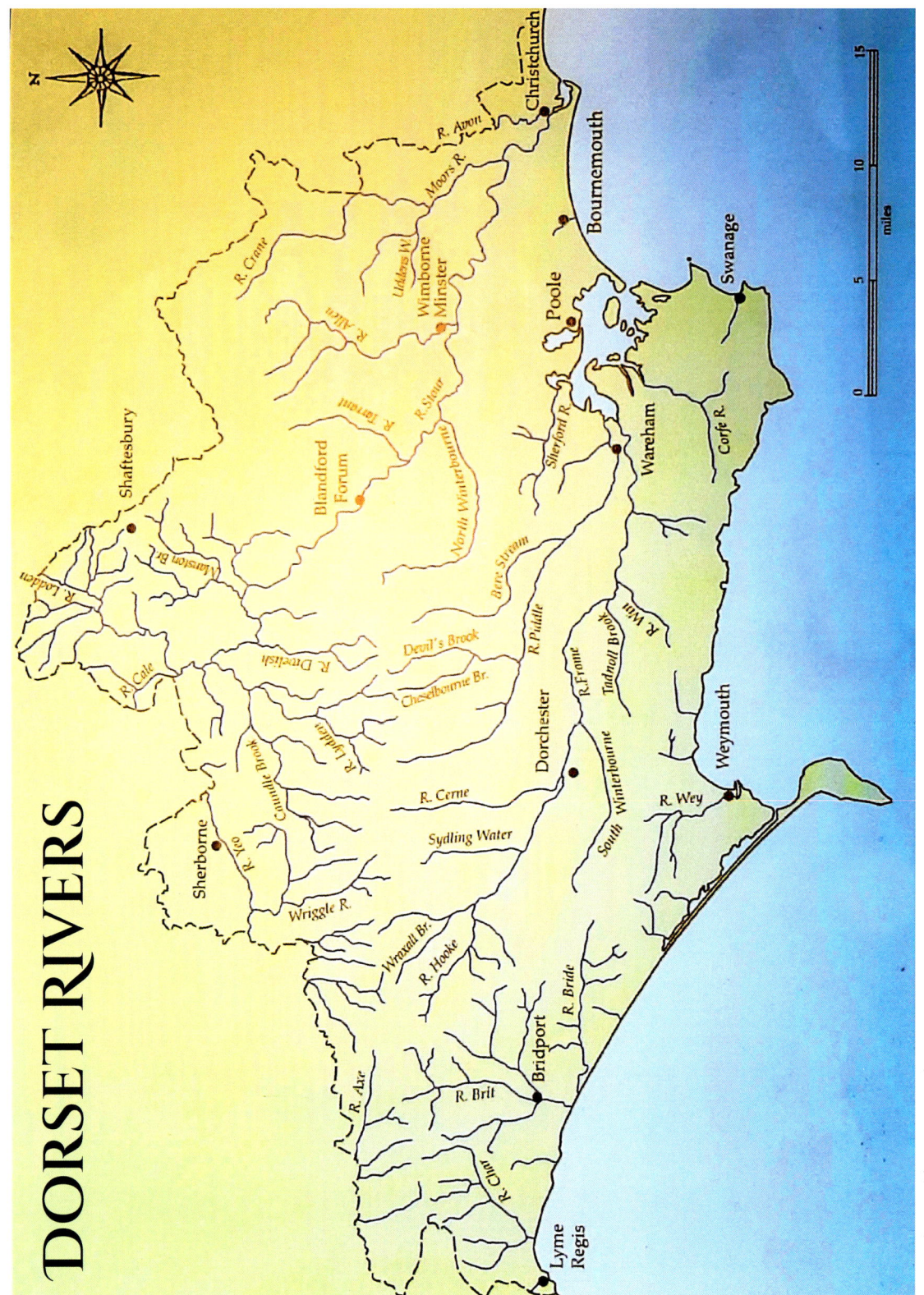

Downstream Dorset – River Tales and Local History

DORSET RIVERS

Map reproduced with kind permission from *Rivers and Streams* by John Wright in the Discover Dorset Series published by Dovecote Press.

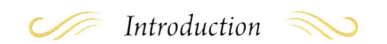

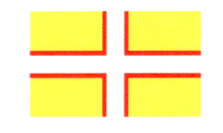

Introduction

Living in Dorset for over 40 years since coming to work at Poole General Hospital, has given me a wealth of wonderful memories. Like many, I have always felt an emotional affinity with flowing waterways, I have been fascinated by the quaint village names and the varied lives of their inhabitants, past and present.

Eleven years ago I married Ryan, who hails from Zimbabwe and together we have explored Dorset. We often stand in awe of God's creation, captivated by the breath-taking views of chalk hills rolling across the countryside and spacious farmland criss-crossed by hedgerows - never far from flowing water. We are amazed at the infinite varieties and colours of birds, plants and animals living and breeding in their diverse habitats. We wonder at the human endeavour that has built fortified castles, church spires and the ramparts of iron-age forts without the equipment and resources that we have today.

As Pet Home Boarders we have a succession of dogs and other animals staying with us. Many of the dogs love splashing around in water when we walk along the local rivers and streams!

At the time of writing the world is coming through the coronavirus pandemic and we are grateful for the scientists and hospitals who are working to combat the disease. When writing about the Black Death in the 14th century, I imagined the fear and devastation without the hope of a vaccine.

Downstream Dorset: River Tales and Local History is an attempt to share my love for this beautiful county with its streams and rivers that have been its life blood for centuries. I have included towns and villages in West Dorset that may be considered to be in south Dorset. This is only to make it easier to divide the county into sections for the purposes of this book, with no intention of causing offence or confusion!

So come with me now and follow the Piddle – or Stour, or Char, or Wriggle. As you dive, or just dangle your toes, into the chapters of this book you will follow Dorset's waterways and read about their villages and towns with the origins of their place names. Perhaps, like me, you will wonder about families in the past, working and playing to the accompaniment of the same river music that we hear today.

Barney and Millie enjoying a paddle in Bourne Stream

NORTH DORSET

Following the rivers and streams that flow through north Dorset

'Sherborne in the early evening was rain-washed cobbles, glistening eves, mellow stone buildings dripping with excess rainwater and, behind it all, the magnificent backdrop of the abbey…'

Spare The Rod by Rosie Lear

Downstream Dorset – River Tales and Local History

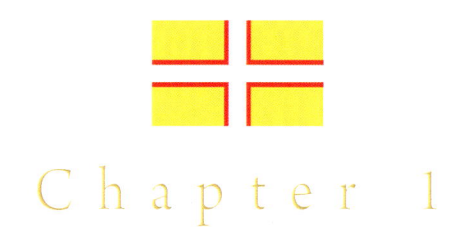

Chapter 1

RIVER YEO
(DORSET REACHES ONLY)

AT A GLANCE

SOURCE
Seven Sisters Wells in Seven Wells Down, Poyntington and springs around Henstridge Bowden, Somerset.

MOUTH
Confluences with the River Parrett near Langport, Somerset.

LENGTH
Approximately 12km (7.5 miles) within Dorset; 46km (28.5 miles) from source to confluence with the River Parrett.

TRIBUTARIES (DORSET ONLY)
River Wriggle confluences with the River Yeo near Bradford Abbas.
Gascoigne River confluences with the River Yeo at Sherborne Lake (rises in Somerset).

The River Yeo, also known as the River Ivel, is a tributary of the River Parrett. It flows mostly through the county of Somerset but begins its journey in North Dorset. The name Yeo comes from the Old English word for water, *ea*. The alternative name, Ivel, derives from Old Celtic word *gifl*, meaning forked river.

River Yeo passing through the village of Oborne

North Dorset – River Yeo

VILLAGES AND TOWNS IN DORSET AND THE ORIGINS OF THEIR NAMES
(from source to the Somerset border)

POYNTINGTON
1122 Puntintuna
Old English:
Punt – personal name
ing – associated with
tun – a farm or estate
'a farm or estate associated with a family named Punt'

Angel's wing
All Saints Church displays a carved wing of an angel. During the First World War, Amiens Cathedral in France was bombed. Major Hugh Munro Warrand picked up the wooden carving and brought it home to Dorset. In 1961, his daughter presented it to the church where it hangs today with the permission of the Bishop of Amiens.

OBORNE
1086 (Domesday Book) Wocburne
Old English:
woh – crooked or winding
burna – a stream
'a settlement near a winding stream'

Opera in Oborne
In January 2012, a chance meeting between Oborne residents Sir Robert and Lady Susan Corbett and the musical director of an opera group resulted in a fundraising event for St Cuthbert church *(below)*. A concert of opera excerpts was held in the church.. By 2014, the Sunday concert had evolved into a weekend event. An abridged performance of Mozart's The Magic Flute on Saturday was followed by the concert on Sunday.

Today, international opera singers come to the village of Oborne every year for a weekend performance in the diminutive 19th century church of St Cuthbert.

Old Sherborne Castle viewed across the lake in the grounds of the New Sherborne Castle
(right) Sherborne Abbey showing some of the vaulted ceiling

SHERBORNE
1086 (Domesday Book) Scireburne
Old English:
scir – clear or bright
burna – a stream
'a settlement near a clear water stream'

Fallen out of favour
Sir Walter Raleigh was a favourite of Queen Elizabeth l. In 1592, she gave him 12th century Sherborne Castle. However, Sir Walter fell out of favour when he married Elizabeth's lady-in-waiting Bess Throckmorton without the queen's permission. They were both confined to the Tower of London for several years but eventually returned to Sherborne. The castle proved too expensive to maintain so Sir Walter and his family moved into the hunting lodge in the deer park. They developed it into a stately home that became known as New Sherborne Castle. The castle has been improved over the centuries. Today it is owned by the Digby family and is open to the public.

The gardens, including the creation of Sherborne Lake, were landscaped by Sir Lancelot (Capability) Brown in the 18th century.

Sherborne Abbey and many of the buildings in the town are built of warm, honey-coloured limestone known as hamstone. It is quarried in Ham Hill, Somerset.

THORNFORD

1086 (Domesday Book) Torneford
1249 Thorneford
Old English:
thorn – a thorn
ford – a ford, river crossing
'a settlement near a ford crossing with thorn trees growing'

BRADFORD ABBAS

1086 (Domesday Book) Bradeford
1386 Braddeford Abbatis
Old English:
brad – broad
ford – a ford, river crossing
abbas – an abbot
'a settlement by a wide ford crossing, owned by Sherborne Abbey'

Footbridge across the River Yeo in Bradford Abbas

Downstream Dorset – River Tales and Local History

Chapter 2

WRIGGLE RIVER

AT A GLANCE

SOURCE
Several springs forming streams in the chalk downs near Hilfield and Batcombe, including the Friary of St Francis.

MOUTH / OUTLET
Confluence with the River Yeo near Bradford Abbas, which then flows into the Bristol Channel.

LENGTH
Approximately 15km (9.5 miles).

The Old English word *wrigian*, meaning 'to twist', gives this river its name. It's a river that wriggles its way through the Dorset countryside until reaching its confluence with the River Yeo.

Stone pillar near Batcombe

North Dorset – Wriggle River

VILLAGES AND TOWNS IN DORSET AND THE ORIGINS OF THEIR NAMES
(from source to mouth of the river)

HILFIELD
934 Hylfelde
Old English:
hyll – a hill
feld – a field or open land
'a field or open land situated near a hill'

The secret garden
In the grounds of the Friary of St Francis, an Anglican community, Brother Vincent has planted a lovely secret garden with magnificent magnolias and camellias.

On the day Ryan and I visited the friary we were delighted to find Brother Vincent *(below and right)* tending his garden. He was happy to engage in conversation and tell us about many of his 'friends', which was how he referred to all the plants in his garden. Some of them he had brought as seedlings from distant countries, including China and New Zealand. Others were harvested closer to home in Wales and Scotland.

The garden was full of plants, with footpaths winding between them – rhododendron, palms, bamboo, juniper, myrtle. There is no doubt Brother Vincent's passion and loving care for each tree and shrub has made it the fascinating and peaceful garden it is today.

Brother Vincent died in May 2020 aged 87. He has moved on to be with his Lord and Saviour, Jesus Christ – and perhaps to tend more heavenly gardens.

BATCOMBE
1201 Batecumbe
Old English:
Bata – personal name
cumb – a valley
'a settlement in a valley owned by a person named Bata'

Stone pillar
On a roadside overlooking Batcombe there is a stone pillar, about one metre (3.3 feet) in height, known as the 'Cross and Hand' or the 'Cross in Hand'. It is probably a Saxon landmark but the pillar is associated with local legends of murder and miracles.

WOOLCOMBE
1086 (Domesday Book) Wellecome
1219 Wulecomb
Old English:
wella – a spring
cumb – a valley
'a settlement in a valley alongside a spring'

MELBURY BUBB
1086 (Domesday Book) Meleberie
1244 Melebir Bubbe
Old English:
maele – multi-coloured
burh – a fortified place
Bubbe – personal name
'a colourful, fortified settlement owned by a man named Bubbe'

Topsy-Turvy
The font in the church of St Mary is beautifully carved with animals and intricate designs – but they are all upside down! Perhaps the stone that was used for the font was originally intended for a different purpose?

STOCKWOOD
1221 Stocwode
Old English:
stoc – a secondary settlement
wudu – a wood
'secondary or outlying settlement beside a wood having a church dedicated to St Edwold'

Smallest church
The church of St Edwold is said to be the smallest in Dorset and the second smallest in England. It measures only 9m x 4m, lies in a beautiful woodland setting and can be reached by crossing a small stone bridge.

The church of St Edwold in Stockwood is reached via a small stone bridge

CHETNOLE
1268 Chatecnolle
Old English:
Ceatta – personal name
cnoll – a hilltop
'a settlement on the top of a hill owned by a person named Ceatta'

LEIGH
1228 Lega
Old English:
leah – a wood
'a wooded area (possibly cleared for cultivation)'

RYME INTRINSECA
1160 Rima
1611 Ryme Intrinsica
Old English:
rima – a rim or border
Latin:
intrinseca – inner
'a settlement inside the county border'

YETMINSTER

1086 (Domesday Book) Etiminstre
1226 Yateminstre

Old English:
Eata – personal name
mynstre – a church
'a settlement with a church, owned by a person named Eata'

Ringing out the national anthem

Since Queen Victoria's jubilee celebrations in 1897, the chimes of St Andrew's clock ring out the national anthem six times each day!

When Ryan and I visited in July 2016 we were curious to know if this still rang true. A friendly Yetminster resident informed us that parts of the clock were being repaired by a blacksmith and the national anthem was noticeable by its absence!

Discovering smallpox inoculation

Benjamin Jesty (1736-1816) lived most of his life in Yetminster. His scientific experiments led to his discovery of immunisation against smallpox in 1774. He tested his theories on his wife Elizabeth and their two sons, using a darning needle to inoculate them with pus from cowpox pustules.

Jesty did not publish his work, and in 1796 Edward Jenner was given credit for this major advancement in preventative medicine.

The Wellcome Library has now recognised Jesty's scientific discovery and purchased the only portrait of Benjamin Jesty, painted in oils by Michael William Sharp in 1805.

The same villager who told us about the national anthem chimes also talked about Benjamin Jesty. Apparently the other villagers believed that what Jesty had done to his wife and sons was akin to black magic so the family was forced to leave Upbury Farm. The gravestones of Benjamin and Elizabeth Jesty can be found in the churchyard of Worth Matravers.

Upbury Farm, Yetminster

St Andrew's, Yetminster

KNIGHTON
1288 Knytheton
Old English:
cniht – a knight or retainer
tun – a farm or estate
'a farm or estate owned by retainers'
Retainers were men who undertook a specified form of work for the lord of the manor in return for a fee. This could be domestic or household service, military service, legal advice or any other service required by the lord.

BEER HACKETT
1176 Haket de Bera
1362 Berehaket
Old English:
baer – a woodland grove
Haket – personal name (probably Norman)
'a woodland grove owned by a family named Haket'

THORNFORD
951 Thornford
1086 (Domesday Book) Torneford
Old English:
thorn – a thorn tree
ford – a ford, river crossing
'a settlement at a river crossing where thorn trees grow'

BRADFORD ABBAS
(see also River Yeo)
1086 (Domesday Book) Bradeford
1386 Braddeford Abbatis
Old English:
brad – broad
ford – a ford, river crossing
Latin abbas – an abbot
'a settlement at a river crossing owned by Sherborne Abbey'

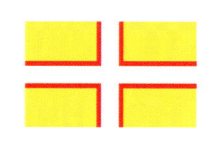

Chapter 3

RIVER PARRETT
(DORSET REACHES ONLY)

AT A GLANCE

SOURCE
Thorney Mills springs, near Chedington.

MOUTH / OUTLET
The Bristol Channel near Burnham-on-Sea, Somerset.

LENGTH
Approximately 60 km (37 miles) mostly in Somerset, upper reaches in Dorset.

TRIBUTARIES (DORSET ONLY)
The main tributaries are the rivers Tone, Isle, Yeo and Cary. Only the River Yeo passes through Dorset, see separate chapter.

The name Parrett comes from the Old English word *pedr*, meaning 'four', and the Old Celtic word *rit*, meaning a 'stream'. This refers to the four main tributaries of the river – the River Tone, River Isle, River Yeo and River Cary. The River Parrett rises in Dorset and flows northward into Somerset.

CHEDINGTON
1194 Chedinton
Old English:
Cedda – personal name
ing – associated with
tun – a farm or estate
'a settlement associated with or named after a man named Cedda'
The River Parrett Trail starts in Chedington and its footpaths and cycle tracks follow the route of the River Parrett, which rises in the hills around the village.

MOSTERTON
1086 (Domesday Book) Mortestorne
Old English:
Mort – personal name
thorn – a thorn tree
'a settlement with a thorn tree owned by a man named Mort'

VILLAGES AND TOWNS IN DORSET AND THE ORIGINS OF THEIR NAMES
(from source to mouth of the river)

SOUTH PERROTT
1086 (Domesday Book) Pedret
1268 suthperet
Old English:
suth – south
pedr – four
Celtic:
rit – flow
'a settlement by the River Parrett, south of North Perrott (in Somerset)'
The River Parrett then crosses the county border into Somerset.

River Parrett flowing through the village of South Perrott

WEST DORSET

Following the rivers and streams whose waters flow through west Dorset to the English Channel

'Hill-warded haven, creek well found
To sailors on thy stormy shore,
When midst the waters deafning roar
They step on this thy peaceful ground,
As blest with happy homes at hand,
Or strangers on a foreign land.'

Bridport Harbour by Rev William Barnes
(Dorset dialect poet)

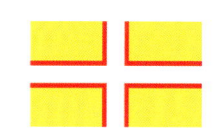

Chapter 4

RIVER AXE

AT A GLANCE

SOURCE
Springs in farmland south of Chedington

MOUTH / OUTLET
Seaton, Devon

LENGTH
Approximately 35km (22 miles) in total, half its course is in Dorset and along its county border

TRIBUTARIES (WITHIN DORSET)
- Little Axe, Drimpton
- Temple Brook, confluences with the River Axe north of the B3165 in Somerset
- Procer's Lake, confluences with the River Axe near the railway between Winsham and Wayford in Somerset
- River Synderford, confluences with the River Axe west of the B3162, south of Winsham in Somerset
- Blackwater River, confluences with the River Axe south of Broom Lane

The River Axe rises from springs south of Chedington. It travels west passing through Dorset, Somerset and Devon, following the county border from Oathill to Broom. It enters the English Channel near Seaton in Lyme Bay.

The name Axe derives from *isca*, the word for 'water' in the ancient Celtic language.

River Axe forms the county border near Forde Abbey

Villages and Towns within Dorset and the Origins of their Names
(from source to mouth of the river)

CHEDINGTON
1194 Chedinton
Old English:
Cedd – personal name
ing – associated with
tun – a farm or estate
'a farm or estate associated with, or named after, a man named Cedd'
The River Parrett Trail starts in Chedington and follows the course of the River Parrett.

MOSTERTON
1086 (Domesday Book) Mortestorne
Old English:
Mort – personal name
thorn – a thorn tree
'a settlement with a thorn tree owned by a man named Mort'

BROADWINDSOR
1086 (Domesday Book) Windesore
1324 Brodewyndesore
Old English:
windels – a windlass
ora – a bank or slope
brad – broad to distinguish it from Littlewindsor
'a settlement on a river bank with a windlass or winch'

LITTLEWINDSOR
1086 (Domesday Book) Windresorie
1279 Little Windesore
Latin:
parva – little, to distinguish it from Broadwindsor

Schematic diagram of the River Axe and its tributaries in Dorset

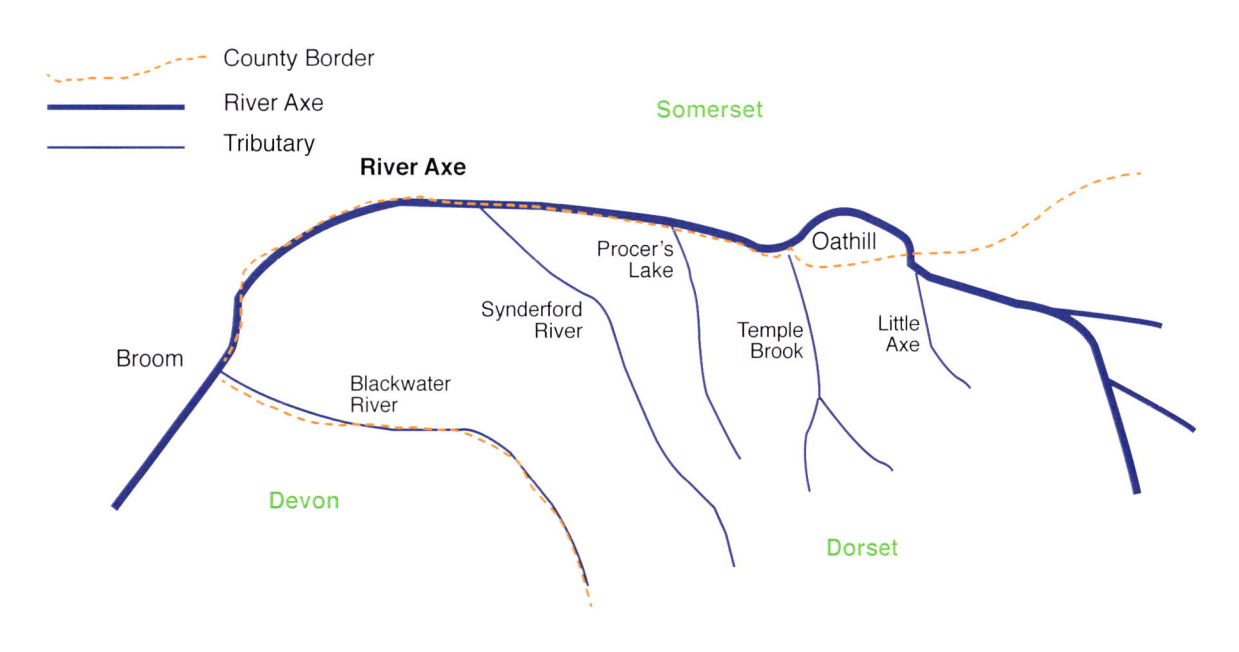

SEABOROUGH

1086 (Domesday Book) Seveberge

Old English:
seofon – seven
beorg – a hill
'a settlement near seven hills'

Ducking stool
There was a ducking stool in Seaborough near a small stone bridge that crosses the River Axe. By court order, nagging wives were seated on a stool at the end of a wooden arm and dunked in the water.

Pity the poor pigs
In March 2013, approximately 900 pigs were killed in a fire at Seaborough Manor. The 100m (330ft) piggery was destroyed despite the efforts of 50 firefighters.

River Axe in Seaborough

It would be easy to miss Temple Brook in Greenham Lane as it flows towards Oathill and its confluence with the River Axe

OATHILL

In the 13th century there was a division between Up Oathill and Nether Oathill.

Old English:
nether – lower
'a settlement on a hill where oats are grown'
Oathill probably indicates the type of crops grown on hills in the area.

DRIMPTON

1244 Dremeton

Old English:
Dreama – personal name
tun – a farm or estate
'a farm or estate owned by a man named Dreama'
Drimpton is a settlement on a small tributary of the River Axe. In 2005, villagers voted to name the stream 'Little Axe'.

West Dorset – River Axe

FORDE ABBEY
1189 Ford
Old English:
ford – a ford across a river
abbey – a Cistercian monastery founded in 1141
'a settlement by a ford with an abbey'

Visiting Forde Abbey
The Cistercian monastery at Forde Abbey *(above)* was dissolved in 1539 during the reign of Henry VIII. In the 17th century it was converted into a sumptuous private residence. The present owner, Mark Roper, has opened the house to the public along with its 30 acres of beautiful gardens.

THORNCOMBE
1236 Thorncumbe
Old English:
thorn – a thorn tree
cumb – a valley
'a settlement in a valley where thorn trees grow'

HOLDITCH COURT
1219 Holedich
Old English:
hol – a hollow
dic – a ditch
'a settlement in a hollow with a ditch nearby'

Medieval manor
Holditch Court was built as a medieval manor house during the reign of Edward II (1284-1327). The original building no longer exists except for the ruins of one tower and the keep. Beyond the courtyard is the site of what is thought to be a fish pond, a source of food for the manor house.

MARSHALSEA
1344 Mareschalesheighes
Old English:
Mareschal – personal name
haeg – an enclosure
'an enclosure owned by a man named Mareschal'
An enclosure is a piece of land the owner has surrounded with a fence or other barrier.

MARSHWOOD
1188 Merswude
Old English:
mersc – a marsh
wudu – a wood
'a settlement in a wood near a marsh'

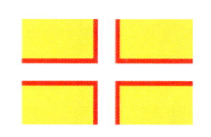

Chapter 5

RIVER LIM

AT A GLANCE

SOURCE
Springs in woodlands and farmland north of Yawl and a spring near Raymond's Hill in Devon

MOUTH / OUTLET
Lyme Regis flowing into Lyme Bay

LENGTH
Approximately 5km (3 miles)

The River Lim, also known as the River Lyme, rises in Devon and crosses the county border into Dorset just north of Lyme Regis.

Its catchment area is mostly pastoral with some woodland and, during heavy rains, is prone to flooding, especially in the Lyme Regis area.

There were once 13 mills along the course of the river. Today, The Town Mill is once again producing flour.

River Lim as it flows towards Lyme Bay

West Dorset – River Lim

THE ONLY TOWN IN DORSET ON THE RIVER LIM

LYME REGIS
774 Lim
1285 Lyme Regis

Old Celtic
lim – a stream
Regis – a royal charter granted by Edward I
'a settlement on a stream with a royal charter'

Salty monks
In 774 Cynewulf, King of Wessex, permitted a settlement of monks to extract salt from sea water, which was then exported.

Town charter
In 1284 the town of Lyme was granted a charter by King Edward I giving it the right to use the suffix Regis. It was an important base for the king's naval fleet during the wars against the French.

Lepers' Well
In the 14th century there was a hospital for lepers on the site of Lepers' Well. Leprosy was a term used for any skin disease and led to the sufferer being shunned. The well's waters were used as a cure and as a separate water supply from the other inhabitants of Lyme Regis.

Monmouth Rebellion
Following the death of King Charles II in 1685, his brother succeeded him as King James II. Charles' illegitimate son, the Duke of Monmouth, attempted to seize the throne. In June 1685 he landed in Lyme Regis with 82 followers and raised the support of more than 4,000 men. However, he was defeated at the Battle of Sedgemoor in Somerset. Monmouth attempted to flee but was captured and was executed on July 15th 1685.

Banksy
In April 2012, renowned graffiti artist Banksy painted an origami crane catching a goldfish on a concrete wall beside the River Lim. It appeared overnight at a place known as the Lynch and was later confirmed by Banksy to be one of his creations. Sadly, the crane has faded over time and the goldfish is barely discernible.

Flour mill restoration
Lyme Regis had a working flour mill from the early 14th century. In 1644, during the English Civil War, it was almost destroyed and had to be rebuilt. Most of its buildings date to that time and it was a working mill until 1926.

In 1991 the mill was threatened with demolition but local residents raised thousands of pounds to restore it. Today there are guided tours to see the grain milled into flour. There are also artists' studios and a cafe that serves an excellent bread and butter pudding!

The lettering on the sign is faded, it reads: "THE LEPERS WELL Near This Spot Some 700 Years Ago A Hospital for Lepers Was Dedicated To St Mary and The Holy Spirit"

The Town Mill courtyard

23

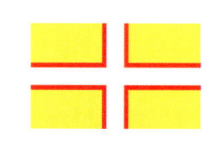

Chapter 6

RIVER CHAR

AT A GLANCE

SOURCE
Springs north of Bettiscombe and Blackney, streams coming together in the Marshwood Vale

MOUTH / OUTLET
Charmouth beach

LENGTH
Approximately 15km (9 miles)

TRIBUTARIES
Monkton Wyld Stream flows almost parallel with the Monarch's Way footpath until it reaches its confluence with the Wootton Fitzpaine Stream.

Wootton Fitzpaine Stream and the Monarch's Way then turn south, passing through Wootton Fitzpaine Gwyle until the stream reaches its confluence with the River Char on the western outskirts of Charmouth town.

Both streams have several small, unnamed tributaries.

The Char Valley offers rich grassland for dairy cattle and fields where maize is grown. It is a typical English pastoral landscape with trees, hedgerows and green fields. There are ancient hill forts on surrounding hills. This small river has footpaths along its length but the catchment area is prone to erosion so the River Char carries stones and gravel to the sea.

West Dorset – River Char

VILLAGES AND TOWNS AND THE ORIGINS OF THEIR NAMES
(from source to mouth of the river, divided into four sections)

Mouth of the River Char at Charmouth beach

1. From springs and streams to their confluence with the River Char:

MONKTON WYLD
1189 La Wilae
1535 Monkynwyll
Old English:
wil – a wile, trick
munec – a monk
tun – a farm or estate
possibly *'a farm or estate owned by the monks of Forde Abbey where there are traps or snares'*

Traditional farming skills
Monkton Wyld Court, originally a vicarage, houses a charity that provides courses for the traditional skills of scything, hedge-laying, herbal medicine and straw-bale building.

The vicarage was designed in neo-Gothic style by greatly respected Victorian architect Richard Cromwell Carpenter. He also designed the village church.

FISHPOND BOTTOM
Bottom – a broad floor of a valley (geographical term)
'a fish pond in a wide valley'

WOOTTON FITZPAINE
1086 (Domesday Book) Wodetone
1392 Wotton Fitz Payn
Old English:
wudu – a wood
tun – a farm or estate
Fitz Payn – personal name
'a farm or estate owned by a family named Fitz Payn'

Lambert Castle and Coney's Castle
About 1.5km (1 mile) apart, they are both Iron Age hill forts owned by the National Trust and offering lovely walks and views. Cattle graze in the fields so take care when letting dogs run free. There are three hill forts in the area, the other is Pilsdon Pen further to the north east. They all command extensive views across Marshwood Vale.

2 Upper reaches of River Char, from hills north of Bettiscombe to Marshwood Vale:

BIRDSMOORGATE
1663 Birds Moore
Old English:
Bird – probably a personal name
mor – moorland
'a settlement on an area of moorland owned by a family named Bird'

MARSHALSEA
1344 Mareschalesheighes
Old English:
Mareschal – personal name
haeg – an enclosure
'an enclosure owned by a family named Marischal'

MARSHWOOD
1188 Merswude
Old English:
mersc – a marsh
wudu – a wood
'a settlement in a wood near a marsh'

Poet's refuge
William Wordsworth and his sister Dorothy lived at Racedown House in Marshwood for about two years from September 1795. John Penney, of Bettiscombe Manor, offered the house to them rent-free. Wordsworth was impoverished and desperate to escape London life so accepted the offer gratefully.

Before living in London, Wordsworth had been in France with his mistress Annette Vallon, who gave birth to their daughter Caroline in 1792. He returned to England to earn money to support them. Unfortunately, the French Revolution started and then France declared war on England. Wordsworth didn't see his daughter again until she was ten years old. Annette Vallon is reported to have been a courageous lady who helped many prisoners escape the guillotine.

Pew with a view
If you visit St Mary's church and stand in the churchyard looking south *(above)*, you have a wonderful vista of Marshwood Vale across the hills to the sea. Thoughtfully, a seat has been provided to enjoy the view at one's ease. St Mary's is a Grade II-listed historic building.

BETTISCOMBE
1129 Bethescomme
Old English:
Betti – personal name
cumb – a valley
'a settlement in a valley owned by a man named Betti'

Ghosts at Bettiscombe Manor?
There are legends concerning a human skull that is housed at Bettiscombe Manor. They differ in detail but all tell of the last wish of a Jamaican slave.

One version of the legend is as follows:
As he lay dying, this faithful servant said his body would never rest in peace until it was returned to his homeland. John Penney, owner of Bettiscombe Manor, refused to spend money on such an expensive funeral arrangement and organised his burial in St Stephen's churchyard.

Not long after his burial locals said they heard loud screams emanating from the cemetery, while at the manor house there were reports of doors slamming and windows rattling. The body was moved to the manor house, where the skull remains to this day.

In 1963 a member of the Royal College of Surgeons stated the skull was not of Jamaican origin but that of a European lady aged about 25 – what could the story be concerning this young woman?

PILSDON
1086 (Domesday Book) Pilesdone
Old English:
pil – a peak
dun – a hill
'a settlement near a hill with a peak (probably Pilsdon Pen)'

SHAVE CROSS
1220 la Shaghe
Old English:
sceaga – a copse
'a settlement near a woodland or copse (later 'Cross', indicating crossroads, was added)'

Shaved heads?
We had the pleasure of staying a couple of nights at Shave Cross Inn *(below)* in 2019. The weather was wet but we were given a warm welcome by our hosts, Joe and Louise Baron. Shave Cross Inn celebrated its 700th anniversary in 2020, the flagstones in the bar date to the 14th century. Once used by pilgrims to break their journey to St Wite's shrine in Whitchurch Canonicorum, it was said the monks would have their tonsures shaved at the inn, giving rise to its name. However, the landlord told us this wasn't the origin as can be proved from its original 13th century name, la Shaghe *(see above)*.

MARSHWOOD VALE
1319 Merswodeuaal
Old English:
mersc – a marsh
wudu – a wood
Middle English:
vale – a broad valley
"a broad valley with wooded areas and marshland"

3 Upper reaches of the River Char, from hills north of Blackney to the Marshwood Vale:

BLACKNEY
1327 Blakenhay
Old English:
blaec – dark or black
haeg – an enclosure
'an enclosure, possibly blackened by fire'

MONKWOOD
1244 Munkewode
Old English:
munuc – monks
wudu – a wood
'a wood owned by monks (reference to Sherborne Abbey)'

4 Lower reaches from Marshwood Vale to Charmouth:

WHITCHURCH CANONICORUM
1086 (Domesday Book) Witcerce
1231 Witechurch
1262 Whitchurch Canonicorum
Old English:
hwit – white
cirice – a church
Latin:
conanicorum – of the canons
probably *'a settlement with a white church owned by the canons of Salisbury'*
However, the church is dedicated to St Candida, also known as St Wite.

MORCOMBELAKE
1240 Mortecumb (see also River Winniford)
1558 Morecombelake
Old English:
mor – moorland
cumb – a valley
lacu – a stream
'a settlement near a stream through a moorland valley'

Charmouth beach showing the mouth of the River Char

CATHERSTON LEWESTON

1268 Chartreston
1316 Lesterton
1576 Katherston Lewson

Old English:
tun – a farm or estate
Charteray and Lester – possibly adjacent estates owned by the Charteray and Lester families
'farms or estates owned by the Charteray and Lester families'

Methodists' ancestor

Bartholomew Westley, the great-grandfather of John and Charles Wesley, founding fathers of the Methodist Church, sometimes preached at St Mary's in the 1600s.

CHARMOUTH

737 Cearn
1086 (Domesday Book) Cernemude

Old Celtic:
cearn – a pile of stones or cairn

Old English:
mutha – a mouth
'a settlement near the mouth of a stony river'

Fossil hunting

Charmouth Heritage Coast Centre is the place to visit to find out about fossil hunting on Charmouth beach. Fossils may be taken home but no hammers are permitted to be used on the cliffs... happy hunting!

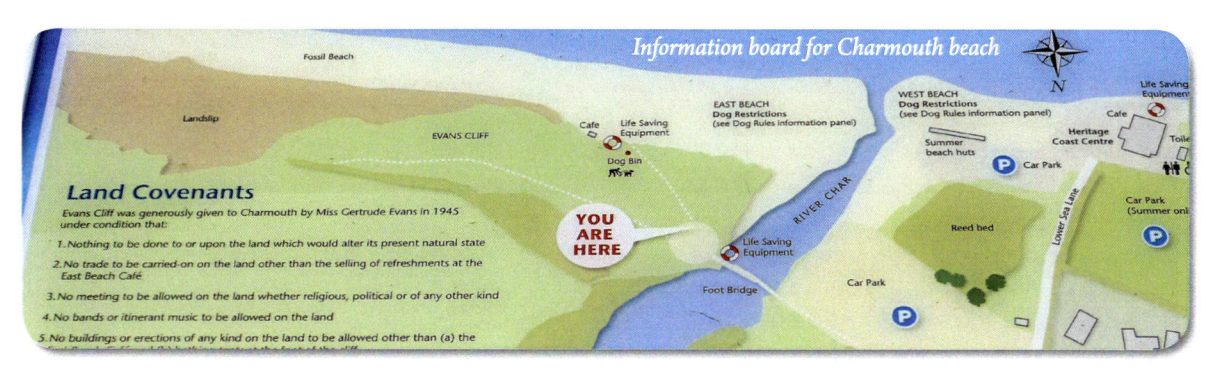

Information board for Charmouth beach

Chapter 7

RIVER WINNIFORD

The River Winniford is a short river flowing south to the English Channel at Seatown on the South West Coastal Path. Seatown lies west of Golden Cap, a favourite beauty spot for walkers. The name Winniford is taken from *winn*, the old Celtic word for 'stream' – a stream with a ford crossing.

AT A GLANCE

SOURCE
Springs in the hills around Ryall

END / MOUTH
English Channel at Seatown beach

LENGTH
Approximately 5km (3 miles)

River Winniford having passed under the A35 in Chideock

Villages and towns and the origins of their names
(from source to mouth of the river)

RYALL
1240 Rihull
Old English:
ryge – rye
hyll – a hill
'a settlement on a hill where rye grows'

MORCOMBELAKE
1240 Mortecumb
(See also River Char)
1558 Morecombelake
Old English:
mor – moorland
cumb – a valley
lacu – a stream
'a settlement near a stream passing through a moorland valley'

CHIDEOCK
1086 (Domesday Book) Cidihoc
1240 Cidioc
Celtic:
ced – a wood
'a settlement near or in a wood'

What a clanger!
An inscription on one of the old bells in St Giles Church still bears the spelling error from when it was cast in 1602. Instead of 'Love God' it exhorts parishioners to 'Love Dog'.

SEATOWN
1469 Setowne
Old English:
sae – sea
tun – a farm or estate
'a farm or estate near the sea'

Golden Cap
To the west of Seatown is a 40-minute walk along the South West Coast Path to Golden Cap, the highest point on the south coast of England. Golden Cap takes its name from the greensand rock that forms the uppermost layer. When the sun shines, it reflects a beautiful golden colour.

Monmouth Rebellion of 1685
An advance party of the Monmouth Rebellion landed at Seatown ahead of the rest of the Duke of Monmouth's troops at Lyme Regis. Among them was cavalry commander Colonel Venner, who was wounded at the battle of Bridport during the first engagement with the king's soldiers.

Fossil hunting
The most common fossil found on Seatown beach is the ammonite. Fossils lie within nodules on the shingle and can often be picked up without the need for tools. You need to extract them gently without hammering as the fossils are easily damaged. Hammering on the cliffs is forbidden.

Contraband
Fishing and farming were the main occupations for Seatown villagers. In the past smuggling supplemented their income. Rowing boats would bring the illicit cargo ashore at night, hiding it in St Gabriel's Chapel, now a ruin. It was carried by horse and cart, possibly along the same path present-day walkers use to reach the Golden Cap.

Chapter 8

RIVER BRIT

AT A GLANCE

SOURCE
Springs in the hills north of Beaminster, around North Bowood

MOUTH / OUTLET
English Channel, West Bay south of Bridport

LENGTH
Approximately 6.3km (4 miles)

TRIBUTARIES
- Stoke Water, confluences with the River Brit at Netherbury
- River Simene, confluences with the River Brit near St Mary's Playing Field in Bridport
- River Asker, confluences with the River Brit near Palmers Brewery, Bridport

The River Brit was originally called the River Woth, an Anglo Saxon word meaning 'melody', a lovely description of the sound of water flowing over stones and gravel on the riverbed. The name changed to Brit, probably taken from the town of Bridport.

The River Brit is found in southwest Dorset and flows southward until it reaches Bridport. Here it confluences with its tributaries the River Simene and the River Asker. Together they empty into the harbour at West Bay.

The Brit's catchment area is mostly fields for grazing cattle and sheep, and wooded areas. Approaching Bridport it becomes more urban.

Work has been undertaken to improve the quality of the water, which was polluted in the past by the hemp and flax industries. Today many varieties of fish breed in its waters, including trout, loach and minnows.

West Dorset – River Brit

VILLAGES AND TOWNS AND THE ORIGINS OF THEIR NAMES
(from source to mouth of the river)

West Bay harbour

BEAMINSTER
862 Bebingmynster
1086 (Domesday Book) Beiminstre
Old English:
Beage – personal name
mynster – a church
'a church founded by a woman named Beage'

Cognac
Thomas Hine was born in Beaminster but moved to France at the age of 17 to seek his fortune. It was the time of the French Revolution followed by the Napoleonic Wars against England, but Thomas found work at a brandy distillery. He married the owner's daughter, became a partner in the business and eventually owned it outright. Before he died, aged 42, he changed the name of the business to Cognac Hine. Cognac Hine became recognised among brandy connoisseurs as one of the finest cognacs in the world.

Parnham House
Originally owned by Stephen de Parnham, the first Parnham House dates to 1400 when it was built by the influential Gerard family. They married into the Strode family, who became owners in the mid-1500s and lived there for 200 years.

During the English Civil War (1642-1651), Lady Anne Strode was killed by a sword as she tried to stop soldiers under the command of General Fairfax entering the house. More recently, the house was a country club in the 1920s and an army hospital during the Second World War. In 1976, John Makepeace established his School for Craftsmen in Wood and in 2001 it became the home of Michael and Emma Treichl. It is open to the public during the summer months.

33

BUCKHAM
1086 (Domesday Book) Bochenhamm
Old English:
bucca – a male goat
or bucc – a buck (male deer)
hamm – pasture land
'pasture with he-goats or bucks'

Martin Clunes' Buckham Fair
Competitions, displays, food and fun! Hosted by well-known actor Martin Clunes with his wife Philippa and dedicated support from Buckham villagers, all proceeds support local charities. At the time of writing it has been suspended because of the coronavirus pandemic but we're looking forward to Buckham Fair returning soon.

On a personal note... in 2018 one of our Dog Home Boarding clients, Butch, won dog of the day – what a star!

STOKE ABBOTT
1086 (Domesday Book) Stoche
1273 Stok Abbatis
Old English:
stoc – a secondary settlement
Latin:
abbatis – of the abbot
'a secondary settlement owned by Sherborne Abbey'

Last public hanging in Dorset
In 1858 a cottage caught fire in the village and a woman's body was found. Sarah Guppy's throat had been cut. John Seale was found guilty of her murder. His execution at the gates of Dorchester Prison was the last public hanging in Dorset.

NETHERBURY
1086 (Domesday Book) Niderberie
Old English:
neotherra – lower
burh – a fortified place
'a lower fortified place'

SILKHAY
1332 Selkeheye
Old English:
Selk – personal name
haeg – an enclosure
'an enclosure owned by a man named Selk'

WAYTOWN
1626 Wayetowne
Middle English:
wei – a thoroughfare
toun – a village or hamlet
'a village beside a thoroughfare between two settlements, Beaminster to Bridport'

OXBRIDGE
Probably derived from a bridge crossing a small tributary of the River Brit where oxen grazed.

MELPLASH
1155 Melpleys
1312 Melepleisch
Old English:
maele – multi-coloured
plaesc – a pool
Possibly... *'a settlement near a pool or pond reflecting many colours'*

Melplash Manor and a night to regret
Sir Thomas More was the Sheriff of Dorset in the time of Henry VIII – not *the* Sir Thomas More who was executed in 1535. After a drunken night,

River Brit entering the sea at West Bay

Sir Thomas opened the doors to Dorchester jail and released all the prisoners – sheep stealers, pickpockets, highwaymen! After sobering up he realised he had to ask for the king's pardon for being so reckless. He sought the help of Lord Paulet and the pardon was granted. In return Lord Paulet demanded one of Thomas' daughters should marry one of his sons, bringing with her a large dowry. The Paulet family became owners of Melplash Manor, their family motto can be seen above a fireplace 'Aimez Loyaulte', 'Love Loyalty'.

WOOTH
1276 Woth Traunceys
Old English:
woth – a melody or sound (the original name of the River Brit)
Norman:
Frauncey – personal name
'a settlement by the river Woth owned by the Traunceys family'

PYMORE
1236 Pimore
Old English:
pie – insects
mor – marshy ground
'a place near marshland probably infested with mosquitoes'

ALLINGTON
1086 (Domesday Book) Adelingtone
Old English:
aetheling – princes
tun – a farm or estate
'a farm or estate owned by princes'

BRIDPORT

1086 (Domesday Book) Brideport

Celtic:
bridie – a fast-flowing stream

Old English:
port – a harbour with a market

'a market town with a harbour with a fast-flowing stream or river'

Money for old rope

Rope-making and net-making have been part of Bridport life for centuries. Ropes were used on naval and fishing boats and for hangman's nooses. Nets have been on Wimbledon tennis courts for many years. Flax and hemp, used to make rope, were grown in the area and there were several flax mills, one being at Netherbury.

Fleeing for his life

Following the Battle of Worcester in 1651, young Prince Charles (later King Charles II) was fleeing to France disguised as a servant. He rested for a meal at the George Inn, East Street. A painting by Francis Henry Newbery hangs in Bridport Town Hall depicting Parliamentarian troops searching for Charles, who can be seen in the background escaping with his horse.

Confluence of the River Asker with the River Brit near Palmers Brewery in Bridport

WATTON

1228 Wutton
1256 Wottune

Old English:
woth – a melody or sound (river name, see Wooth above)
tun – a farm or estate
'a farm or estate on the River Woth'

BOTHENHAMPTON

1285 Bothenamtone
bothm – a valley bottom
ham-tun – a home farm
'a home farm situated in the bottom of a valley'

WYCH

1481 la Wiche
wic – a dwelling place
or wice – wych elm (ulmus glabra)
'a dwelling place' or 'a place near wych elm trees'

Shipbuilding
West Bay was known as Bridport Harbour until 1884. It was the centre of the shipbuilding industry. Many ships built at West Bay were essential to the Napoleonic Wars (1799-1815).

West bay from the pier

Chapter 9

RIVER SIMENE

AT A GLANCE

SOURCE
Several springs near North Bowood

MOUTH / OUTLET
Confluences with the River Brit near St Mary's Playing Field in Bridport

LENGTH
Approximately 9.5km (6 miles)

The River Simene flows in a south easterly direction from North Bowood towards Bridport, where it joins with the River Brit. It is often more stream than river and has several villages and hamlets along its length. The catchment area is predominantly grassland for cattle and sheep grazing, with some maize crops.

River Simene along Filford lane

West Dorset – River Simene

VILLAGES AND TOWNS AND THE ORIGINS OF THEIR NAMES
(from source to its confluence with the River Brit)

BOWOOD NORTH AND SOUTH
1086 (Domesday Book) Bovewode
Old English:
bufan – above
wudu – a wood
'a settlement above a wood'

FILFORD
1327 Filleforde
Old English:
filethe – hay
leah – a clearing in a wood
ford – a ford, river crossing
'a settlement by a ford near a clearing where hay is grown'

SALWAYASH
1332 Shouleweye
1682 Shallways Ash
Old English:
scofl – narrow/hollow
weg – a way
ash – an ash tree
'a settlement on a narrow way close to ash trees'

ATRIM
1086 (Domesday Book) Atrem
unknown origin

The Monarch's Way
Atrim is a village close to Monarch's Way, a footpath that starts in Worcester and ends at Shoreham-by-Sea, near Brighton.

It is approximately 1,000km (620 miles) long and is the route that Charles II used to escape Oliver Cromwell's men. The king fled to France where he lived until the restoration of the monarchy in 1660.

During his escape Charles hid in an oak tree to avoid capture, which is included on the footpath's symbol.

Monarch's Way enters Dorset north of Sherborne, travels south and follows the southwest coast path from Charmouth to West Bay before turning north again towards Somerset.

SYMONDSBURY
1086 (Domesday Book) Simondesberge
Old English:
Sigemund – personal name
beorg – a barrow or hill
'a settlement on a hill belonging to a man named Sigemund'

ALLINGTON
1086 (Domesday Book) Adelingtone
1227 Athelington
Old English:
aethel – princes
ing – associated with
tun – a farm or estate
'a farm or estate associated with princes'

BRIDPORT
1086 (Domesday Book) Brideport
Celtic:
bridie – a fast-flowing stream
Old English:
port – a harbour with a market
'a market town with a harbour with a fast-flowing stream or river'

Chapter 10

RIVER ASKER

AT A GLANCE

SOURCE
Several springs in the hills near Askerswell and Eggardon Hill

MOUTH / OUTLET
Confluences with the River Brit near Palmers Brewery, Bridport

LENGTH
Approximately 12km (7.5 miles)

TRIBUTARIES
Mangerton Brook, confluences with the River Asker in Bradpole

Two tributaries combine and flow west through the Loders villages until the River Asker reaches Bradpole. Here it is joined by its main tributary, Mangerton Brook.

The river continues its journey to Bridport, confluencing with the River Brit.

The catchment area of the Asker is mainly dairy and arable agriculture.

The name Asker is taken from Askerswell, while Lodres was an earlier Celtic name for the river. The name was changed after the Norman invasion of 1066.

VILLAGES AND TOWNS AND THE ORIGINS OF THEIR NAMES
(from source to mouth of the river)

ASKERSWELL
1086 (Domesday Book) Oscherwille
Old English:
Osgar – personal name
wella – a spring
'a settlement by a spring owned by a man named Osgar'

Buzzed by bees
Canon Edward Daniell was rector of the Church of St Michael's & All Angels during the Second World War. He lived in the rectory until it was requisitioned by American troops preparing for the D-Day invasion of France on Omaha Beach. Canon Daniell was an enthusiastic bee keeper and tended many hives in the churchyard. It is said one Sunday a swarm of bees invaded the church during morning service causing a hurried exit by preacher and congregation!

EGGARDON HILL
1086 (Domesday Book) Giochresdone
Old English:
Eohhere – personal name
dun – a hill
'a hill owned by a man named Eohhere'

Fort with a view
Eggardon hill fort is partly owned by the National Trust (the southern aspect) with the rest privately owned. The Iron Age fort is 2,500 years old. Before the fort was built there were two Bronze Age burial mounds at the summit of Eggardon Hill.

UPLODERS
1086 (Domesday Book) Lodres
1445 Uppelodres
Old English:
upp – higher or upstream
Celtic:
lo-dre – a homestead
or loch – a pool
dour – water
'a homestead upstream from Loders'

YONDOVER
1454 Endouer
1544 Yendover
Old English:
begeondan – beyond
ofer – a river bank
'a settlement beyond the banks of a river'

LODERS
(ALSO KNOWN AS LOWER LODERS)
Celtic:
lo-dre – a homestead
or loch – a pool
dour – water
'a homestead by water'

Mangerton Mill

MANGERTON
1207 Mangerton
Old English:
mangere – merchants
tun – a farm or estate
'a farm or estate owned by merchants'

Rural bygones
Mangerton Mill dates to the 17th century as a water mill for grinding barley. Restoration began in 1986 to bring the mill to full working order – the 12ft x 4ft solid oak and cast iron wheel is magnificent. Why not enjoy a cup of tea and visit the craft centre and Museum of Rural Bygones?

BRADPOLE
1086 (Domesday Book) Bratepolle
Old English:
brad – broad
pol – a pool
'a settlement with a wide pool or pond'

River Asker in Asker Meadows, Bridport

BRIDPORT

1086 (Domesday Book) Brideport
Celtic:
bridie – fast-flowing stream
Old English:
port – a harbour with a market
'a market town with a harbour and fast-flowing stream or river'

Twisted flax
Rope-making has been part of Bridport's history for centuries, dating to the reign of King John (1199-1216).

Hemp and flax were grown in the surrounding fields and today's high street is noticeably wide because this was where the ropes were dried after they had been twisted together. The manufacture of netting continues to supply the fishing and aerospace industries.

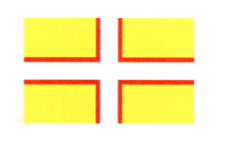

Downstream Dorset – River Tales and Local History

Chapter 11

RIVER BRIDE

The River Bride emerges from the Bridehead Lake over a small, pretty waterfall. The Celtic word *bride* means a 'gushing stream'. It flows west through rolling hills and open fields, travelling parallel to Bredy Road until it reaches the sea at Burton Bradstock on the western end of Chesil Beach.

AT A GLANCE

SOURCE
Springs forming Bridehead Lake in the grounds of Bridehead House

MOUTH / OUTLET
Burton Bradstock, the western part of Chesil Beach

LENGTH
Approximately 12km (6 miles)

Waterfall flowing from Bridehead Lake

West Dorset – River Bride

VILLAGES AND TOWNS AND THE ORIGINS OF THEIR NAMES
(from source to mouth of the river)

Little Bredy, Bridehead lake

LITTLE BREDY OR LITTLEBREDY
1086 (Domesday Book) Litelbride
Celtic:
bride – gushing or surging stream
Old English:
lytel – little
'a small settlement near a gushing stream – the River Bride'

Bridehead House
The original manor house was built in 1600 but the house today is predominantly 19th century. It is owned by the Williams family, originally wealthy bankers and MPs. The source of the River Bride lies within the estate and was dammed to create the lake that is free to visit.

LONG BREDY
987 Bridian
1086 (Domesday Book) Langebride
Celtic:
bride – a gushing stream
Old English:
lang – long
'a long settlement near a gushing stream – the River Bride'

Kingston Russell House
The medieval seat of the Earls of Bedford. The first earl also owned Woburn Abbey, one of England's stately homes.

Vice-Admiral Sir Thomas Masterman Hardy was born in Kingston Russell House on 5th April 1769. He was a long-standing

45

comrade and friend of Admiral Horatio Lord Nelson. Nelson appointed Hardy to be flag captain of HMS Victory during the Battle of Trafalgar. They were walking together on the deck of the Victory when Nelson received his fatal gunshot wound.

Kingston Russell Stone Circle
Also known as the Gorwell Circle, Kingston Russell Stone Circle was probably built during the Bronze Age, about 2000 BC, and is the largest stone circle in Dorset. The 18 standing stones have all fallen.

Grey Mare and Colts
Near the stone circle is a Neolithic long barrow, the Grey Mare and her Colts. It is possibly so named because of the massive grey sarsen stones that mark the barrow. This chambered barrow was excavated in the early 1800s with numerous human bones and pottery uncovered.

LITTON CHENEY
1194 Lidinton
Old English:
hlyde – a noisy stream
tun – a farm or estate
Cheyne – personal name, 14th century
'a farm or estate near a noisy stream owned by the Cheyne family'

PUNCKNOWLE
1086 (Domesday Book) Pomacanole
Old English:
cnoll – a hilltop
Puma – personal name
'Land on the top of a hill owned by a man named Puma'

Invention of shrapnel
In the early 19th century Colonel Henry Shrapnel lived in Puncknowle manor house. His

Puncknowle Manor viewed from St Mary's churchyard

Ryan on the National Trust cliff walk from Hive Beach to Burton Bradstock, looking down on the mouth of the River Bride

name lives on as the inventor of an artillery shell containing numerous small lead balls. He designed the fuse to be shortened or lengthened so the shell would explode above the heads of the enemy, spreading shot over a wide area. Today the dictionary term for shrapnel is 'fragments of a bomb, shell or other object thrown out by an explosion'.

SWYRE
1086 (Domesday Book) Svere
Old English:
sweora – a col or gap between two peaks
'a settlement on a neck of land between two peaks'

From farmer to earl
In 1506, the life of Swyre farmer John Russell changed greatly thanks to his ability to speak Spanish. He was taken to Wolfeton House near Dorchester to translate for a Spanish princess recently wed to the Archduke of Austria. The couple had been sailing to London but bad weather meant they landed in Weymouth for an overnight stay. Russell travelled with the couple to London and so began his rise in the royal court. He became the first Earl of Bedford and a wealthy landowner.

BURTON BRADSTOCK
1086 (Domesday Book) Bridetone
Celtic:
bride – a gushing or surging stream
Old English:
tun – a farm or estate
Bradstock's name derives from the Abbey of Bradenstoke in Wiltshire, which owned the manor from the 13th century.
'a farm or estate on the River Bride owned by the Abbey of Bradenstoke'

Fossil hunting
Burton Bradstock is situated along the Jurassic Coast so there is always the possibility of finding a fossil on the beach that has fallen from the sandstone cliffs above.

Smuggling
In the 18th century, well-known Bournemouth and Poole-based smuggler Isaac Gulliver expanded his business to the West Country. The beaches at Burton Bradstock were ideal for unloading contraband, which was then moved to his farm near Eggardon Hill, about 8km (5 miles) inland. Gulliver planted pine trees on the summit of this Iron Age hill fort to guide his ships towards the shore. His farm was visited by customers from as far afield as Bristol and Bath.

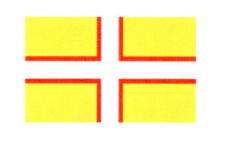

Downstream Dorset – River Tales and Local History

Chapter 12

FLEET LAGOON

West Dorset – Fleet Lagoon

Chesil Beach stretches about 30km (18 miles) from Portland to West Bay. Between the beach and the mainland lies Fleet Lagoon. The lagoon starts at Portland in the east and continues 13km (8 miles) to Abbotsbury.

Fed by freshwater streams as well as the sea, it has slightly salted, brackish water and is a haven for many species of wildlife. Abbotsbury is famous for its swannery, the only managed nesting colony of mute swans in the world.

The name Chesil Beach comes from the Old English word *cisel* meaning 'shingle'. The pebbles on the shingle beach gradually reduce in size from Portland, where they are about 8cm (3in), to West Bay, where they are only 1cm (0.3in) in diameter.

Fleet Lagoon and the strip of Chesil Beach taken from Abbotsbury Hill

STREAMS ENTERING FLEET LAGOON FROM ABBOTSBURY TO PORTLAND
(and villages along those streams)

COWARDS LAKE
Cowards Lake is a small stream that rises near Cowards Lake Farm and from springs in Abbotsbury Hill flowing through Abbotsbury Gardens. The two streams confluence and enter Fleet Lagoon at its most western end.

Old English:
cuhyrde – a cow herdsman

Cowards Lake Farmhouse
A guest house dating back about 300 years. Some of the building materials were taken from Abbotsbury Abbey after it was demolished in the 16th century during the Dissolution of the Monasteries in the reign of Henry VIII.

PORTESHAM STREAM AND MILL STREAM
Portesham Stream rises from streams around the village of Portesham near the South Dorset Ridgeway. It flows south-westward from Portesham and enters Fleet Lagoon to the east of the swannery.

Mill Stream is a tributary that is fed by springs as it travels from Portesham towards Abbotsbury, entering the Fleet Lagoon at the swannery.

PORTESHAM
1024 Porteshamme
Old English:
port – a port or harbour town
ham – a homestead
'a homestead near a harbour town (probably Abbotsbury)'

Hardy's Monument (photograph reproduced with kind permission of Ian Paterson)

Vice-Admiral Thomas Masterman Hardy
Portesham was home to Sir Thomas Masterman Hardy who served under Lord Horatio Nelson and was walking with him on the deck of the Victory when Nelson was shot (see also River Bride, Kingston Russell House).

A couple of miles north of Portesham the tall monument erected in memory of Sir Thomas towers over the landscape. It is sited on Black Down Hill and was intended to be a landmark to help ships safely navigate the dangerous waters of Portland.

The monument is 22m (72ft) high and is visible from a distance of 100km (62 miles). It was built in 1844 and has been on navigation charts since 1846.

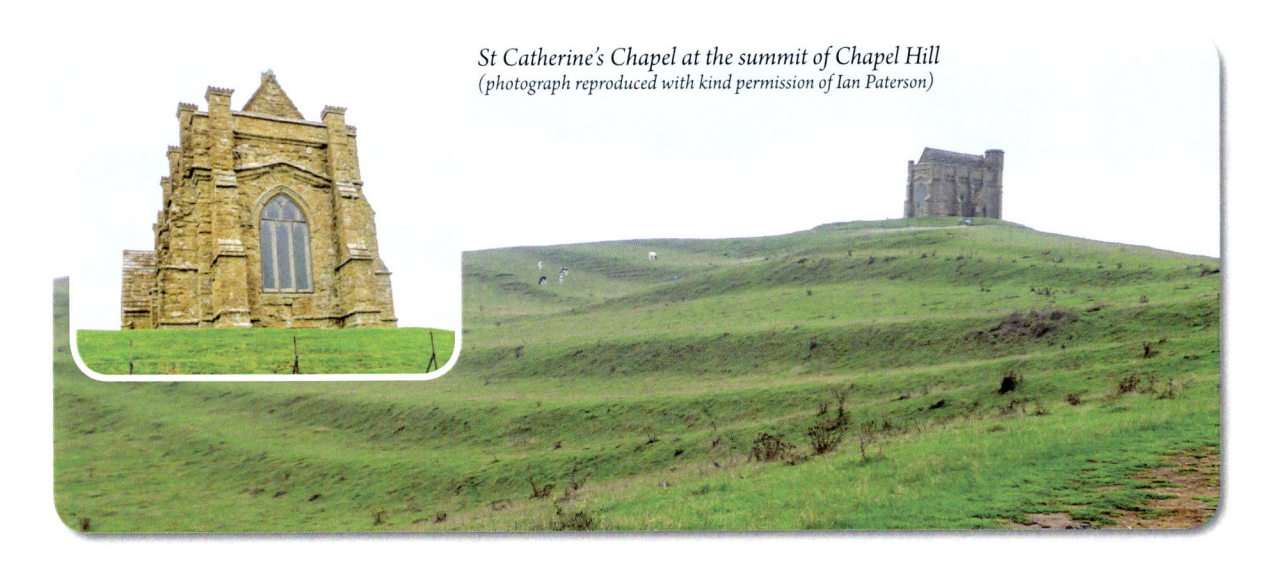

St Catherine's Chapel at the summit of Chapel Hill
(photograph reproduced with kind permission of Ian Paterson)

ABBOTSBURY
946 Abbedesburie
Old English:
abbod – an abbot
burh – a fortified place
'a fortified place belonging to the abbot (of Glastonbury)'

St Catherine's Chapel
This chapel was a place of pilgrimage for the monks of Abbotsbury Abbey. It survived the Dissolution of the Monasteries Act in 1539, probably because it was also a landmark for shipping and a beacon used to warn of foreign attack. The monks would use the chapel as a place of retreat during Lent. In later years a light was permanently lit at the top of its turret.

My son, Ian, and I explored Abbotsbury and St Catherine's Chapel on a blustery day in August. The chapel was open but seemed to be occupied. On the floor were a collapsed tent and an empty pizza box. In a small alcove in the wall there were beer bottles, neatly stored. The monks used the chapel as a place of retreat to meditate. Perhaps this time it had been used by campers as a retreat from the wild weather?

Abbotsbury Swannery
This unique swannery features 10 hectares (25 acres) of natural wildlife habitat and is the breeding area for about 600 mute swans. It was established by Benedictine monks at the Abbotsbury monastery in the mid 11th century. They bred swans as food for extravagant banquets.

RODDEN STREAM (RODDEN BROOK)
Rodden Stream is about 4km (2.5 miles) in length, rising at West Elworth and passing through the village of Rodden. There are also springs around Langton Herring. Rodden Stream enters Fleet Lagoon at Rodden Hive. The stream and its tributaries travel through agricultural land mainly used for dairy farming.

EAST ELWORTH
1086 (Domesday Book) Aleurde
1221 Elleworthe
Old English:
Ella – personal name
worth – an enclosure
'an enclosure owned by a man named Ella'

RODDEN

1221 Raddun
Old English:
read – red
dun – a hill
'a red hill' – possibly sandstone in the area

LANGTON HERRING

1086 (Domesday Book) Langetone
1336 Langeton Heryng
Old English:
lang – long
tun – a farm or estate
Harang – personal name
'a long farm or estate owned by a family named Harang' as in Chaldon Herring and Winterborne Herringston

RODDEN HIVE

as in Rodden above
Old English:
hive – a landing place or harbour
'the harbour near the settlement named Rodden' or 'the harbour at the mouth of Rodden Stream'

HERBURY STREAM

The small Herbury Stream rises near Bagwell Farm and enters the lagoon in a bay west of Herbury Peninsula.

HERBURY

Old English:
Here – personal name, as in Herston near Swanage
burh – a fortified place.
'a fortified place owned by a man named Here'

WEST FLEET AND EAST FLEET STREAMS

West Fleet and East Fleet streams rise slightly west of the village of Chickerell and flow into the lagoon at the village of East Fleet and further west near the Moonfleet Manor Hotel.

CHICKERELL

1086 (Domesday Book) Chicherelle
The derivation of this name has never been discovered, which is very unusual.

West Dorset – Fleet Lagoon

Approaching Moonfleet Manor Hotel with views of Fleet Lagoon and Chesil Beach

Celtic Christian church
St Mary's Church (*left*) dates to about 1260. However, there is evidence of earlier Celtic Christianity and there probably would have been a wooden Saxon church on the site before the present one.

FLEET
1086 (Domesday Book) Flete
Old English:
fleot – an estuary or inlet
East and West Fleet villages take their names from the Fleet Lagoon.
'a settlement beside the Fleet Lagoon'

Moonfleet Manor Hotel
Once called Fleet House, it was the manor house of the Mohun family who owned the estate. The name Moonfleet is a combination of the name Mohun and the villages of Fleet. At the entrance to the estate two columns can be seen featuring the symbols of the family's coat of arms.

Moonfleet Manor Hotel overlooking Fleet Lagoon and Chesil Beach

Chapter 13

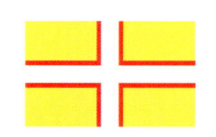

CULVERWELL STREAM

The stream rises near Portland Bill headland and flows through narrow ditches, beneath Portland Bill Road and a wooden footbridge and finally over the edge of the south-east cliff as a waterfall. This is a winterbourne stream so the waterfall often dries up in the summer months.

AT A GLANCE

SOURCE
Culverwell, north-east of Portland Bill

MOUTH / OUTLET
Waterfall into the sea

LENGTH
Approximately 300m (984 feet)

Footbridge over a dry Culverwell Stream

West Dorset – Culverwell Stream

VILLAGES AND TOWNS AND THE ORIGINS OF THEIR NAMES
on the Isle of Portland

Portland Bill headland

PORTLAND, ISLE OF
9th century Port
862 Portlande
Old English:
port – a harbour
land – land or estate
'land or estate with a harbour'

FORTUNESWELL
Recorded as Fortuneswell in 1608
probably *'a well or spring that would bring you good fortune'*

EASTON
1323 Eston
Old English:
east – east
tun – a farm or estate
'an eastern farm or estate'

WAKEHAM
1608 Wacombe
Old English:
wacu – a watch or lookout
cumb – a valley
'a valley where there was a watchman keeping guard'

Blowhole with safety precautions

WESTON
1324 Westone
Old English:
west – west
tun – a farm or estate
'a western farm or estate'

SOUTHWELL
1608 Southwelle
Old English:
suth – south
wella – a spring
'a spring to the south'

CULVERWELL
Old English:
culfre – a dove or pigeon
possibly *'a well or spring where there are many pigeons or doves'*

Important Mesolithic site
There is an archaeological site near Culverwell in which about 25 dwellings existed during the Mesolithic period, 8,000 years ago. The site was given a major archaeological recognition in 2004, the Pitt Rivers Award. A replica of a dwelling and a dinosaur footprint can be seen on open days.

The cave beneath the blowhole

PORTLAND BILL
Old English:
bile – a bird's bill or beak
'a headland that is tapering like the beak of a bird'

Cave hole and blowhole
A ten-minute walk from Portland Bill leads you to a large cave with a blowhole in its roof through which waves can be seen crashing on to the rocks below. At times they shoot up through the blowhole creating a geyser of sea water.

Attempts have been made to place concrete slabs across the blowhole to stop unwary walkers from falling through. However, the sea was too powerful. Today there are steel bars weighed down by Portland stone to prevent accidents.

Shipwrecked in cave hole
In 1949 Frank and Ann Davison were shipwrecked at the mouth of the cave having set sail from Lancashire for the West Indies. Frank drowned but Ann was able to scramble ashore. Three years later she became the first woman to sail single-handed across the Atlantic.

Chapter 14

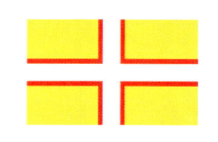

RIVER WEY

AT A GLANCE

SOURCE
Springs in the chalk hills around Upwey, including Upwey Wishing Well tea rooms

MOUTH / OUTLET
Weymouth Harbour

LENGTH
14km (8.5 miles)

TRIBUTARIES
Small tributaries including Pucksey Brook, which rises near Portesham and confluences with the River Wey at Broadwey

The River Wey is one of the smaller chalk rivers in Dorset. Its name derives from the old Celtic word *ueis*, meaning 'water' or the Anglo Saxon word *ea* meaning 'river'. The River Wey had been an important route to transport supplies from Weymouth to Dorchester since Roman times.

The Wey flows through the suburbs of Weymouth, which were once separate villages. It fills the Radipole Lake in the centre of town and then empties into Weymouth Harbour. There were once at least five working mills on the river. There is a fish farm at Upwey, which is also famous for its watercress beds.

Radipole Lake has been managed by the RSPB (Royal Society for the Protection of Birds) since 1979 and is open to visitors, bird watchers, cyclists and anglers.

VILLAGES AND TOWNS AND THE ORIGINS OF THEIR NAMES
(from source to mouth of the river)

UPWEY
1086 (Domesday Book) Waie
1241 Uppeweie
Old English:
upp – upper or higher
Old Celtic:
ueis – water
or Old English:
ea – a river
'a settlement on the upper reaches of the River Wey'

Early settlers and Lucille Ball
Award-winning American actress and comedienne Lucille Ball (1911-1989) could trace her ancestors back to the Sprague family of Upwey. In 1628 and 1629, the family sailed to settle in New England. William Sprague was one of the founders of the city of Charlestown in Massachusetts, while another Sprague relative became governor of Rhode Island.

Upwey Wishing Well
Upwey Wishing Well tea rooms, with its lovely water gardens, is 'well' worth a visit, if you excuse the pun. Good food, friendly owners and staff, and treats on sale for dogs!

BROADWEY
1086 (Domesday Book) Waia
1249 Bradeweye
Old English:
brad – broad
Old Celtic:
ueis – water
or Old English:
ea – a river
'a settlement where the river is wider'

The spring where the River Wey rises in the gardens of Upwey Wishing Well tea rooms

NOTTINGTON
1212 Notinton
Old English:
Hnott or Hnotta – personal name
ing – associated with
tun – a farm or estate
'a farm or estate associated with or named after a man named Hnott(a)'

Remedy for gout
The Spa House (circa 1830) in Nottington was built around a sulphurous spring. Guests came to partake of the waters to alleviate gout and jaundice among other physical complaints.

Nothe Fort

RADIPOLE
1086 (Domesday Book) Retpole
Old English:
hreod – a reed
pol – a pool
'a settlement near a pool or lake of reeds'

MELCOMBE REGIS
1223 Melecumb
1336 Melcoumbe Regis
Old English:
meoluc – milk
cumb – a valley
Latin:
regis – of the king
'a valley owned by the king where milk was produced'

Black Death arrives
In 1348 the bubonic plague, or Black Death, arrived in England at the port of Melcombe Regis. Within two years more than half the population of England had died.

WEYMOUTH
934 Waimouie
1248 Weymuth
Old Celtic:
ueis – water
mouie – a mouth
or Old English:
ea – a river
mutha – a mouth
'a settlement at the mouth of the river'

Spanish Armada arrives
In 1588, ships carrying more than 200 Weymouth men put to sea. They fought with the Spanish Armada off Portland and captured a 25-gun galleon, the San Salvador, after its gunpowder magazine exploded. It was towed by the Golden Hind into Weymouth Harbour.

King George III
King George III was a regular visitor to the town between 1789 and 1805. He would swim in Weymouth Bay after changing in one of the first bathing machines. He purchased Gloucester

Tribute to King George III

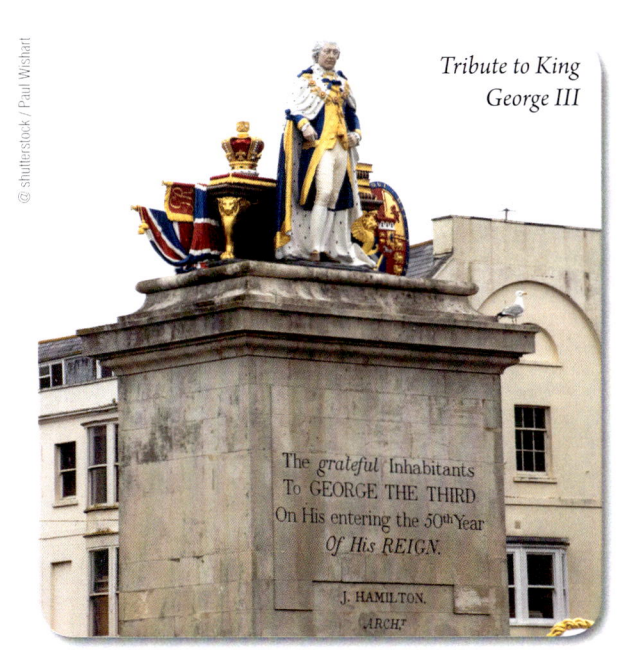

The Jubilee Clock

Memorial to D-Day

Lodge, which was owned by his brother, the Duke of Gloucester. It has since been a hotel and, more recently, luxury apartments.

Jubilee Clock

The clock, which has been standing on the promenade at the end of King Street since 1887, commemorates Queen Victoria's Golden Jubilee. She had succeeded to the throne 50 years earlier after the death of William IV in 1837.

Nothe Fort

The fort was built in 1860 by the Royal Engineers and some of the inmates of Portland Prison. It was used as part of Britain's coastal defences until 1956. The fort has been restored through the dedicated work of the Weymouth Civic Society and is now open to visitors.

D-Day memorial

On June 6th 1944 a memorial was erected on the promenade opposite the Royal Hotel. It commemorates those who lost their lives during the preparations and assault on the Normandy beaches. A bell inside the monument rings at 11am, while the light in the globe is lit permanently.

Downstream Dorset – River Tales and Local History

Chapter 15

RIVER JORDAN

AT A GLANCE

SOURCE
Hills around Sutton Poyntz and Osmington

MOUTH / OUTLET
Bowleaze Cove

LENGTH
Approximately 5km (3 miles)

The River Jordan is a small, pretty river that meanders through the village of Preston and flows on to the beach at Bowleaze Cove.

The upper catchment area is mainly agricultural, becoming urban closer to the sea. There are several caravan holiday sites near the coast.

Mouth of the River Jordan in Bowleaze Cove

West Dorset – River Jordan

VILLAGES AND TOWNS AND THE ORIGINS OF THEIR NAMES
(from source to mouth of the river)

OSMINGTON
934 Osmyntone
Osmington Mills
Old English:
Osmund – personal name
ing – associated with
tun – a farm or estate
'a farm or estate owned by a man named Osmund'

King George on horseback
The figure of King George III on horseback was cut into the limestone on Osmington Hill (*above*) in 1808. The king enjoyed visiting Weymouth during his reign but, strangely, the figure is riding away from the town not towards it.

It is thought the king was insulted by the carving and never visited Weymouth again.

Sutton Poyntz

SUTTON POYNTZ
891 Suttone
1314 Sutton Pointz
Old English:
suth – south
tun – a farm or estate
Poyntz – personal name from the 13th century
'a southern farm or estate owned by a family named Poyntz'

Transportation to Australia
Mary Lawrence, nee Mary Butt, was indicted on 24th March 1813 for stealing a watch owned by Thomas Courtin, of Melcombe Regis. She was a widow and 22 years old when found guilty. After months in prison, Mary was transported to Australia for seven years, arriving in Sydney in July 1814. In Australia, Mary married a fellow convict who had also been transported and they had children. Years later some of Mary's family emigrated to join her and start a new life.

Brutal murder
John Cox was a servant to a butcher's family and, in 1862 he bludgeoned Dr Adam Puckett to death and then dismembered his body. Cox knew that Dr Puckett was going to commit him to the asylum in Forston. Instead, he became one of the first patients in Broadmoor.

PRESTON
1228 Prestun
Old English:
preost – a priest
tun – a farm or estate
'a farm or estate owned by a priest or abbey'

Wesley's grandfather arrested
Evangelist and non-conformist preacher John Westley lived in Manor Cottage in Preston until his death in 1678 at the age of 42. During his life of ministry he was imprisoned more than once for not using the Book of Common Prayer in church services. He and his family were impoverished but their plight came to the attention of local landowners the Gollop family, who offered Manor Cottage rent-free.

In later years the family name was changed to Wesley. John Westley's grandchildren, John and Charles Wesley, were the 18th century co-founders of the Methodist Church.

BOWLEAZE COVE
1461 Bolheys
Old English:
bula – bulls
haeg – an enclosure
'a settlement by a cove with an enclosure for bulls'

Art Deco hotel
The striking Art Deco arches of the Grade II-listed Riviera Hotel can be seen overlooking the bay. It was built in the 1930s with a second storey of white arches added at a later date.

Roman temple
Hoards of coins were uncovered during excavations at the site of a 4th century Roman temple. Some of them can be seen in Dorset County Museum in Dorchester.

The Riviera Hotel overlooking Bowleaze Cove

Site of the Roman temple at Bowleaze

River Jordan approaching Bowleaze Cove

Exploring the River Jordan

Ryan and I visited Sutton Poyntz in a quest to find the source of the River Jordan. Following a path upstream we walked for about ten minutes before we discovered Wessex Water had erected railings that stopped us getting any closer to the springhead.

Returning to the village we met a gentleman walking his two red setters. He told us the pumping station used to be steam-powered and the original filtration system included a funnel from the SS Great Eastern.

It had been retrieved and put to good use after an onboard explosion near Portland in 1859. Many thanks to our anonymous friend. If we meet again, the drinks are on us!

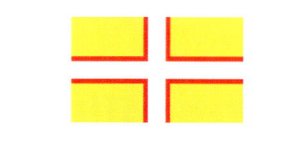

Chapter 16

SMALLER STREAMS

Several small streams flow into the English Channel between Lyme Regis and Ringstead Bay along the Jurassic Coast, including Westhay Water, Ridge Water, St Gabriel's Stream, Eype Stream, Swyre Stream, West Bexington Stream, Osmington Stream and Ringstead Stream.

WESTHAY WATER AND RIDGE WATER

These are two small streams that rise south of Chardown Hill and enter the sea separately between Charmouth and St Gabriel's Mouth.

The South West Coastal Path crosses the streams near their outlets. This section of the path is known as Monarch's Way, part of the route Charles II took when escaping Oliver Cromwell's army after the Battle of Worcester.

ST GABRIEL'S STREAM

This stream is almost 3km (1.8 miles) in length. It passes through Morcombelake and flows south to the sea at a small bay St Gabriel's Mouth.

EYPE STREAM

The village of Eype dates to the 14th century when it was called Yepe, from the Old English word geapes meaning 'spacious' or geap meaning 'steep'.

Defending our beaches

In November 1940, the local Home Guard was on duty at the Eype Mouth pillbox when a German Heinkel He 111 bomber made an emergency landing on the beach. The Home Guard captured the crew so proving Sir Winston Churchill's inspiring speech "we shall fight them on the beaches".

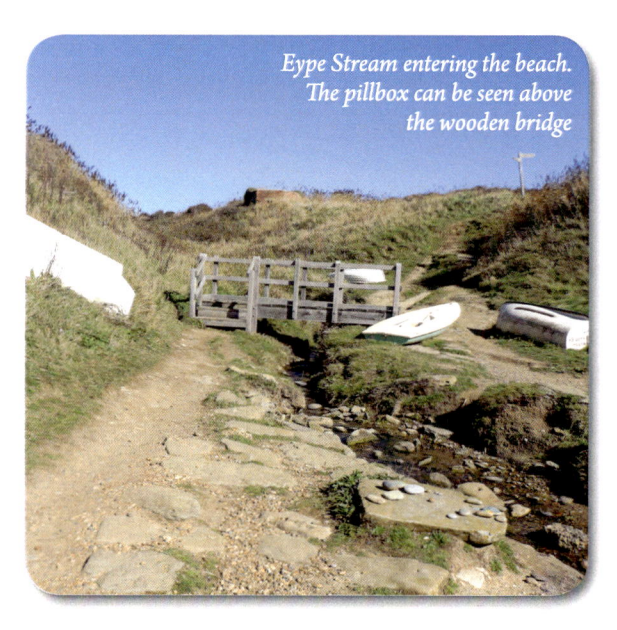

Eype Stream entering the beach. The pillbox can be seen above the wooden bridge

Looking down on Eype Mouth from the car park

BURTON MERE

Burton Mere is a small lagoon separated from the sea by Chesil Beach. It is surrounded by reeds and is a haven for wildlife.

The name Burton probably derives from nearby Burton Bradstock (River Bride). Mere is Anglo Saxon for a 'lake or sea'.

SWYRE STREAM

Swyre is mentioned in the Domesday Book (1086) and by the 12th century was known as Swere. Old English *sweora* means a 'col or gap between two peaks'.

WEST BEXINGTON STREAM

This is a small stream rising in West Hill and flowing through West Bexington. There is a nature reserve nearby with a lake, Bexington Mere. This lagoon is separated from the sea by Chesil Beach and depends on rainfall. The stream empties into Chesil Beach just west of the nature reserve.

UPPER TAMARISK

This is a small settlement on Swyre Road, probably named after the tamarisk trees often found in coastal areas and cultivated for windbreaks.

WEST BEXINGTON

1086 (Domesday Book) Bessintone

Old English:
byxen – boxwood
tun – a farm or estate
'a farm or estate where box trees grow'

OSMINGTON STREAM

Osmington Stream flows through Poxwell and Upton. The chalk figure of King George III on horseback can be seen along the Osmington to Poxwell road.

POXWELL

1066 (Domesday Book) Poscheswelle

Old English:
Poc or Poca – personal name
swelle – steep ground
or wella – a spring of water
'steep land owned by a man named Poc or Poca'
or *'a spring owned by a man named Poc or Poca'*

Cairn Circle
At the edge of Poxwell village are two small stone circles, one within the other, called Cairn Circle. It is only 4m (5 yards) in diameter and is thought to be a place of pagan worship. There are wonderful views from the top of the hill.

Poxwell Cairn Circle

Poxwell Manor
This manor house was used by Thomas Hardy as the home to Anne Garland, his heroine in The Trumpet-Major. It was built in the 17th century so is Jacobean in style and is surrounded by walled gardens with ten acres of land.

UPTON

1361 Upton

Old English:
upp – higher
tun – a farm or estate
'a higher farm or higher part of the estate' – probably referring to the high ground to the south of the village

OSMINGTON

1066 (Domesday Book) Osmentone

Old English:
Osmund – personal name
tun – a farm or estate
'a farm owned by a man named Osmund'

Craig's Farm Dairy shop and tea room
Enjoy a cup of tea and cake at Craig's Farm Dairy tea room. The family-run dairy serves home-cooked food at the tea room from breakfast to afternoon tea.

It offers seating indoors and outside and is dog friendly. The adjoining farm shop sells local produce ranging from home-made chutney and jam to locally grown fruit and vegetables.

Smugglers Inn, Osmington
The Smugglers Inn dates to the 13th century when it was named The Crown Inn, with its own brewery in the back yard. It was headquarters for profitable smuggling activity over several centuries. In the 17th century it was the landing place for French smuggler Pierre Latour.

The Smugglers Inn, Osmington

In the late 18th and 19th centuries it was the home of Emmanuel Charles and his family. Charles was the leader of the notoriously ruthless Charles Gang.

Apparently the gang imported brandy that tasted so bad even the local inhabitants refused to drink it.

Precarious future

In 2016, Osmington Stream had to be diverted for several months so that its banks could be strengthened alongside The Smugglers Inn. However, the cottages along the stream may eventually succumb to the effects of the gradual but constant coastal erosion.

John Constable (1776–1837)

The famous landscape painter spent many holidays, including his honeymoon, in Osmington. He was friends with the Reverend John Fisher, vicar of Osmington, and created many of his most famous paintings while staying with him, including Weymouth Bay and A Mill At Gillingham.

RINGSTEAD STREAM

This stream is formed by two smaller streams that confluence above Ringstead village. One rises at South Down Farm and travels through grassland, the other flows through woodland.

Osmington Stream after the walls had been strengthened where it flows past The Smugglers Inn

Ringstead Stream flows southward to reach the sea at Ringstead Bay, passing the medieval village of Ringstead, which no longer exists.

RINGSTEAD

1086 (Domesday Book) Ringestede
Old English:
hring – a ring or circuit
stede – a place or site
possibly *'the site of a stone circle'*
There are well-preserved earthworks at the site of the medieval West Ringstead village. The Black Death in the 14th century is one possible reason for the village being abandoned.

ISLE OF PURBECK

Following the rivers and streams on the Isle of Purbeck

'They followed no road or path, but rode where they pleased. There were great stretches of wiry grass, masses of heather springing up afresh, and, blazing its gold everywhere on this lovely April day, was the gorse.'

Five Go To Mystery Moor (Stoborough Heath) by Enid Blyton

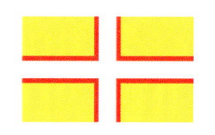

Chapter 17

PURBECK STREAMS
STREAMS OF THE ISLE OF PURBECK FROM ST OSWALD'S BAY TO POOLE HARBOUR

Poole Harbour extends from its entrance between Sandbanks and South Haven Point inland to Wareham. Many of Dorset's rivers and streams empty into the harbour, which is the second-largest natural harbour in the world, only beaten by Sydney Harbour in Australia. Some of the streams that drain the Purbeck Hills have their outlets along the southern coastline of the harbour. The rest empty into the English Channel further to the south.

Lulworth Stream approaching Lulworth Cove

RIVERS AND STREAMS FLOWING INTO THE ENGLISH CHANNEL

ST OSWALD'S BAY STREAMS

The streams are of special interest to scientists as they are highly acidic and sulphurous, creating conditions close to those found on Mars.

Limestone stacks

Durdle Door is a limestone arch formed thousands of years ago when the sea pierced the Portland stone. In the bay there are limestone stacks showing where the coastline used to be.

LULWORTH STREAMS

One stream flows through West Lulworth village and on to the beach at Lulworth Cove. It is about 1.5km (1 mile) in length. Another rises near Lulworth Camp and travels about 2.5km (1.5 miles) to the sea at Arish Mell.

Lulworth comes from an Anglo Saxon personal name, *Lulla*, and *worth*, which means 'an enclosure'.

Tourist trap

Lulworth Cove was formed by the sea eroding through Portland stone to reach clay, which washed away more easily. The cove is the shape of a horseshoe and has a pebbled beach. It's a very popular destination for visitors to Dorset.

Fossil forest

East of Lulworth Cove lies an area featuring the fossilised remains of a forest that was growing when dinosaurs roamed the Earth about 45 million years ago. The forest floor was wet and marshy, a perfect environment for algae to flourish. The algae grew around the base of the trees and became fossilised. The tree trunks rotted away leaving hollows defining their outline in the fossilised thrombolites.

TYNEHAM STREAM

Tyneham Stream rises in the hills around North Egliston, flows through woodland and grassland within the army ranges, and enters the sea at Worbarrow Bay. Its length is about 2km (1.2 miles).

Its name translates from the Old English word *Tyneham*, which means a 'homestead where goats are tended'.

Requisitioned

The villages of Tyneham and North and South Egliston were requisitioned by the Ministry of Defence (MoD) in 1943 during the Second World War.

Many villagers had lived there for generations but believed they were serving their country by evacuating the area with the promise they would return after the war. The MoD failed to honour its promise so today the cottages lie abandoned and in ruins. Tyneham village is open to the public – when the firing ranges aren't in use. The village school and church now house memories and information about village life in the past.

Tyneham Stream widens into the village pond before continuing through woodland to Worbarrow Bay

Broad Bench viewed from Kimmeridge Bay

EGLISTON STREAM

Egliston Stream rises in the hills around the ruins of Egliston, flows through Egliston Gwyle (pronounced goyle) until it reaches the sea at the English Channel between Hobarrow Bay and Kimmeridge Bay. In the Dorset dialect a *gwyle* is a 'wooded valley with a stream'.

EGLISTON GWYLE

Eggelin – Germanic personal name
Old English:
tun – a farm or estate
Dorset dialect:
gwyle – a wooded valley with a stream
'a wooded valley with a stream owned by a man named Eggelin'

Broad Bench

The sea has been gradually eroding a band of limestone (dolomite) in the cliffs of the headland over thousands of years until it has formed a platform known as Broad Bench.

KIMMERIDGE STREAM

Kimmeridge Stream flows from springs around Kimmeridge village to the beach in Kimmeridge Bay. It is about 1.2km (0.75 miles) in length.

In the Domesday Book of 1086, Kimmeridge village was named Cameric after a wealthy man named Cyme. The Old English word ric means a rich ruler.

Nodding donkey

Oil has been drilled from above Kimmeridge Bay since 1961, with the help of a 'nodding donkey' *(below)*. The original daily yield of 350 barrels has reduced to about 60 barrels. The oil is taken by tanker to Wytch Farm oil processing plant on the edge of Poole Harbour. From there, it is piped underwater to storage tanks near Southampton before being taken to Fawley for further refining.

Marine wildlife reserve

Kimmeridge Bay is a popular area for scuba divers and snorkellers. The waters in the bay have a plethora of marine plants and creatures and is designated a marine wildlife reserve.

Kimmeridge Bay

KIMMERIDGE NEW BARN STREAM

Kimmeridge New Barn Stream rises in the Smedmore hills and enters the sea at the eastern end of Kimmeridge Bay. It is about 2km (1.2 miles) in length.

Smedmore House
Smedmore House was a school before being used by the US Army for D-Day preparations during the Second World War. Today, owner Sir Philip Mansell lives in the house, which can be hired for holidays and events.

A 'War Room' displays letters and other memorabilia belonging to sisters Marcia and Juliet Mansell, who served as nurses on the Western Front during the First World War.

Wedding celebrations
On a personal note, my son Ian and his lovely wife Pamela held their wedding reception at Smedmore House in September 2018. Family and friends had a happy time together preparing the wedding breakfast in the huge kitchen and celebrating in a marquee on the front lawn. What a wonderful experience staying in this Georgian house with beautiful grounds.

Clavell's Tower
Rev John Clavell-Richards (1759-1833) built a folly, Clavell's Tower *(above)*, on cliffs overlooking Kimmeridge Bay. The tower was moved in 2008 to prevent it being lost to the sea because of landslides. It is now owned by the Landmark Trust and can be booked for holidays.

ENCOMBE VALLEY STREAM
The stream that passes through Encombe Valley flows from two lakes in the grounds of Encombe House.

It travels to the sea through South Gwyle and cascades over the cliff at Egmont Bight.

EGMONT BIGHT
Old English:
biht – a corner, angle or bay
Probably *'a bay owned by a man named Egmont'*

Chapman's Pool

Emmetts Hill Memorial

Mouth of Chapman's Pool Stream as it enters the cove

The village pond at Worth Matravers

CHAPMAN'S POOL STREAM (THE LAKE)

The stream rises in North Hill near Renscombe Farm and travels southward to Chapman's Pool. In 948 it was recorded in Anglo Saxon as schort mannes pol – *sceort* meaning 'short', *gemana* is 'common property' and *pol* means 'pool'. Chapman's Pool, therefore, is a 'small pool used by the community'.

Lifeboat decommissioned
The cove has been created over thousands of years by the sea washing away the shale and limestone of the cliffs to make a horseshoe-shaped bay, very similar to Lulworth Cove.

A lifeboat station was built on the beach in 1867. However, the station closed only 13 years later because of maintenance costs and landslides from the cliffs above. Today the boathouse is used as a fisherman's hut.

Emmetts Hill Memorial
A memorial dedicated to Royal Marines who lost their lives between the end of the Second World War and 1990 lies along the South West Coast Path towards St Aldhelm's Head. A service is held at the memorial each year on 19th August.

The inscription invites us to: 'Rest awhile and reflect that we who are living can enjoy the beauty of the sea and countryside.'

SEACOMBE VALLEY STREAM AND WINSPIT VALLEY STREAM

Both streams rise in the hills around Worth Matravers. They flow southwards towards the sea where there are disused quarries. Both streams disappear underground before reaching the shore.

Worth Matravers means 'an enclosure owned by a family named Matravers'

Benjamin and Elizabeth Jesty's graves

Medical breakthrough
Benjamin and Elizabeth Jesty are buried in St Nicholas churchyard. Benjamin discovered cowpox could inoculate against the virulent disease smallpox (for more information see Yetminster, River Yeo).

The inscriptions on the gravestones read: *Sacred to the Memory of Benj:m Jesty of (Downshay) who departed this life April 16th 1869… Particularly noted for being the first person (known) that introduced Cow Pox by inoculation and who from his great strength of mind made the experiment from the (cow) on his wife and two sons in the year 1774. Sacred to the Memory of Elizabeth Jesty… who departed this life January 8th 1824 aged 84 years. 'This time we have allotted here We highly ought to prize And strive to make salvation sure Ere death doth close our eyes.'*

Winspit. Reproduced by kind permission of Ian Paterson

Winspit Quarry

This disused quarry provided Purbeck limestone for many buildings in the area and as far away as London. It was quarried from the cliff in caves and tunnels. Some of them can still be explored by the public while others are closed for safety reasons and to preserve colonies of mouse-eared and greater horseshoe bats.

William Bower, known as 'Billy Winspit', lived in Winspit Cottage and worked the quarry for as long as he was physically able. He died in 1966 aged 80. Winspit means 'a pit (or quarry) with a winch installed'.

Ancient chapel's beacon for shipping

St Aldhelm's Head lies between Winspit and Chapman's Pool. The tiny St Aldhelm's chapel has been standing on the headland since the 12th century. The cross on the roof was originally a fire brazier used as a beacon to mark the headland for ships.

ULWELL STREAM

This small stream rises in springs near Ulwell Village and enters the sea in Swanage Bay.

The Old English word *ule* means 'owl', so this was originally 'a spring where owls live'.

STUDLAND STREAM

Studland Stream drains into Studland Bay. Studland means an area of land with a herd of horses, from Old English word *stod*.

Old Harry

At Handfast Point, tall chalk stacks, known as Old Harry Rocks, have been separated from the mainland by erosion from the sea. The name is possibly taken from notorious Poole smuggler Harry Paye.

Fort Henry

Studland beaches feature several Second World War defences, including Fort Henry. The fort is a concrete lookout bunker from where King George VI, Sir Winston Churchill, General Eisenhower, Field Marshall Montgomery and Admiral Mountbatten watched the D-Day rehearsals in Studland Bay in 1944.

Good news for seahorses thanks to coronavirus lockdown!

There was a thriving seahorse breeding ground amid the seagrass in Studland Bay. Alas, The Seahorse Trust and Dorset Wildlife Trust reported that the anchors of small boats had all but destroyed their specialised seagrass habitat.

However, there's good news thanks to the

Old Harry Rocks viewed from Studland. A cruise ship lies anchored during the coronavirus pandemic

coronavirus lockdown! Seahorse Trust founder Neil Garrick-Maidment says the numbers are beginning to increase. During a single dive he spotted 16 seahorses, including pregnant males and two babies.

GODLINGSTON STREAM

Godlingston Stream drains Godlingston Heath into Brand's Bay at Mead Point. *Godelin* **is an Anglo Saxon personal name while** *tun* **means 'farm or estate', so this was 'a farm or estate owned by a man named Godelin'.**

There are numerous streams on the various heathlands that lie south of Poole Harbour.

Fort Henry and a view of the bay through the observation slits that the war leaders would have seen – but with warships and troops, not paddle boards and sunbathers!

79

DERIVATION OF THE NAMES OF HEATHS, VILLAGES AND TOWNS

Grange Arch

STOBOROUGH
1086 (Domesday Book) Stanberge
Old English:
stan – stony
beorg – a hill or barrow
'a settlement with a stony hill or barrow'
A barrow is an ancient burial mound.

CREECH BARROW
1086 (Domesday Book) Cric and Crist
1224 Crich
Celtic:
crug – a hill or mound
Old English:
beorg – a hill or barrow
'a hill used for burial'

Twin peaks?
At the summit of Creech Barrow, the highest point of the Purbeck heathlands, there is a Bronze Age round barrow, which gives the impression the hill has two summits. The hill gives its name to Creech Heath, Creech Grange and the villages of West Creech and East Creech.

Creech Grange in Steeple
Sir Oliver Lawrence, an ancestor of first American president George Washington, built Creech Grange in the 16th century. The estate was bought in the 17th century by Nathaniel Bond, who was related to the family that developed Bond Street in London.

In 1746 Denis Bond built the Grange Arch as a folly on Ridgeway Hill overlooking the house and gardens and enjoying magnificent views across the fields to the sea.

Norden Station

Norden Station ticket office

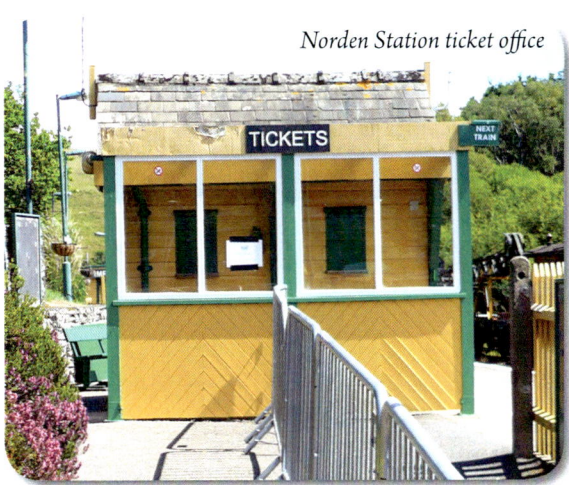

MIDDLEBERE
1291 Middlebere
Old English:
middle – middle
bearu – a wood
'middle wood'

SLEPE
1244 Slepe
Old English:
slaep – slippery
'a slippery place'

RIDGE
1431 Rygge
Old English:
hrycg – a ridge, long narrow hill or bank
'a settlement near a river bank (of the River Frome)'

NORDEN
1291 Northdon
Old English:
north – north
dun – a hill
'a settlement on or near a north hill'

Steam power
Dedicated volunteers and full-time staff have lovingly restored the heritage railway line from Swanage. Steam trains travel from Swanage to Norden Station. The track has been extended to Wareham, where it will eventually connect with mainline trains to Weymouth and London.

REMPSTONE
1280 Rameston
Old English:
hramsa – garlic
tun – a farm or estate
'a farm or estate where garlic grows'
or possibly **Old English:**
hring – a ring
stun – stone
'a ring of stones' relating to the Bronze Age stone circle

OWER
934 Ore
1316 Oure
Old English:
ora – a border or edge
'a place on the edge of the harbour'

Chapter 18

CORFE RIVER

East and West Corfe rivers flow northward, uniting to form the Corfe River just north of Corfe Castle.

West Corfe River is also known as the Wicken Stream or Steeple Brook.

East Corfe River is also called Byle Brook.

Both rivers resemble streams today. Over several thousands of years they have carved gaps in the ridge of hills either side of the castle, forming the prominent Castle Hill, on which Corfe Castle was built.

Corfe River was once known as the River Wych, taken from the wych elm trees growing in the area. The name Corfe comes from the Anglo Saxon word *corf*, meaning 'cutting' or 'pass'.

The castle was built in Saxon times and extended by William the Conqueror after 1066.

Schematic diagram of the flow and confluence of East and West Corfe rivers

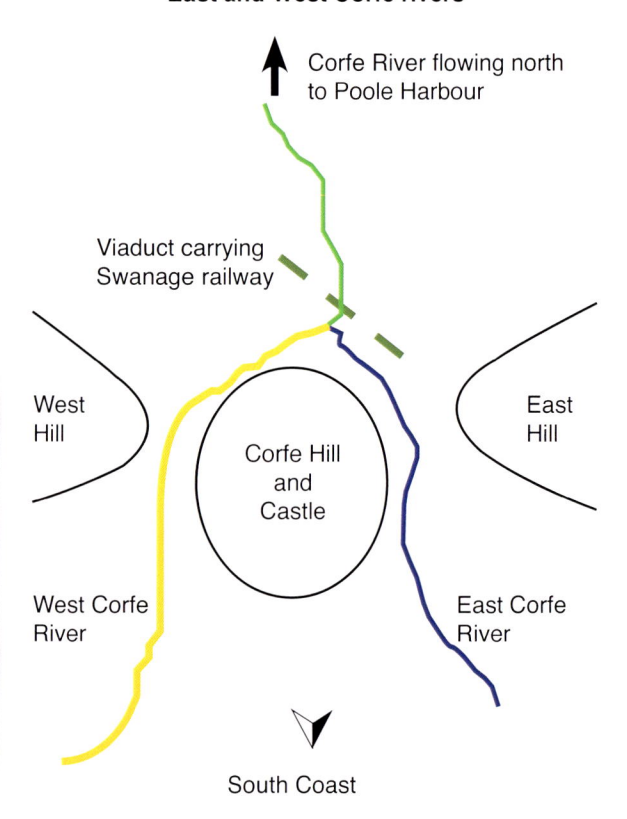

AT A GLANCE

SOURCE
Many springs in the chalk hills south of Corfe village

MOUTH / OUTLET
Wych Lake in Poole Harbour

LENGTH
Approximately 3km (2 miles) after the East and West rivers converge

Isle of Purbeck – Corfe River

East Corfe River (Byle Brook) viewed from the road entering Corfe Castle village

VILLAGES AND TOWNS AND THE ORIGINS OF THEIR NAMES
(from source to mouth of the river)

WEST CORFE RIVER

NORTH EGLISTON
1202 Egelineston
Egglin – personal name, probably Germanic
Old English:
tun – a farm or estate
'a farm or estate owned by a man named Egglin'

LUTTON
1288 Lutteton
Old English:
Lutta – personal name
tun – a farm or estate
'a farm or estate owned by a man named Lutta'

Lutton Gwyle is an area of woodland near the village to the north. In the Dorset dialect, *gwyle* is the word for a 'wooded stream valley'. Towards the Purbeck coast, Egliston Gwyle and Tyneham Gwyle use the same name.

STEEPLE
1086 (Domesday Book) Stiple
1222 Stepel
Old English:
stiepel – steep or tower
'a settlement on a steep slope'

Stars and stripes
Two wealthy families in Lancashire inter-married in 1390 when Edmund Lawrence wed Agnes de Wessington. Their family crests became united, with the crusader cross of the Lawrence family quartered with the mullets and bars (stars and stripes) of the Wessingtons. The Lawrence-Wessington family coat of arms can be seen in St Michael and All Angels church in Steeple.

Sir Oliver Lawrence moved from Lancashire to Steeple in 1540, and in 1559 he built Creech Grange, which became the family's country seat.

One of Agnes' descendants, John, emigrated to America and settled in Virginia. His great-grandson, George Washington, became the first president of the United States of America. His signet ring bore the Lawrence-Wessington coat of arms – the flag of the US capital, Washington DC, was designed from that ring.

A Washington DC flag was presented to the villagers of Steeple in 1977 by Walter Washington, mayor of Washington DC, and hangs in the church.

West Corfe River at the foot of Castle Hill

Bond Street connection
Nathaniel Bond gave a barrel organ to the church in Tyneham in the 19th century. It was moved to Steeple when Tyneham was evacuated in 1943 for military training. Several members of the Bond family were vicars at Steeple. Nathaniel Bond is from the same family that developed Bond Street in Mayfair on boggy fields near the River Tyburn, London.

BRADLE FARM
1086 (Domesday Book) Bradelage
Old English:
brad – broad
leah – a wood or clearing in a wood
'a wide clearing in a wood'

CHURCH KNOWLE
1086 (Domesday Book) Cnolle, Chenolle
1346 Churchecnolle
Old English:
cnoll – a hilltop
cirice – a church
'church on top of a hill'

Margaret Green Animal Rescue Centre
This charitable centre was founded in 1968 to care for homeless pets. Our granddaughter loved stroking the donkeys but was startled by the appearance of a pony with only one eye. We explained to her Dan the pony was just like granddad, who also has only one working eye. Her compassion held sway and, by the time we were ready to leave, she wanted to adopt Dan and take him home. Thank you Margaret Green for helping her understand outward appearances aren't always important.

KINGSTON
1086 (Domesday Book) Chingeston
1212 Kingeston
Old English:
cyning – belonging to a king
tun – a farm or estate
'the king's estate' or *'royal manor'*
(probably owned by King Eadred, who reigned from 946 until his death in 955. Kingston is mentioned in a Saxon charter dated 948)

A true-life love story
John Scott was born in Newcastle in 1751, the son of a coal merchant. He won a scholarship to University College Oxford and was awarded a fellowship. While still a young man he met and fell in love with Bessie Surtees, a banker's daughter. The parents of both John and Bessie opposed their wedding so, with the aid of a rope ladder, they eloped to Scotland. On their return they were reconciled to both families and John continued his law studies.

Later in life he became MP for Wembley (1783) and Lord Chancellor (1801). By 1821 he had become the 1st Earl of Eldon. In 1806, John Scott bought Encombe House, south of Kingston, where he and his beloved Bessie lived until she died in 1831. Many said John grieved for Bessie until his own death in 1837. They are buried together in the older church in Kingston, which is surprising as the Scotts built the newer church – a landmark when approaching Kingston from many directions.

The gap created over many centuries by East Corfe River (Byle Brook) and the heritage railway

EAST CORFE RIVER

HARMAN'S CROSS
Armons Cross
'crossroads or a crossing of paths on land owned by a man named Harmon'
(see Swanbrook River for more information)

WOOLGARSTON
1086 (Domesday Book) Orgarestone
1213 Wulgareston
Old English:
Wulfgar – personal name
tun – a farm or estate
'a farm or estate owned by a man named Wulfgar'

CORFE CASTLE
955 Corf
11th century Corfesgeat
1302 Corffe Castell
Old English:
corf – a cutting, gap or pass
geat – a gap
'a castle in a cutting or gap between hills'

Brave Dame Mary
Lady Mary Bankes earned her reputation as Brave Dame Mary when she defended Corfe Castle against two major sieges by Oliver Cromwell's Parliamentarian troops during the English Civil War. The second siege was in 1646 and lasted 48 days, only ending when one of her officers

Photograph above reproduced with kind permission of Kari Culver

opened the castle gates to Cromwell's men. The castle was subsequently blown up using gunpowder, leaving the remains we see today. Dame Mary was allowed to keep the keys to the ruined castle! Her estate was confiscated but was returned after the monarchy was restored in 1660.

Royal murder
Edward the Martyr succeeded his father, King Edgar, in 975. In 978 Elfreda (Aelfthryth), his ambitious stepmother, invited King Edward to the royal residence at Corfe Castle.

As Edward approached on horseback he was greeted by servants offering him wine. One of them grabbed his leg while another stabbed him in the chest. The horse bolted through the woods, dragging the dying Edward whose foot had become caught in a stirrup.

King Edward was buried without ceremony in Wareham's churchyard. Miracles were reported immediately after his death, including a blind woman regaining her sight. A freshwater spring appeared near his grave resulting in more stories of healing. A year after his death, Edward's body was moved to St Edward's Abbey in Shaftesbury. In 1008, King Edward the Martyr was canonised as a saint and pilgrims travelled from afar to venerate relics at his shrine.

Famous purchase
Enid Blyton, the well-known author of children's books, was a regular visitor to Dorset and the Purbeck Hills. Corfe Castle became Kirrin Castle in her Famous Five series of books.

In 1950 she and husband Kenneth Waters bought the Isle of Purbeck Golf Club (then called the Studland Bay Golf Club) for the princely sum of £1.00.

CORFE RIVER
(AFTER THE CONFLUENCE OF EAST AND WEST CORFE RIVERS)

WYTCH HEATH
12th century Wicha
Old English:
wice – supple or pliant
or a wych elm tree
'an area where wych elm trees grow'
The wych elm tree (ulmus glabra) grew in this area. Its wood has long been used for making boats, furniture, wheel hubs and coffins.

Black gold
Wytch Farm oil field is said to be the largest onshore oil field in west Europe and pumps oil through pipelines beneath Poole Harbour. The oil field is well camouflaged and screened by conifer trees. Oil from the 'nodding donkey' wells at Kimmeridge is processed at Wytch Farm.

In search of the confluence!
Ryan and I headed for the village of Corfe Castle to discover the confluence of East Corfe River and West Corfe River. Armed with an Ordnance Survey map and a camera, we crossed a field grazed by sheep we later identified as the ancient Herdwick breed,

Isle of Purbeck – Corfe River

Bankes Arms

originally from the Lake District.

We followed footpaths and streams but found no confluence.

After a welcome drink in the Bankes Arms we visited the village museum, which was once the smallest town hall in the country.

Still searching for the confluence, we left the village in the direction of Wareham. Crossing the road at the foot of Castle Hill we investigated the road bridge that passed over a stream. A viaduct towered above us carrying the steam trains from Swanage.

Success at last as we found the East and West rivers converging near the bridge, well hidden by shrubs and vegetation.

Chapter 19

SWANBROOK RIVER
(OR SWAN BROOK)

The Swanbrook River, also known as Swan Brook, is one of the shorter rivers in Dorset. It drains the chalk hills east of Corfe Castle and north of Langton Matravers flowing eastwards to the coastal town of Swanage.

Several tributaries drain the Swanbrook's catchment area. During heavy rainfall and high tides the land becomes saturated with water, creating the risk of flooding. There have been schemes to alleviate this threat to homes and businesses since Victorian times.

In the 19th century an underground culvert was built from St Mary's church to the seafront at Mowlem Theatre.

Two reservoirs and sluice gates were installed in the late 20th century to divert water from the town centre, while another underground channel was built. This culvert passes under Victoria Avenue and discharges into the sea at the end of Banjo Pier, specifically built for that purpose.

AT A GLANCE

SOURCE

Several springs feeding streams draining into the upper and middle reaches of the river, including:
- springs on Nine Barrow Down
- springs south of Woolgarston
- springs near the B3069 close to Putlake Adventure Farm and Leeson House

MOUTH / OUTLET
Swanage seafront

LENGTH
Approximately 6km (4 miles)

Underground culvert viewed from the seafront near Mowlem Theatre

Langton Matravers Dorset England
Dramatic cliff scenery at Dancing Ledge,
on Dorset's beautiful Jurassic Coast

VILLAGES AND TOWNS AND THE ORIGINS OF THEIR NAMES
(from source to mouth of the river)

WOOLGARSTON

1086 (Domesday Book) Orgarestone
1213 Wulgareston
Old English:
Wulfgar – personal name
tun – a farm or estate
'a farm or estate owned by a man named Wulfgar'

HARMAN'S CROSS

1840 Armon's Cross
Harman – personal name or surname
Cross – crossroads
'crossroads where a man named Harman lived'

There are various stories connected to the name of this village, including:
- A man by the name of Harman hanged himself from a tree close to the present site of the crossroads
- Harman was the only person living at the site of the crossroads
- Harman was hanged for a crime so horrendous he was buried outside the village in a place marked by a cross – Harman's cross

LANGTON MATRAVERS

1165 Langeton
1428 Langeton Mawtravers
Old English:
lang – long
tun – a farm or estate
13th century Mautravers – personal name
'a long farm or estate owned by a family named Mautravers'

Smuggler's stash
In the 19th century Charles Hayward was a respectable village postmaster, quarry manager and clerk of the parish for more than 30 years... he was also the local smuggler.

Hayward used the roof space of St George's church (re-built in 1829) to conceal casks of brandy. Unwisely he failed to realise the weight of the contraband was too heavy for the rafters. The side walls were pushed out of the perpendicular so the church had to be demolished and rebuilt.

Famous pupil
In 1915, Ian Fleming, author of the James Bond books, became a pupil at Durnford Preparatory School aged seven. He 'borrowed' names of wealthy Dorset families to use in his novels, for instance Drax in Moonraker.

Downstream Dorset – River Tales and Local History

Wellington Clock Tower

SWANAGE

9th century Swanawic
1086 (Domesday Book) Swanwic

Old English:

swan – a swan
or: swain – a herdsman or peasant
wic – a dwelling place
'a dwelling place with swans nearby'
or: *'a dwelling place for a herdsman'*

19th century recycling

In the 19th century John Mowlem owned a construction business in Swanage succeeded by his nephew, George Burt. Their company shipped Purbeck stone to London for use in the construction of many buildings. These ships returned to Swanage carrying unwanted building material as ballast, which was recycled to enhance buildings in their home town.

For example:

- The town hall in Swanage High Street – the façade was originally part of Sir Christopher Wren's Mercer House in Cheapside
- Purbeck House Hotel, also in the high street – some of the walls include fragments of coloured marble deemed surplus to requirements for the steps of the Albert Memorial in Kensington Gardens
- Wellington Clock Tower, on the seashore between the pier and Peverell Point – was originally on London Bridge erected in memory of the Duke of Wellington. It was removed when it was considered to be a traffic hazard only ten years after being built.
- A tiny, windowless gaol can be found behind the town hall in Swanage High Street. This lock-up was used to curb antisocial behaviour by people who had imbibed one too many at the local tavern!

The lamp-post to the side of the lock-up was originally in London.

Dancing Ledge

In 1898 Tom Pellatt, headmaster of Durnford Preparatory School in Langton Matravers, created a swimming pool for his pupils by having it blasted out of rock at the quarry. The sea would fill the pool and the boys could swim there safely.

POOLE HARBOUR

Following the rivers that flow into Poole Harbour

'Had I the shillings, pounds and pence
I'd pull up stakes and hie me hence,
I'd buy that small mixed farm in Dorset
Which has an inglenook and faucet –
Kiddles Farm, Piddletrenthide,
In the valley of the River Piddle'

Paradise for Sale by Ogden Nash

Chapter 20

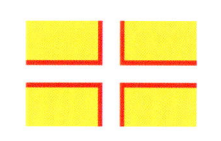

RIVER FROME

AT A GLANCE

TRIBUTARIES
IN THE UPPER REACHES INCLUDE:
- Wraxall Brook, confluences with the River Frome at Sandhills
- River Hooke, confluences with the River Frome near Maiden Newton
- Sydling Water, confluences with the River Frome near Grimstone
- River Cerne, confluences with the River Frome south of Charminster, near Wolfeton Manor

TRIBUTARIES
IN THE LOWER REACHES, SOUTH OF DORCHESTER, INCLUDE:
- River Win, confluences with the River Frome near East Burton
- South Winterborne River, confluences with the River Frome near West Stafford
- Tadnoll Brook, confluences with the River Frome near Broomhill Bridge
- Holy Stream, confluences with the River Frome downstream from Wool

The River Frome derives its name from the Old English word *fram* or *ffraw* meaning 'fine', 'fair' or 'brisk'. It was known to be a beautiful, briskly flowing river.

The Frome rises in Evershot, which is the second-highest village in Dorset. It travels through chalk downland, farmland, flood plains, water meadows and heathland. Further south it flows over sand, clay and gravel until it reaches the ancient town of Wareham.

The water meadows are created by an elaborate system of channels and sluice gates, irrigating the land from early spring onwards. The resulting increase in crops produces more winter fodder for cattle.

As the river approaches Dorchester it separates into smaller streams that reunite a couple of miles further south. On reaching its destination at Wareham, the River Frome joins the River Piddle and empties into Poole Harbour via the Wareham Channel.

The Frome Valley Trail, signposted by an arrowhead, begins in Evershot and ends in Dorchester, with plans to extend the route to Wareham. The arrowhead symbol reflects Bronze Age artefacts found in the valley.

Poole Harbour – River Frome

VILLAGES AND TOWNS AND THE ORIGINS OF THEIR NAMES
(from source to mouth of the river)

EVERSHOT
1286 Evershet
Old English:
eofor – wild boar
holt – a thicket
'a settlement near a thicket with wild boar'

The Acorn Inn
The Acorn Inn *(above)* in Fore Street is a 16th century coaching inn. It appears in Tess Of The D'Urbervilles by Thomas Hardy as The Sow and Acorn. We enjoyed a very tasty home-made Scotch egg as a lunchtime snack when we visited the inn.

CHANTMARLE
1288 Chauntemerle
Norman Chauntmerle – personal name
'land owned by a family named Chauntmerle'
Chauntmerle also means 'blackbird song'

Chantmarle Manor House
Grade I-listed Chantmarle Manor House was built in 1212 and owned by the monastery at Milton Abbey. It was rebuilt in 1612 by John Strode.

The property was bought by the Home Office in 1951 and converted into a training centre for Dorset Police. The Home Office sold the property in 1995 and it was renovated and converted into a private house. In 2002 it was sold again to become a Christian centre that can be hired for weddings and functions.

FROME ST QUINTIN
1086 (Domesday Book) Litelfrome
1288 Fromequintin
Old English:
litel – little
Quintin – personal name
'a small settlement on the River Frome owned by the St Quintin family'

CHALMINGTON
934 Chelmyntone
Old English:
Ceolhelm/Ceolmund – personal name
ing – associated with
tun – a farm or estate
'a farm or estate associated with or named after a man named Ceolhelm'

Fire at the manor house
In April 2020 a major fire broke out in the roof of Chalmington Manor *(below)*. Six fire crews attended, with water pumped from a nearby lake to quench the flames. No-one was in the property at the time and it was believed renovation work was the cause of the blaze.

SANDHILLS
13th century Sandhulle
Old English:
sand – sand
hyll – a hill
'a settlement with sandy hills'

CATTISTOCK
934 Cattesstoke
Old English:
Catt – personal name
or: catt – a cat
stoc – a second settlement
'a secondary settlement owned by a man named Catt'

Cattistock font cover

Knob throwing

Cattistock has hosted Dorset Knob-throwing festivals for several years. Dorset Knobs are savoury biscuits made by Moores Biscuits, a family-owned bakery founded in Dorset in 1880. Apart from the throwing competition other contests have included Knob Darts, Guess The Weight Of The Knob, Knob Putting and a Knob & Spoon Race. In 2012 the record for throwing a Dorset Knob was 29.4m (32 yards).

Font cover and funeral bier

St Peter and St Paul is said to be one of the finest examples of a Victorian church in Dorset. The cover of the font, designed by Temple Moore, is extraordinarily tall, reaching 6m (20ft). A Victorian funeral bier can also be seen, almost hidden between rows of pews.

FROME

1086 (Domesday Book) Frome
1206 Childefrome
Old English:
cild – a young nobleman
'a manor or estate on the River Frome owned by three young noblemen'
(according to the records in the Domesday Book)

MAIDEN NEWTON

1086 (Domesday Book) Newetone
1288 Maydene Newetone
Old English:
maegden – maidens
niwe – new
tun – a farm or estate
'a new farm owned by maidens (or possibly nuns)'
(See also chapter on the River Hooke)

FROME VAUCHURCH

1297 Frome Vaghechurche
Old English:
fah – coloured or decorated
or: **Old French:**
vag – a valley
Old English:
cirice – a church building
'a settlement on the River Frome with a decorative church'
or: *'a settlement on the River Frome with a church standing in the valley'*

CRUXTON

1178 Froma Johannis Croc
1195 Crocston
Old English:
Johannis Croc – personal name
tun – a farm or estate
'a farm or estate owned by a man named Johannis Croc'

Sandway Bridge, also known as the White Bridge, in Frampton

FRAMPTON
1086 (Domesday Book) Frantone
1188 Fromton
Old English:
tun – a farm or estate
'a farm or estate on the River Frome'

Blot on the landscape
In 1840 the Sheridan family, who owned Frampton estate, removed all the cottages on one side of the main street to improve the landscape of Frampton Park, which no longer exists.

SOUTHOVER
1670 Southover
Old English:
suth – south
ofer – a river bank
'a settlement on the south bank (of the River Frome)'

GRIMSTONE
1212 Grimeston
Danish (Viking):
Grim – personal name
Old English:
tun – a farm or estate
'a farm or estate owned by a man named Grim'

MUCKLEFORD
1244 Mukelford
Old English:
Mucela – personal name
ford – a ford
'a settlement with a ford (across the River Frome) owned by a man named Mucela'

STRATTON
1212 Stratton
Old English:
straet – road
tun – a farm or estate
'a farm or estate on a (Roman) road'
(the Roman road between Ilchester and Dorchester)

BRADFORD PEVERELL
1086 (Domesday Book) Bradeford
1244 Bradeford Peuerel
Old English:
brad – broad
ford – a ford
Peuerel – Robert Peverell
'a settlement by a wide ford owned by Robert Peverell'

Looking towards the site of the Roman aqueduct

Poundbury skyline viewed from Maiden Castle car park across harvested fields

Roman aqueduct
The remains of a Roman feat of engineering can be seen in Bradford Peverell and from the A35 Dorchester bypass. An aqueduct, about 9km (5.6 miles) long, stretched from Frampton to Dorchester delivering 60 million litres (13 million gallons) per day!

CHARMINSTER
1086 (Domesday Book) Cerminstre
(see also River Cerne)
Old English:
mynster – a church
Cerne – name taken from the River Cerne
'a settlement with a church near the River Cerne'

BURTON
1204 Burton
Old English:
burh – a fortified place
tun – a farm or estate
'a fortified farm or estate'

POUNDBURY CAMP
1333 Ponebury
Old English:
Puna – personal name
burh – a fortified place
'a fortified place (hill fort) associated with a man named Puna'

Poundbury Camp
Poundbury Camp lies to the south of the River Frome and north west of Dorchester. Dating to the Neolithic period it incorporates an Iron Age hill fort and sections of the Roman aqueduct that supplied Dorchester (Durnovaria) with fresh water. Poundbury Camp covers about six hectares (15 acres) with archaeological evidence of a large Romano-British cemetery just outside the fort.

Royal creation
Poundbury is an 'urban village', an extension of Dorchester town and the creation of HRH Prince Charles. He employed prize-winning architect Leon Krier to create a combination of traditional architecture and modern town planning for a community of people living and working together.

Maumbury Rings amphitheatre

DORCHESTER
Roman Durnovaria
864 Dornwarasceaster
1086 (Domesday Book) Dorecestre.
Old Celtic (Latinised):
Dornovaria – possibly a place with fist-sized pebbles
Old English:
ceaster – Roman fortified town
'a fortified town with stones the size of a man's fist'

Maumbury Rings amphitheatre
The Neolithic Maumbury Rings in the centre of Dorchester date to 2,500BC. During the 1st century AD, the Romans developed the earthworks to create an amphitheatre seating about 10,000 spectators.

In 1642, during the English Civil War, the rings were used as an artillery fort to defend the town from attack by Royalists.

Swimming near Grey's Bridge
Grey's Bridge, built in the mid 18th century, straddles the River Frome as part of London Road (B3150) between Dorchester and Stinsford. It is a stone bridge with three arches and is Grade II-listed.

There is an abandoned outdoor swimming pool not far from the bridge that was enjoyed by families in the 1930s but gradually became silted up and used by grazing cattle. According to a former swimmer who wrote to the Dorset Echo, there was an outbreak of polio in the area that was attributed to cattle.

A fund was launched to pay for a swimming pool in the town and, although land was donated, the project was never realised, probably because the Second World War intervened. Money that had been collected was later used to fund the sports centre and swimming pool at Thomas Hardye School.

STINSFORD
1086 (Domesday Book) Stincteford
1244 Stintesford
Old English:
stint – a sandpiper or dunlin
ford – a ford
'a settlement with a ford (crossing the River Frome) where sandpipers or dunlins can be seen'

Thomas Hardy's heart – and a cat's tale
Thomas Hardy wanted to be buried in Stinsford but his second wife, Florence, was approached with a request to bury him in Poet's Corner, Westminster Abbey. Florence suggested a

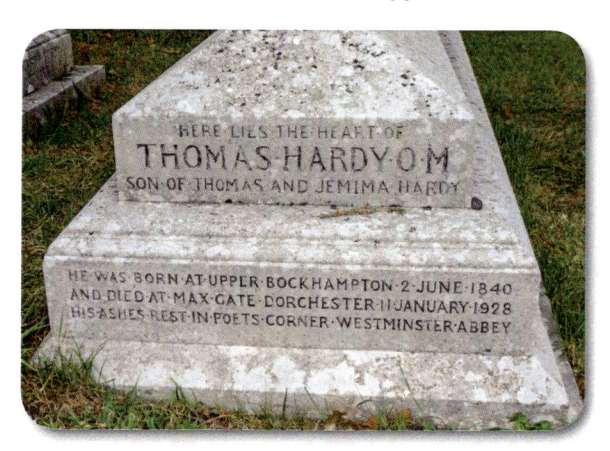

compromise – his heart would be interred at St Michael's Church in Stinsford and his ashes in Westminster Abbey.

There is a story that the doctor was interrupted while removing Hardy's heart and his cat decided to make a meal of it. Consequently, the cat was buried along with the remains of Hardy's heart. However, the National Trust guide at Hardy's Cottage was far from convinced!

The grave nearby

Cecil Day-Lewis (1904-1972), poet laureate and author, greatly admired Thomas Hardy and asked to be buried as close as possible to Hardy's grave.

The epitaph on his gravestone is an extract from his poem Is It Far To Go?:

Shall I be gone long?
For ever and a day.
To whom there belong?
Ask the stone to say.
Ask my song.

His wife's gravestone also has an inscription:
Says the heart to the mind
'Believe me'
Said the shadow to the sun
'Don't leave me'

HIGHER BOCKHAMPTON

1086 (Domesday Book) Bochehamtone

LOWER BOCKHAMPTON

Old English:
boc – a beech tree
ham – a homestead
tun – a farm or estate
'a farm or estate owned by people who had a homestead near beech trees'

Hardy's Cottage

Hardy's Cottage *(above)*, owned by the National Trust, is where Thomas Hardy grew up with his siblings, Henry, Kate and Mary. He lived there until he was 34 and wrote his first novels in his bedroom, which is where his granny used to sleep during his childhood.

KINGSTON MAURWARD

1244 Kingeston
1280 Kyngeston Marlevard

Old English:
cyning – a king
tun – a farm or estate
Mauregard – a personal name
'the king's estate held by the Mauregard family'
(Geoffrey Mauregard 1247)

Kingston Maurward House
Kingston Maurward House was built in 1720, used as a fuel depot in preparation for the D-Day landings in the Second World War, and today is an agricultural college hosting more than 850 students and apprentices. The college undertakes important conservation work with the Rare Breeds Survival Trust. The beautiful gardens are open to the public with an animal park where you can feed sheep, alpacas and chickens.

Singer Motors
George Singer, founder of Singer Motors, was born at Kingston Maurward in 1847.

WEST STAFFORD

1086 (Domesday Book) Stanford
1285 West Stafford

Old English:
stan – stony
ford – a ford
'a settlement with a stony ford'
(There was once an East Stafford near West Knighton)

Stafford House
Stafford House has been sensitively renovated by Lord and Lady Fellowes. Lord Julian Fellowes, historian, author and actor, wrote the highly acclaimed book and television series Downton Abbey. Lady Emma Kitchener-Fellowes is a screenwriter and lady-in-waiting to Princess

Stafford House hosting the village fete

Michael of Kent. Stafford House is one of the finest examples of Stuart architecture in the country and was built in 1633 by Dorset merchant John Gould.

A mantelpiece was fitted in the early 20th century by Henry Hardy, master builder and brother of Thomas Hardy, the novelist and architect. Mr Hounsell, the local stonemason, supplied the stone. According to Henry Hardy's records of transactions, Mr Hounsell later provided the stone for the grave of Thomas Hardy in Stinsford churchyard. Mr Hounsell's descendants live in the village to this day.

Celebrating village life

A few years ago we attended the summer fete in the grounds of Stafford House. It was a beautiful summer's day and the whole village and their friends were there. Lord and Lady Fellowes joined in with enthusiasm, spending time with visitors and judging the dog show. Their own dog didn't seem to mind sharing his garden with other dogs.

There were birds of prey, morris dancing, cake stalls, pony rides and vintage cars. The freshly cooked burgers were well worth the queue. It was a very enjoyable day out and so good to see village life being celebrated.

WOODSFORD

1280 Wyrdesford
Old English:
Weard – personal name
ford – a ford
'a ford (crossing the River Frome) owned by a man named Weard'

Woodsford Castle

Woodsford Castle *(above)* is one of the few remaining examples of a 14th century fortified manor house. Guy de Brian owned the manor from 1367 and was granted permission to add crenellations to the house. Crenellations are extra fortifications with arrow slits.

In 1660 the huge roof was thatched, buildings were demolished and the main house became home to a succession of gentleman farmers.

In 1850 the house was restored by master builder Thomas Hardy, father to Thomas Hardy, Dorset architect, poet and novelist.

In 1977 Woodsford Castle was bought by The Landmark Trust, which restores historic buildings and lets them to holidaymakers.

MORETON

1086 (Domesday Book) Mortune
1195 Moreton

Old English:
mor – a marsh
tun – a farm or estate
'a farm or estate on marshland'

Lawrence of Arabia
After the First World War, TE Lawrence (Lawrence of Arabia) lived near Moreton at Clouds Hill, now owned by the National Trust. Lawrence enlisted as a private in the Tank Corps at Bovington under the name TE Ross, hoping for anonymity. Lawrence died in a motorbike accident in 1935 and is buried in the graveyard near St Nicholas Church.

Beautifully restored church windows
Many people visit St Nicholas Church to gaze on its world-renowned engraved windows *(above)*, created by Laurence Whistler. The original stained-glass windows were destroyed by a German bomber in the Second World War. The engraved glass gives the church light and beauty. I would recommend a visit to experience this work of art and craftsmanship.

EAST BURTON

1212 Bureton
(East and West, Long)
1280 Estburton, Westburton
1460 Langebourton

Old English:
burh – fortified
tun – a farm or estate
'a fortified farm or estate'

WOOL
1086 (Domesday Book) Wille, Welle
1249 Woll
Old English:
wella – a spring
'a settlement by a spring'

EAST STOKE
1086 (Domesday Book) Stoches
1316 Estok
Old English:
stoc – secondary settlement
'a secondary settlement'
East could refer to being situated to the east of Bindon Abbey, now in ruins but once a Cistercian monastery founded in the 12th century.

EAST HOLME
1086 (Domesday Book) Holne

WEST HOLME
1288 Estholn, Westholn

HOLME BRIDGE
1530 Holmebrygge
Old English:
holegn – a holly tree
brygge – a bridge
'a settlement by the holly tree (with a bridge over the River Frome)'

A brave stand
On 27th February 1644, during the English Civil War, Sir Anthony Ashley Cooper and Parliamentarian soldiers from Poole attacked the Royalist town of Wareham.

On Holme Bridge, 45 Royalist men held back 300 Roundheads for more than five hours. Eventually, however, the garrison at Wareham was forced to surrender.

Sir Anthony was created 1st Earl of Shaftesbury in 1672 after the restoration of the monarchy. He had been one of 12 commissioners sent by the House of Commons to Holland to invite Charles II to return to the throne.

The new and old Holme Bridge on the B3070 from Lulworth

Wareham Quay

STOBOROUGH
1086 (Domesday Book) Stanberge
1253 Stabergh
Old English:
stan – stone
beorg – a hill or barrow
'a settlement with a stony hill or barrow'

WAREHAM
9th century Werham
1086 (Domesday Book) Warham
Old English:
wer or waer – a weir
ham – a homestead
'a homestead by a weir (on the River Frome)'

Medieval tax and 'community service'
In the Middle Ages, any tradesman or craftsman not born or apprenticed in Wareham had to pay 3s 4d (17p) for permission to open their shop windows.

All inhabitants of Wareham were required to maintain the quay by "carrying away dirt, stones and rubbish".

Defence against Vikings
The Vikings made frequent use of the River Frome to raid and plunder. In 876 AD, during the reign of Alfred the Great, the residents of Wareham built strong walls to defend their town. The walls protected three sides of the town, the fourth side being the river. These walls are now grassy mounds that create a delightful walk offering views of the rivers Frome and Piddle.

Poole Harbour – River Frome

Surrounded by trees, a footbridge crosses part of the River Frome called the Broad, near Moreton

Downstream Dorset – River Tales and Local History

Chapter 21

Wraxall Brook

AT A GLANCE

SOURCE
Several tributaries flowing from the chalk hills of the Dorset Downs

MOUTH / OUTLET
Confluences with the River Frome near Sandhills

LENGTH
Approximately 8km (5 miles)

Wraxall Brook, a chalk stream tributary of the River Frome, rises in the Dorset Downs and joins the Frome from the west at Sandhills.

A narrow track winds between hedgerows down to Frome St Quintin parish church, below Rampisham Down radio transmitter station on the rolling landscape of England's Dorset Downs

110

Poole Harbour – Wraxall Brook

VILLAGES AND TOWNS AND THE ORIGINS OF THEIR NAMES
(from source to mouth of the river)

A sign warns drivers they are approaching Wraxall Brook ford from the direction of Rampisham

RAMPISHAM
1086 (Domesday Book) Ramesham
Old English:
ramm – a ram
or: Ramm – personal name
or: hramsa – wild garlic
hamm – a water meadow or enclosure
'a water meadow or enclosure where wild garlic grows'
or: *'a water meadow or enclosure grazed by a group of rams'*
or: *'a water meadow or enclosure owned by a man named Ramm'*

Roman artefact
A decorative Roman pavement measuring about 4m x 3m was uncovered in 1799 just north of St Michael's and All Angels church but was removed by treasure hunters.

WRAXALL
HIGHER AND LOWER
1086 (Domesday Book) Wrocheshale
Old English:
wrocc – a buzzard or bird of prey
holh – a hollow
'a settlement in a hollow where buzzards and other birds of prey fly'

SANDHILLS
13th century Sandhulle
Old English:
sand – sand
hyll – a hill
'a settlement surrounded by or built on sandhills'

111

Chapter 22

RIVER HOOKE

AT A GLANCE

SOURCE
Springs near Toller Whelme

MOUTH / OUTLET
Confluences with the River Frome near Maiden Newton

LENGTH
Approximately 10km (6 miles)

TRIBUTARIES
Toller Brook and small streams from surrounding hills

The River Hooke is a tributary of the River Frome. Its former name was the River Toller. Hooke is the Anglo Saxon word for 'sharp bend' or 'angle'. Toller is Anglo Saxon for a 'stream in a valley'.

A stone-carved lion holding a shield bearing the Tudor coat of arms

VILLAGES AND TOWNS AND THE ORIGINS OF THEIR NAMES
(from source to its confluence with the River) Frome

TOLLER WHELME
1035 Tollor aewylman
1268 Tolre Euulme
Old English:
aewielm – a river spring
'a settlement near the source of the River Toller'

HOOKE
1086 (Domesday Book) Lahoc
1209 Hoc
Old English:
hoc – angle
'a settlement near a bend in the river'

Hooke Park
Hooke Park, which lies between Hooke and Beaminster, offers 150 hectares (350 acres) of ancient woodland. Students on the Architectural Association's Design and Make course work with timber from the conifers and broad-leaved trees in on-site workshops.

LOWER AND HIGHER KINGCOMBE
1086 (Domesday Book) Chimedecome
1212 Kendecumb
Old English:
cymed – germander (a plant of the mint family)
cumb – a valley
'a settlement in a valley where germander grows'

TOLLER PORCORUM AND TOLLER FRATRUM
1086 (Domesday Book) Tolre
1340 Tolre Porcorum and Swyne Tolre
1340 Tolre Fratrum
Old Celtic:
tolre – a stream flowing through a valley
Latin:
porcorum – of the pigs
fratrum – of the brothers/brethren
Old English:
swyne – pigs
'a settlement named after the River Toller (now the River Hooke) with a herd of swine/pigs'
and: *'a settlement named after the River Toller (now the River Hooke) owned by the brethren of the Knights Hospitaller'*

Knights Hospitaller
Fratrum, Latin for 'of the brothers', refers to the Knights Hospitaller (The Order of Knights of the Hospital of St John of Jerusalem) who owned the manor from the late 12th century until the dissolution of the monasteries in 1536 during the reign of Henry VIII.

Little Toller Farm fire
Little Toller Farm was built in the mid-16th century. A stone-carved monkey holding a mirror stood between barley-twist chimney stacks.

Above the 19th century porch sits a lion holding a shield that bears the royal Tudor coat of arms. To the east of the courtyard is a thatched barn, which a villager told me was originally the refectory of the Knights Hospitaller.

Sadly the farmhouse and barn almost burned down in 2015, possibly due to unattended

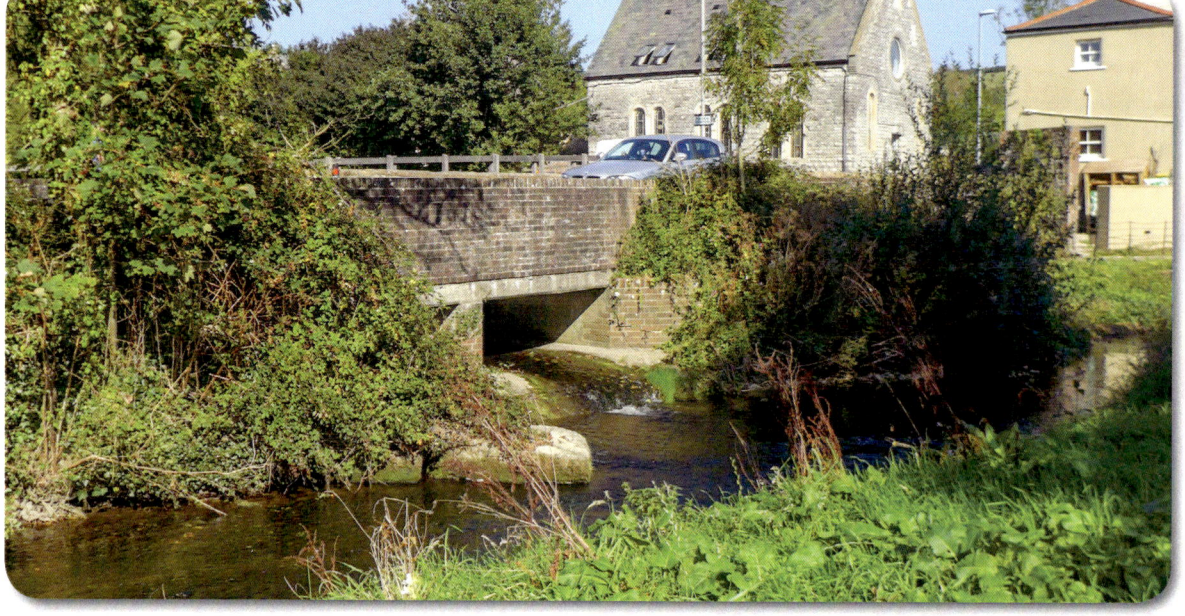

Confluence of the River Hooke with the River Frome

candles in a bedroom. The monkey can no longer be seen but the lion is still in place.

Black Death
Over four days in November 1348, seven priests in parishes between Toller Porcorum and East Morden died of bubonic plague, demonstrating the selfless dedication of the priests and the devastation caused by the 'Black Death' running rampant through the country.

Toller Duckorum
Approaching Toller Porcorum, where the road passes over the River Hooke, there is a noticeable warning *(below left)* to motorists travelling too fast for others' safety. A touch of Toller humour makes the message very effective.

TOLLERFORD
1086 (Domesday Book) Tolreforde
Old Celtic:
tolre – a stream flowing through a valley
Old English:
forde – a ford
'a settlement with a ford crossing a stream in a valley'

MAIDEN NEWTON
1086 (Domesday Book) Newetone
1288 Maydene Newetone
Old English:
maegden – maidens
niwe – new
tun – a farm or estate
'a new farm or estate owned by maidens (or possibly nuns)'

Poole Harbour – River Hooke

An old dark stone bridge across the river Frome in Maiden Newton

Chapter 23

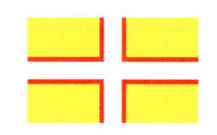

SYDLING WATER

AT A GLANCE

SOURCE
Springs in the hills around Up Sydling

MOUTH / OUTLET
Confluences with the River Frome near Grimstone

LENGTH
Approximately 8km (5 miles)

Sydling Water is a chalk stream tributary of the River Frome that flows parallel with the River Cerne. It travels southwards, fording the road from Maiden Newton to Cerne Abbas just north of Sydling St Nicholas until it reaches Grimstone. There it flows beneath the viaduct to its confluence with the River Frome.

Watercress beds flourish in the clear waters of the chalk stream with trout, heron and egret feeding and nesting along its course.

Ford and footbridge north of Sydling St Nicholas

VILLAGES AND TOWNS AND THE ORIGINS OF THEIR NAMES
(from source to mouth of the river)

UP SYDLING
1230 Upsidelinch
Old English:
sid – a ledge
hlinc – a ridge
up – upper
'a settlement on a ridge or ledge higher up the river from Sydling St Nicholas'

SYDLING ST NICHOLAS
1086 (Domesday Book) Sidelince
1288 Brodesideling
Old English:
sid – a ledge
hlinc – a ridge
brode – broad
'a settlement on a broad ledge or ridge with a church dedicated to St Nicholas'

Sir Francis Walsingham
During the reign of Queen Elizabeth l, the manor was leased to Sir Francis Walsingham, her favourite courtier and principal secretary. Walsingham is sometimes referred to as the queen's spymaster because of his use of codes and secret agents against England's enemies.

Miller Spriggs
Robert Spriggs, the last miller to work and live in Sydling St Nicholas, died in 1919. His grave and that of his wife, Louisa, features one of his millstones as a headstone.

Robert Spriggs' headstone

Sydling St Nicholas Church

MAGISTON
1330 Magereston
Old English:
Malger – personal name
tun – a farm or estate
'a farm or estate owned by a family named Malger'

GRIMSTONE
1212 Grimeston
Danish (Viking) Grim – personal name
Old English:
tun – a farm or estate
'a farm or estate owned by a man named Grim'

Chapter 24

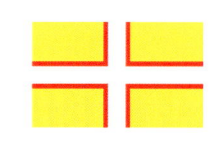

RIVER CERNE

AT A GLANCE

SOURCE
Springs to the north of Minterne Magna

MOUTH / OUTLET
Confluences with the River Frome south of Charminster, near Wolfeton Manor

LENGTH
Approximately 13km (8 miles)

The River Cerne drains the chalk downland north of the county town of Dorchester. The name comes from the Old Celtic word *carn*, which translates as a 'pile of stones' or 'cairn'. The Cerne flows southwards from Minterne Magna until it reaches its confluence with the River Frome.

River Cerne flowing towards Charminster

Poole Harbour – River Cerne

VILLAGES AND TOWNS AND THE ORIGINS OF THEIR NAMES
(from source to confluence with the River Frome)

Minterne Magna
987 Minterne

Minterne Parva
1314 Minterne Parv
1596 Mynterene Magna
Old English:
minte – mint
aern – a house
Latin:
magna – great
parva – small
'the house where mint grows'

Minterne House
Minterne House in Minterne Magna has been the home of the Churchill and Digby families since 1620. The gardens are open to the public and offer lakes and cascades but the house is a private residence. Group tours of the house can be booked and it can be hired for weddings and other events.

The Cerne Abbas Giant

CERNE ABBAS
1086 (Domesday Book) Cernel
1175 Cerne
1288 Cerne Abbatis
Cerne – name taken from the River Cerne
Old Celtic:
carn – a pile of stones or cairn
Latin:
abbas – an abbot
'a settlement with an abbey near the River Cerne'

Giant and fertility
The Cerne Abbas Giant is the largest chalk figure in Britain – 55m (180 feet) high – and lies a short uphill walk from the village. Its origin is unknown but one theory is the figure portrays Hercules while another says it is a mockery of Oliver Cromwell. A more obvious suggestion is a fertility god!

NETHER CERNE
1288 Nethercerne
Cerne – name taken from the River Cerne
Old Celtic:
carn – a pile of stones or cairn
Old English:
neotherra – down river
'a settlement further down the River Cerne'

Dissenter's grave
A stone slab in All Saints Church marks the grave of John Dammer (1675), a well-known dissenter whose body was forbidden from being buried alongside his wife in Godmanstone.

A dissenter, or non-conformist, is an English Protestant who does not conform to the doctrines and practices of the established Church of England

The well-worn inscription, according to a historic survey in 1951, states:
> His will was to be layed with his dear wife
> When he by Death's stroke was bereft of life
> The souls of both are in eternal joy
> Their bodys freed from what did them anoy
> Tho humane force have thus their bodys parted
> They rest in peace, both being upright hearted.

GODMANSTONE
1166 Godemanestone
Old English:
Godmann – personal name
tun – a farm or estate
'a farm or estate owned by a man named Godmann'

120

FORSTON
1236 Fosardeston
Old English:
Forsard – personal name
tun – a farm or estate
'a farm or estate owned by a family named Forsard'

First asylum in Dorset
Francis Browne founded Dorset County Asylum in 1827 in Forston House, originally a private residence built in 1720. The asylum treated both paupers and private patients until a new asylum was built, Herrison House. By 1900, Forston House had once again become a private residence.

CHARMINSTER
1086 (Domesday Book) Cerminstre
Cerne – name taken from the River Cerne
Old Celtic:
carn – a pile of stones or cairn
Old English:
mynster – a church
'a settlement with a church near the River Cerne'

Church flooded
St Mary's church, with its Norman arches and 15th century tower, was built in the 12th century beside the River Cerne.

In 2014 the river flooded its banks, inundating the church and several cottages after a Grade ll-listed bridge impeded the flow of water. The church was closed for repairs.

At time of writing there are other restrictions on church services because of the coronavirus pandemic but there are no restrictions on the good news the church declares.

St Mary's Church

Magnet fishing!
Whilst walking along the river in Charminster I met Belinda with her daughter who was riding her bicycle. This young girl, about 7 years of age, told me that when learning to ride her bike she had fallen into a bunch of stinging nettles. Not deterred by the unpleasant experience, she had remounted and carried on. Not only an intrepid cyclist she was also a discoverer and a protector of wildlife. Whilst magnet fishing in the river with her mum and dad she had found an ancient coin and even better than that, they had fished out some nasty barbed wire. I think we all need to try fishing with magnets!

Wolfeton House
Wolfeton House owner Captain Thimbleby welcomes the public into his home with an informative guided tour. This medieval and Elizabethan manor house surrounded by water meadows was renovated in 1560 with impressive wood panelling and plasterwork.

BURTON
1204 Burton
Old English:
burh – a fort
tun – a farm or estate
'a fortified farm or estate'

Chapter 25

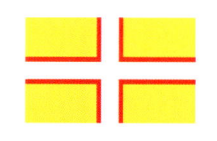

SOUTH WINTERBORNE RIVER

AT A GLANCE

SOURCE
Springs in hills west of Winterbourne Abbas

MOUTH / OUTLET
Confluences with the River Frome near West Stafford

LENGTH
Approximately 15km (9.5 miles)

South Winterborne River, also spelled Winterbourne and a tributary of the River Frome, takes its name from the Old English words *wyntre* and *burna* meaning 'winter stream'. In winter months the river is full but in summer months it can dry completely.

The river gives its name to many surrounding villages although, sadly, several settlements no longer exist.

Poole Harbour – South Winterborne River

VILLAGES AND TOWNS AND THE ORIGINS OF THEIR NAMES
(from source to confluence with the River Frome)

Maiden Castle

WINTERBOURNE ABBAS
1086 (Domesday Book) Wintreburne
1244 Wynterburn Abbatis
'a settlement by the River Winterborne owned by Cerne Abbey'
Winterbourne Abbas was also known as Watreleswyntreburn – a waterless winter stream.

The Nine Stones
An elliptical ring of sarsen stones can be found along the A35 between Winterbourne Abbas and Bridport. They were probably part of an ancient temple, a theory supported by the many barrows (burial mounds) nearby.

WINTERBOURNE STEEPLETON
1086 (Domesday Book) Wintreburne
1244 Wynterburn Stepilton
Old English:
stiepel – a steeple
tun – a farm or estate
'a farm or estate on the River Winterborne with a church having a steeple'

WINTERBORNE ST MARTIN
1086 (Domesday Book) Wintreburne
1280 Wynterburn Seynt Martyn
'a settlement by the River Winterborne with a church dedicated to St Martin'
Winterborne Martin was also known as Martinstown.

Historic heights
Maiden Castle is an ancient Iron Age hill fort to the north of the village. According to English Heritage it is one of the largest and most complex hill forts in Europe.

Between 800 BC and AD 43 its chalk ramparts would have protected hundreds of people living there – the fort covers an area the size of 50 football pitches.

The name comes from the Old Celtic words *mai* and *dun*, meaning 'great hill'.

Excavations uncovered a Romano-Celtic temple from the 4th century and an Iron Age cemetery containing many skeletons showing signs of a violent death.

Winterborne Monkton

1086 (Domesday Book) Wintreburne
1268 Wynterburne Moneketon

Old English:
munuc – a monk
tun – a farm or estate
'a farm or estate owned by monks (the priory of Le Wast, France)'
Winterborne Monkton was also known as Winterborne Wast.

Winterborne Herringston

1086 (Domesday Book) Wintreburne
1288 Wynterburne Heringeston

Old English:
Harang – personal name
tun – a farm or estate
'a farm or estate on the River Winterborne owned by a man named Harang'
Also in Chaldon Herring and Langton Herring.

Winterborne Farringdon

The name probably derives from

Old English:
fearn – ferns
dun – a hill
'a hill covered in ferns near the River Winterborne'

Abandoned village
Winterborne Farringdon is a deserted medieval village dating to 1397. Investigations have shown ten enclosures with possibly eight houses. St German's Church is in the heart of the group of homes. The church's 14th century foundations can be seen as a rectangular earthwork with a 19th century wall still in existence at the eastern end.

Records indicate there was great poverty in the 15th century and villagers moved away to find work and food. By 1650 only three households remained. Rev John Hutchins, the eminent 18th century Dorset historian, recorded that by 1773 no-one was living in Winterborne Farringdon.

Winterborne Came

1086 (Domesday Book) Wintreburne
1280 Winterburn Caam

Old English:
Caam – Caen in Normandy
'a settlement on the River Winterborne owned by St Stephen's Abbey in Caen'

Whitcombe

1086 (Domesday Book) Widecome

Old English:
wid – wide
cumb – a valley
'a settlement in a broad valley'

William Barnes
In 1847, Dorset dialect poet William Barnes became minister of the church in Whitcombe. His parish clerk, Arthur Cooper, was perhaps the "thorn in his side". Apparently Cooper often told Barnes: "You've got to take notice of I. I be the second man in the church I be."

William Barnes later became rector of Winterborne Came as well as Whitcombe. A comfortable rectory came with the job so he no longer had to travel from Dorchester. He lived there until his death in 1886.

Medieval painting
A painting thought to date to the 15th century was found hidden under layers of paint during restoration of Whitcombe church in 1912. The painting is faded but depicts St Christopher carrying Christ as a young child. Nearby is a painting of a mermaid combing her hair, a strange addition to a Christian church.

Poole Harbour – South Winterborne River

WEST STAFFORD

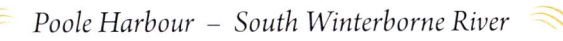

1086 (Domesday Book) Stanford
1285 West Stafford

Old English:

stan – stony
ford – a ford

'a settlement with a stony ford'

There was once an East Stafford near West Knighton (see also chapter on the River Frome).

Talbothays Lodge and Cottages

Thomas Hardy is famed as a novelist and poet but was also a qualified architect. While writing Tess Of The D'Urbervilles he was designing a home for his brother and sisters, along with nine other cottages, in the village of West Stafford on the road to Woodsford. They were built by Thomas' brother Henry Hardy who, like his father, was a master builder. Henry also built the bungalow intending it to be a home for himself and his fiancée, but sadly the wedding never took place.

The lodge was requisitioned by the army during the Second World War, while in 1987 it was registered as a Grade II-listed building.

Modest peal

The three bells in St Andrew's church are referred to in Thomas Hardy's Tess Of The D'Urbervilles after the wedding of Tess to Angel Clare: "As they came out of the church the ringers swung the bells off their rests, and a modest peal of three notes broke forth – that limited amount of expression having been deemed sufficient by the church builders for the joys of such a small parish."

Top to bottom: Whitcombe church; hidden medieval painting at the church; Talbothays Lodge; Talbothays Cottages

Chapter 26

TADNOLL BROOK

AT A GLANCE

SOURCE
Springs around Broadmayne, West Knighton, Empool Bottom and Tadnoll Mill

MOUTH / OUTLET
Confluences with the River Frome near Broomhill Bridge, west of Wool

LENGTH
About 7km (4.5 miles)

Tadnoll Brook is a chalk stream tributary of the River Frome. It flows in an easterly direction towards its confluence with the Frome near Broomhill Bridge, west of the small town of Wool. Tadnoll Brook's journey takes it between Tadnoll and Winfrith Heath nature reserves, both areas of heathland and wetland, ideal nesting territory for Dorset's rare Dartford warbler. The Dartford warbler, almost extinct in the 1960s, now has 3,000 pairs breeding in Devon, Dorset, the New Forest, Suffolk and Surrey.

The name Tadnoll comes from two Old English words – *taden* meaning 'toads' and *hol* meaning 'hollow' or 'depression'.

VILLAGES AND TOWNS AND THE ORIGINS OF THEIR NAMES
(from source to mouth of the river)

WEST KNIGHTON
1086 (Domesday Book) Chenistetone
1208 Cnititon
Old English:
cniht – a servant or retainer (after 1066 – a knight)
tun – a farm or estate
'a farm or estate owned by retainers. In 1066 it was owned by two retainers or knights, probably land granted to them as a result of their service to the king or lord of the manor'
A retainer owes their service to a household and is often a long-standing servant.

BROADMAYNE
1086 (Domesday Book) Maine
1288 Brodemaynne
Old English:
brad – broad
Celtic:
main – a stone or rock
'a large settlement (compared with Little Mayne) where many sarsen stones can be found'

Maine, USA
Sir Ferdinando Gorges (1565-1647), an officer in the army of Elizabeth I, owned an estate in the area of Broadmayne. As founder of the state of Maine in the USA, it is thought he named the state after the village of Broadmayne or Little Mayne.

Stand and deliver
Bill Watch, a highwayman, stabled his horse in Broadmayne. He was notorious for robbing travellers on their journey between Weymouth and London. The barn he used has been converted into a private dwelling.

Tadnoll Brook inside the entrance to Moignes Court, Owermoigne, winding its way downstream

EMPOOL BOTTOM AND HEATH
There is no settlement here
Old English:
emn – smooth or undisturbed
pol – a pool
botm – a valley bottom
'a tranquil pool in the bottom of a valley'

WARMWELL
1086 (Domesday Book) Warmewelle
Old English:
wearm – warm
wella – a spring
'a settlement close to a spring of warm water'

Spitfires and Frank Muir
RAF Warmwell airfield protected the naval base at Portland during the Battle of Britain in the

The Watercress Company, Warmwell Mill (18th century, miller's house added in 19th century)

Second World War. Squadrons 102 and 609 flew Spitfires and were based at Warmwell with other squadrons flying Hurricanes, Typhoons, Whirlwinds and Walruses. One of those Spitfires is now suspended from the ceiling in London's Science Museum.

Frank Muir CBE (1920-1998), comedy writer and raconteur, was stationed at RAF Warmwell before being posted to Iceland. His autobiography, A Kentish Lad, recounts some of his humorous and interesting memories of that time. As a teenager, I loved listening to him on the radio.

Crossways village is built on part of the airfield, while gravel is quarried from other areas.

Watercress

Numerous watercress beds flourish around the village of Warmwell. Watercress thrives in slightly alkaline chalk streams such as Tadnoll Brook.

Prophetic?

Warmwell House has been home to many influential Dorset families, including the Trenchards and Newburghs.

In the 17th century John Sadler lived in the manor house. He was an academic, fluent in Oriental languages and master of Magdalene College, Cambridge. In 1661, as he lay seriously ill, he spoke of an epidemic in London, a terrible fire and three ships landing in the west that would cause havoc. Could this have been a foretelling of the plague in London in 1665, the Great Fire of London in 1666 and the Monmouth Rebellion that landed at Lyme Regis in 1685?

OWERMOIGNE

1086 (Domesday Book) Ogre
1314 Oure Moyngne

Old Celtic:

ogrodust – a wind gap between hills
Moigne – personal name, probably Norman
'a settlement owned by the Moigne family between chalk hills that funnel the wind blowing from the sea'

Cottage at the entrance to the driveway of Warmwell House

The Old Rectory, Owermoigne

Betrayal and murder

In the 16th century the owner of Moignes Court, Charles Stourton, 8th Baron Stourton, was involved in a lawsuit with John Hartgill and his son.

On 12th January 1557, Sir Charles invited the Hartgills to Stourton Castle in Wiltshire to express his regret for his part in the proceedings. Father and son accepted the invitation but never returned home. Their bodies were found buried beneath the cellar floor. At Sir Charles' trial it was revealed he had ordered his servants to club them and cut their throats while they were seated at the dining table.

Sir Charles and his four servants were found guilty of murder and sentenced to death. He appealed to Queen Mary I to rescind the sentence on the grounds of his nobility and Catholicism, knowing Queen Mary was a devoted Roman Catholic. The queen responded by giving permission for him to be hanged with a silken halter. Sir Charles was buried in St Mary's Chapel in Salisbury Cathedral.

Plunder

In 1588, one of the ships from the defeated Spanish Armada came ashore in Ringstead Bay, about three miles from Owermoigne. The crew was murdered and the ship plundered, with some of the timber used as beams in the dining room of Owermoigne's rectory.

WINFRITH

1086 (Domesday Book) Winfrode

Old Celtic:

winn – white or bright

frud – a stream

'a settlement on a clear, bright stream'

Decommissioned

Winfrith Nuclear Power Station operated from the 1950s for about 40 years, employing 2,000 people and covering an area of 950 hectares (2,350 acres). Today the site is divided between a science and technology park, Dorset Police headquarters and heathland.

BROOMHILL BRIDGE

1791 Brumel Bridge

Old English:

brom – a broom bush

hyll – a hill

'a settlement on a hill where broom bushes grow'

Chapter 27

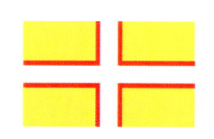

RIVER WIN

AT A GLANCE

SOURCE
Springs in the hills around Chaldon Herring (East Chaldon)

MOUTH / OUTLET
Confluences with the River Frome near East Burton

LENGTH
6.7km (4 miles)

The River Win, a small chalk stream in south Dorset, flows from the hills above Winfrith Newburgh and empties into the Frome near East Burton. The name comes from an old Celtic word meaning 'bright' or 'white', probably a description of the river's waters.

East Burton, R. Win confluence with R. Frome

East Burton, Ryan crossing the R. Win with Tommy, heading for the confluence

Villages and Towns and the Origins of Their Names
(from source to mouth of the river)

Chaldon Herring
1086 (Domesday Book) Calvedone
1243 Chaluedon Hareng
Old English:
cealf – a calf
dun – a hill
Harang – 12th century family name
'a settlement on a hill with calves grazing owned by a family named Harang' as in Langton Herring and Winterborne Herringston

Five Marys and stag antlers
A Bronze Age cemetery known as Five Marys lies on a ridge between Chaldon Herring to the south and Galton Heath to the north. The cemetery includes seven bowl barrows, two bell barrows and one pond barrow.

Two of the barrows were excavated in the 19th century. One contained the skeletons of a man and woman, both in a seated position. The second also contained a skeleton. On the shoulders of all three were stag antlers. The seated position of the skeletons and the stag antlers indicate they had been people held in high esteem.

The name 'Five Marys' is a corruption of the word meer, meaning 'boundary marker'. In 1765, Taylor's map of Dorset marks the site as 'Five Meers'.

Marley Wood
1390 Meryl
Old English:
myrge – pleasant
leah – a wood or clearing
'a settlement near a wood in pleasant surroundings'

Winfrith Newburgh
1086 (Domesday Book) Winfrode
1288 Wynifred Neuburgh
Old Celtic:
winn – white or bright
frud – a stream
Newburgh – 12th century family name
'a settlement on a sparkling stream owned by the Newburgh family'
See chapter on Tadnoll Brook

East Knighton
1244 Knytteton
Old English:
cniht – a knight
tun – a farm or estate
'a farm or estate owned by knights'

East Burton
1212 Bureton
(East, West, Long)
1280 Estburton, Westburton
1460 Langebourton
Old English:
burh – fortified
tun – a farm or estate
'a fortified farm or estate'

Chapter 28

RIVER PIDDLE

AT A GLANCE

SOURCE
Four springs near the church at Alton Pancras

MOUTH / OUTLET
Wareham Channel flowing into Poole Harbour

LENGTH
32km (20 miles)

TRIBUTARIES
- Plush Brook, rises in the hills north east of Plush, confluences with the River Piddle in Piddletrenthide
- Cheselbourne Stream, rises near Ansty, confluences with Devils Brook south of Dewlish Park
- Devils Brook, rises near Higher Ansty, confluences with the River Piddle near Burleston Farm and Athelhampton House
- Bere Stream, rises near Milborne St Andrew, confluences with the River Piddle south of Lower Stockley Farm and north east of Woodlands

The River Piddle, also known as the Trent or North River, is a small rural river whose name Piddle is a derivation of the Anglo Saxon word *pedelen*, meaning 'marshy land' or 'fen'. The alternative name, Trent, is probably taken from the village of Piddletrenthide.

Leaving Alton Pancras the Piddle flows south and turns eastwards at Puddletown towards its outlet into Poole Harbour.. The middle and lower reaches of its course run almost parallel with the Frome and the two rivers enter the harbour via the Wareham Channel.

Some of the place names along the Piddle have been taken from its name but altered to Puddle. A popular theory is that the Victorians were offended by the name Piddle. A more likely reason is a simple spelling mistake, as can be seen in the name Puddletown. Its former name in the 13th century was changed from Pideletun to Pudeletun in less than 70 years.

Water meadows lie to the north of Puddletown and areas of woodland to the south, with watercress farms in the Piddle catchment area. There are weirs and sluices to the north of Wareham to control the flow of water. Crayfish and otters are flourishing in the clear fresh waters of the Piddle.

Fishing rights can be traced to Alfred the Great, King of Wessex (871-899).

Villages and towns with the origins of their names
(from source to mouth of river)

Alton Pancras
1012 Awultone
1226 Aweltone Pancratii
Old English:
aewiell – source of a stream
tun – a farm or estate
Latin:
Pancratius – St Pancras
'a farm or estate at the source of a stream with a church dedicated to St Pancras'

Plush
891 Plyssch
Old English:
plysc – a pool
'a settlement near a pool of water'

Ansty
1219 Anesty
Old English:
anstig – a narrow track, usually linking other paths or routes
'a settlement along a narrow track'

Cheselbourne
870 Chiselburne
1086 (Domesday Book) Ceseburne
Old English:
cisel – gravel
burna – a stream
'a settlement near a gravel stream'

The Black Death
Cheselbourne village may have originally been sited further away from the stream, on a hillside south west of St Martin's Church. Local tradition suggests it was moved to its present location after the plague, also known as the Black Death, in the 14th century. In the upper slopes of Church Field there are plague pits in which victims were buried.

Pandemic thieves
During the coronavirus pandemic in 2020, when all villagers were confined to their homes, thieves took the opportunity to strip the lead from the church roof. Father Butcher said: "Such an attack upon our building is an attack upon the shared communal life of the villagers of Cheselbourne."

Dewlish
1086 (Domesday Book) Devenis
1194 Deueliz
Old Celtic:
river name meaning 'dark stream'
'a settlement near a dark stream'
Also the derivation of Devils Brook, a tributary of the River Piddle

River Piddle at Piddletrenthide

PIDDLETRENTHIDE
966 Uppidelen
1212 Pidele Trentehydes
Old English:
up – upstream
pidelen – a marsh or fen
Old French:
trente – thirty
Old English:
hid – a hide of land
'a settlement on the River Piddle valued (in the 1086 Domesday Book) at 30 hides'

Early numerals
All Saints Church boasts the earliest-recorded Arabic numerals on any building in England. They can be viewed on the west door of the church tower. The inscription reads: 'Est pydeltrenth villa in dorsedie comitatu Nascitur in illa quam rexit Vicariatu 1487.'
Translation:
'It is in Piddletrenthide, a town in Dorset (where) he was born (and) is Vicar, 1487.'

The use of Roman numerals continued in Europe for at least another century so it is special to find Arabic numerals inscribed over a doorway in a small village in Dorset.

WHITE LACKINGTON
1354 Wyghtlakynton
Old English:
Wihtlac – personal name
ing – associated with
tun – a farm or estate
'a farm or estate associated with or named after a man named Wihtlac'

PIDDLEHINTON
1086 (Domesday Book) Pidele
1244 Hinepidel, Pidel Hineton
Old English:
pidelen – a marsh or fen
higna – a religious community
tun – a farm or estate
'a farm or estate on the River Piddle owned by a religious community'

River Piddle at Piddlehinton

Piddlehinton village hall-school

Villagers' outburst
In 1838 the vicar ended an ancient village tradition of distributing mince pies, bread and a pint of ale to all parishioners on 6th January (the original date for Christmas Day). The villagers were so angry they smashed the church windows.

Village hub
Piddlehinton Village Hall was once the village school, founded in 1831. In 1875 Kate and Mary, sisters of Thomas Hardy (Dorset author and poet), were teachers at the school. Mary was headmistress.

Caring for the wounded
Mrs Ann Winzer (1791-1873) nursed the wounded during the Battle of Waterloo in 1815. She is buried alongside her husband, James.

'She was a Waterloo heroine who assisted at that famous battle AD 1815 by aiding and assisting the sick and wounded. She endured many hardships having followed the British Army from Brussels to Paris. From Paris to Duney. Returned to England and from thence to the Rock of Gibraltar where she remained four years. She afterward resided in this parish where she received a pension through the

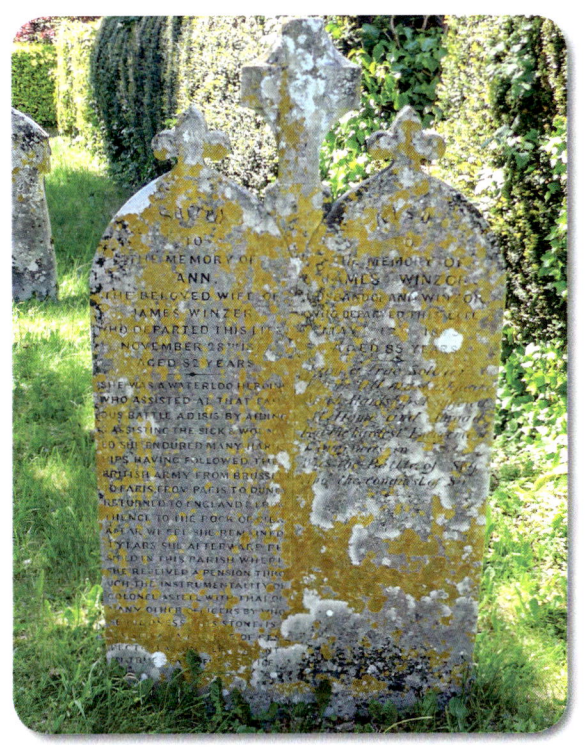

The headstones of James and Ann Winzer in the churchyard of St Mary the Virgin

instrumentality of Colonel Astell with that of many officers by whose kindness this stone is raised as a tribute of respect to a long life spent in true and faithful service.'

The words on her husband's gravestone show he endured his own battles:

To the Memory of James Winzer who
Departed this Life
May 12th 1875 aged 85 years.
'I am a true Soldier
Whom all must applaud
Midst hardships I suffered
At home and abroad
But the hardest engagement
I ever was in
Was the battle of Self
and the Conquest of Sin'

Puddletown

HIGHER/LOWER WATERSTON
1086 (Domesday Book) Pidere
1227 Walterton
1268 Pydele Waltereston
Old English:
Walter – a personal name
tun – a farm or estate
originally: *'a settlement on the River Piddle'*
by 1227: *'a farm or estate owned by a man named Walter'*

PUDDLETOWN
1212 Pideleton
1280 Pudeleton
Old English:
pidelen – a marsh or fen
tun – a farm or estate
'a farm or estate on the River Piddle'

ATHELHAMPTON
1086 (Domesday Book) Pidele
1285 Pidele Athelhamston
1303 Athelhameston
Old English:
pidelen – a marsh or fen
Aethelhelm – Saxon personal name
tun – a farm or estate
'a farm or estate on the River Piddle owned by a man named Aethelhelm'

Athelhampton House – history and ghosts
Athelhampton House *(below)* is a privately owned manor house built in the 15th century. Original features include a dovecote and the Great Hall with its stained-glass windows and huge fireplace. As with many old houses there are tales of ghosts, including a headless man, a monk and a monkey!

In the 19th century, master builder Thomas Hardy was involved in the restoration of the roofs to the Great Hall and West Wing. He was the father of Dorset poet, novelist and architect Thomas Hardy.

BURLESTON

934 Bordelestone
1212 Burdelston
Old French:
Burdel – personal name
Old English:
tun – a farm or estate
'a farm or estate owned by a man named Burdel'

TOLPUDDLE

1086 (Domesday Book) Pidele
1210 Tollepidele
Old English:
pidelen – a marsh or fen
Tola – personal name
'a settlement on the River Piddle owned by a woman named Tola'
(Tola was the Danish widow of Edward the Confessor's bodyguard or housecarl)

The Tolpuddle Martyrs

In 1834 six farm labourers living in Tolpuddle set up a small agricultural union and swore an illegal oath, giving birth to today's trade unions. They were arrested and prosecuted.

During their trial George Loveless stated: "We have injured no man's reputation, character, person or property; we were uniting together to preserve ourselves, our wives and children from utter degradation and starvation." All were found guilty and transported to Australia for a period of seven years. However, there was such a public outcry after the sentences that the martyrs were pardoned a few years later.

Every year, in commemoration of the six martyrs, the Trades Union Congress holds a rally in the village. The sycamore tree *(above)* that the men used to meet beneath still stands on the small village green.

Tolpuddle Martyrs' cottages

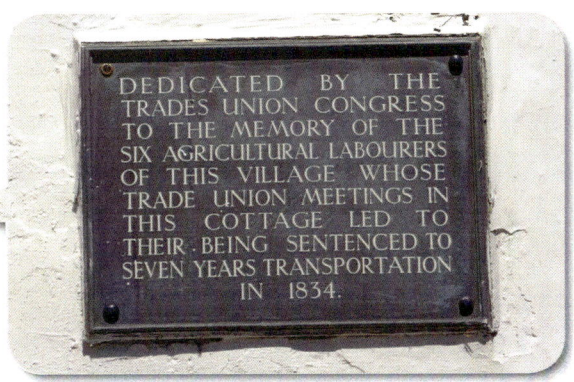

DEDICATED BY THE TRADES UNION CONGRESS TO THE MEMORY OF THE SIX AGRICULTURAL LABOURERS OF THIS VILLAGE WHOSE TRADE UNION MEETINGS IN THIS COTTAGE LED TO THEIR BEING SENTENCED TO SEVEN YEARS TRANSPORTATION IN 1834.

Briantspuddle Debenham Cottages

AFFPUDDLE
1086 (Domesday Book) Affapidele
Old English:
Aeffa – personal name
pidelen – a marsh or fen
'a settlement on the River Piddle owned by a man named Aeffa'

BRIANTSPUDDLE
1086 (Domesday Book) Pidele
14th century Pudele Turberville
1465 Brianis Pedille
Old English:
Brian de Turbeville – personal name
pidelen – a marsh or fen
'a settlement on the River Piddle owned by Brian de Turbeville'

Debenham's farming innovations
Ernest Debenham, grandson of the founder of Debenhams department store William Debenham, launched an agricultural enterprise to promote self-sufficiency for Dorset. Initial work was delayed by the First World War but, by 1929, forty cottages had been built to house estate workers. Every home had an inside toilet and bath, while a quarter of an acre was provided to grow their own vegetables.

This innovative farming estate included pasteurisation of milk, electricity generation, bee keeping, veterinary care, selective breeding and forestry.

When Ernest Debenham died in 1952, the estate was divided and sold.

THROOP
1237 La Trop
(near Turners Puddle)
1268 Thrope
Old English:
throp – an outlying farm or secondary settlement
'an outlying farm or secondary settlement'
(see River Stour for a different Throop)

TURNERS PUDDLE
1086 (Domesday Book) Pidele
1268 Tonerespydele
Old English:
Toner – personal name
pidelen – a marsh or fen
'a settlement on the River Piddle owned by a man with the family name Toner'

Wareham, St Martin's-on-the-Walls Church

WOODLANDS
1244 Wodelande
Old English:
wudu – a wood
land – area of land possibly cleared for cultivation
'a tract of land near or within a wooded area'

CAREY
1220 Keire
1318 Carry
Origin and meaning uncertain but possibly a Celtic river name

WAREHAM
9th century Werham
1086 (Domesday Book) Warham
(see River Frome for more information)
Old English:
wer or waer – a weir
ham – a homestead
'a homestead by a weir'

Saxon beauty
St Martin's-on-the-Walls is the finest example of a Saxon church in Dorset. It has many interesting features. Here are just some of them:

- Red stars are a memorial to every person in Wareham who died during the 17th century plague.
- Ancient paintings were discovered during restoration work, with one depicting the story of St Martin. He is on horseback having torn his cloak in two and given one half to a naked beggar. Later, St Martin dreams he sees Jesus Christ wearing the half of the cloak he had given away. Jesus says: "Truly I tell you, whatever you did for one of the least of these brothers and sisters of mine, you did for me." (New International Version.)
- An effigy of TE Lawrence (Lawrence of Arabia) takes up significant space in the church. Lawrence, a respected archaeologist and great friend of the writer Thomas Hardy, was a brilliant army officer. He lived at Clouds Hill and died in a motorbike accident (see Moreton) near Bovington. Official war artist Eric Kennington sculpted the effigy in 1935. It was intended for St Paul's Cathedral and offered to Westminster Abbey and Salisbury Cathedral but all declined. It seems fitting that Wareham is now the proud owner of this beautiful work of art.

Chapter 29

DEVILS BROOK

AT A GLANCE

SOURCE
Springs in the hills above Ansty and Melcombe Bingham

MOUTH / OUTLET
Confluence with the River Piddle at Burleston Farm

LENGTH
About 14.75km (9 miles)

The names of Devils Brook and the village of Dewlish, once spelled Develish, come from an Old Celtic word meaning 'dark stream'.

Devils Brook, a tributary of the River Piddle, travels southwards through Blackmore Vale to join the Piddle at Burleston Farm.

The course of Devils Brook has been modified by the installation of several hatches (floodgates) and impoundments (dams) to control the irrigation of water meadows. Some are still in use, channelling water to promote the growth of grass as early grazing for livestock. These water meadows are important for the conservation of wading birds.

Poole Harbour – Devils Brook

VILLAGES AND TOWNS AND THE ORIGINS OF THEIR NAMES
(from source to confluence with the River Piddle)

ANSTY
INCLUDING LITTLE ANSTY, HIGHER ANSTY, LOWER ANSTY, ANSTY CROSS

1219 Anesty

Old English:
anstig – a narrow track, a track that links other routes
'settlements on a track that links other routes'
Little Ansty is also called Pleck, probably a Middle English word meaning 'plot of land'.

Brewery origins
The Fox Inn is more than 250 years old and was the original home of the Woodhouse family. In 1777, Charles Hall founded a brewery opposite the inn and, by the mid 19th century, Robert Hall and Edward Woodhouse had become business partners.

Edward fell in love with Charles Hall's granddaughter, Hannah Dodge, and independent brewer Hall & Woodhouse was born. Now based in Blandford Forum, the company owns many pubs and inns that sell its popular Badger beers.

ALLER

1332 Alre

Old English:
alor – an alder tree
'a settlement where alder trees grow'

Melcombe Bingham, Bingham's Melcombe and Melcombe Horsey

1086 (Domesday Book) Melecome
1412 Bynghammes Melcombe
1535 Melcombe Horsey

Old English:
meoluc – milk
cumb – a valley
Bingham – personal name, 13th century
Horsey – personal name, 16th century
'settlements in a valley owned by the Bingham and Horsey families where there is dairy farming'

Hilton

1086 (Domesday Book) Eltone
1212 Helton

Old English:
hielde – a slope
tun – a farm or estate
'a farm or estate on sloping land'

Cheselbourne

870 Chiselburne
1086 (Domesday Book) Ceseburne

Old English:
cisel – shingle or small stones
burna – a stream
'a settlement near a gravel stream'

Dewlish

1086 (Domesday Book) Devenis
1194 Deueliz
an old Celtic name meaning 'dark stream'
'a settlement near Devils Brook'

Heart of the village

The Oak at Dewlish (*above*) stands along a country lane in the beautiful Dorset Downs, with Devils Brook flowing nearby. Once a welcome stop for passing coaches and horses in need of refreshment, it is now the heart of the village of Dewlish. The Oak has more than survived covid restrictions thanks to creative thinking by Roy the landlord. We stayed for bed and breakfast and treated ourselves to an evening meal cooked by their superb chef, Will. Ali, his mum, works part-time and gave us a typically warm Dorset welcome. If you enjoy excellent traditional meals in a friendly country pub, seek out The Oak at Dewlish, only a few miles from Dorchester and Blandford Forum.

Mammoths and a mouse
Once upon a time, a tiny field mouse decided to make his home in the hills above Dewlish. The clever little chap had discovered an area of sand amid the chalk ideal for his tunnelling. One day a visiting geologist became curious when he spotted this sandy mouse hole and dug deeper.

Lo and behold he found fossils of willow trees beneath the sand but that wasn't all, there were gigantic bones! In a huge trench were the skeletal remains of two woolly mammoths that stood 5m (17ft). They had lived on these hills among the willow trees before the last Ice Age and become bogged down in the marshes where they died. The bones were excavated after the First World War and are on display in Dorchester Museum.

What a story, beginning with a tiny creature looking for somewhere to live and ending with the discovery of massive mammoths who died thousands of years ago. Life is never predictable!

CHEBBARD FARM
1335 Scaborthe
Old English:
bord – a plank of wood denoting a boundary
The first part of Scaborthe is probably from a personal name.
'a settlement on a boundary line'

BURLESTON
1212 Burdelston
Old French:
Burdel – personal name
Old English:
tun – a farm or estate
'a farm or estate owned by a man named Burdel'

Dewlish, Devils Brook

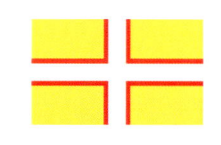

Chapter 30

BERE STREAM

AT A GLANCE

SOURCE
Springs in the hills above Milborne St Andrew

MOUTH / OUTLET
Confluences with the River Piddle south of Lower Stockley Farm and north east of Woodlands

LENGTH
17km (10.5 miles)

A tributary of the River Piddle, Bere Stream rises in the chalk hills above the village of Hilton. Its clear waters travel south through the towns of Milborne St Andrew and Bere Regis, emptying into the River Piddle south of Lower Stockley Farm. Watercress beds have flourished around Bere Regis for more than 200 years.

A watercress bed, Bere Regis

VILLAGES AND TOWNS AND THE ORIGINS OF THEIR NAMES
(from source to mouth of the river)

HILTON
1086 (Domesday Book) Eltone
1212 Helton
Old English:
helde – tansy
tun – a farm or estate
'a farm in an area where tansy flowers grow'

MILTON ABBAS
934 Middeltone
1268 Middelton Abbatis
Old English:
middle – middle
tun – a farm or estate
Latin:
abbatis – of the abbot
'a middle farm owned by the abbey'

Milton Abbey
The Gothic-style Milton Abbey *(above)* dates to the 12th century. Next door is Milton Abbey House, once a magnificent home to the Hambro and Damer families. Today it is an independent co-educational boarding and day school.

In the 1770s the owner of Milton Abbey House, Joseph Damer, Lord Milton and 1st Earl of Dorchester, considered Middleton village a blot on the landscape. He removed the villagers, mostly estate workers, out of sight to a new village, Milton Abbas. With 36 almost identical cottages of whitewashed cob and thatch, each was designed to house two families. Today the village is often photographed as the epitome of an idyllic Dorset village. The original village of Middleton lies beneath the lawns and lake of Milton Abbey, landscaped by Sir Lancelot 'Capability' Brown.

145

The 111 steps

The Great Stair is the name Capability Brown gave to the grass steps that lead to St Catherine's Chapel *(above)* in the woods above Milton Abbey. The chapel dates to 1190 and has many Norman characteristics.

I was told Benedictine monks from the abbey would walk up the 111 steps every morning for prayer in the chapel. It is a captivating picture but one that remains unverified.

MILBORNE ST ANDREW

934 Muleburne
1294 Muleburne St Andrew

Old English:
myln – a mill
burna – a stream
'a settlement on a mill stream with a church dedicated to St Andrew'

BERE REGIS

1086 (Domesday Book) Bere
1264 Kyngesbyre
1495 Bire Regis

Old English:
bearu – woodland or a forest

Latin:
regis – of the king
'a settlement in a royal wood or forest'

Refuge for a murderous queen

Queen Alfrida came to live in Bere Regis after she had her stepson, Edward the Martyr, assassinated outside Corfe Castle in 978 (see Corfe Rivers for more information).

What's in a name?

The Turberville family has lived in Bere Regis for hundreds of years. Dorset novelist Thomas Hardy adapted the name for his well-known tome Tess Of The D'Urbervilles.

Poole Harbour – Bere Stream

Bere Regis during Covid regulations

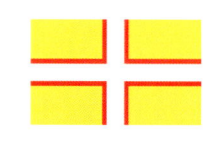

Chapter 31

SHERFORD RIVER

AT A GLANCE

SOURCE
Springs in Wareham Forest and others near Whitefield, south of Morden

MOUTH / OUTLET
Sherford River flows into Lytchett Bay, Poole Harbour, as Rock Lea River

LENGTH
About 12km (7.5 miles)

TRIBUTARIES
Small streams and one main tributary that rises from springs in Lytchett Matravers and confluences with Sherford River near Slepe Farm

Sometimes known as the River Sherford, this small Dorset river starts life as two streams that confluence in Morden Park to form Morden Park Lake. The river flows out of the lake and heads eastward, passing under Sherford Bridge, Organford Bridge and Kings Bridge until it reaches Poole Harbour at Lytchett Bay. Before reaching the sea, its name changes to Rock Lea River.

Poole Harbour – Sherford River

VILLAGES AND TOWNS AND THE ORIGINS OF THEIR NAMES
(from source to mouth of the river)

BLOXWORTH
987 Blacewyrthe
Old English:
personal name – Blocc
worth – an enclosure
'an enclosure owned by a man named Blocc'

WHITEFIELD
1422 Whytewell
Old English:
hwit – white or bright
wiella – a spring
'a settlement with a spring flowing with bright, clear water'

MORDEN
1086 (Domesday Book) Mordune
East and West Morden
Old English:
mor – a marsh
dun – a hill
'a settlement on a hill in marshy ground'

Morden ancient and modern
Morden Park Lake and Morden Bog are Areas of Outstanding Natural Beauty, nesting places for osprey and popular with bird watchers.

Morden Mill was built in the 18th century and is a Grade ll-listed building. Once a thriving mill producing flour for the surrounding area, it is now derelict.

We were disappointed not to be able to see Morden Mill but, to our delight, we found a footpath opposite the mill that led us to the river flowing under the A35. The sound of the stream accompanying the birdsong was a peaceful moment to be enjoyed and remembered.

149

The Old Button Shop

SHERFORD
1244 Sireford
1311 Shyreford
Old English:
scir – clear or gleaming
ford – a ford
'a settlement with a ford of clear water'

SLEPE
1315 Slape
Old English:
slaep – sleep
Possibly *'a quiet, remote settlement'*

ORGANFORD
1194 Argent
1593 Organforde
Old English:
ford – a ford or river crossing
possibly Old French:
argent – silver
Possibly *'a settlement with a ford of silvery waters'*

LYTCHETT MATRAVERS
1086 (Domesday Book) Lichet
1280 Lichet Mautrauers
Celtic:
led – grey
ced – a wood
Matravers – personal name
'a settlement near a grey wood owned by a family named Matravers'
Lytchett Matravers was originally sited around the church. After the Black Death in the late 14th century the population had drastically reduced and the village was relocated further up the hill.

LYTCHETT MINSTER
1244 Licheminster
Celtic:
led – grey
ced – a wood
Old English:
mynster – a monastery or large church
'a settlement near a grey wood with a large church'
(probably St Mary's in Sturminster Marshall)

St Peter's Finger

Gates to the South Lytchett Manor which are now the entrance to the Caravan and Camping Park

Unusual pub name

St Peter's Finger is the unusual name of a well-known pub in the area. The original Latin, St Peter ad Vincula, meaning St Peter in Chains, has been corrupted over time.

The Old Button Shop is not far from St Peter's Finger. More than 100 years ago local women would hand-craft Dorset buttons and bring them to the button shop to sell.

Anyone for tea?

South Lytchett Manor House, once the home of Lord John and Lady Madeline Lees, is now Lytchett Minster School. Part of the grounds are a caravan and camping site.

On one memorable occasion Lady Madeline set up a refreshment stall at the gates to the manor house and served tea to villagers and passers-by using the family silver.

HOLTON

1086 (Domesday Book) Holtone

Old English:

holt – a thicket or wood
tun – a farm or estate
'a farm near a wood'

Underground munitions

Holton Heath is now a trading estate and nature reserve but during the First World War it was the site of the Royal Navy Cordite Factory, most of which was housed underground. During the Second World War it was once more used as a munitions factory, this time making propellants for Royal Navy guns.

UPTON

1463 Upton

Old English:

upp – upper or higher
tun – a farm or estate
'a higher farm'

Chapter 32

Luscombe Valley Stream

This small stream flows from Canford Cliffs towards Sandbanks through very affluent areas of Poole.

It begins its short journey south of Lilliput Road and west of Compton Acres. It travels through Parkstone golf course and Luscombe Valley Nature Reserve, beneath Shore Road and empties into Poole Harbour.

Luscombe Valley

1822 Loscomb
Old English:
hlose – a pigsty
cumb – a valley
'a valley with a pigsty'

Luscombe Valley Nature Reserve

The nature reserve is a 4 hectare (10 acre) Site of Special Scientific Interest. Its diverse habitat of wetland, grassland, streams, ponds and reed beds is home to several rare species. Access is gained through two gated entrances in Shore Road.

Fox watch

I went for a walk through the reserve with one of our doggy clients, a shih tzu named Barney. It was a very windy day so the kite-surfers were enjoying themselves in Poole Harbour. The leaves of silver birches were rustling gently as the rain began to fall. I was grateful for the boardwalks that bridged the wetter areas – saving us from muddy shoes and paws. As the path turned a corner, I caught sight of a fox in the long grass. He watched us as we came closer but moved off quickly and silently before Barney had even spotted him.

Poole Harbour – Luscombe Valley Stream

Above: Luscombe Valley Stream
Left: Fox in the long grass
Below: Entrance to nature reserve with kite-surfers enjoying a very windy day in Poole Harbour

153

THE RIVER STOUR AND ITS TRIBUTARIES

Following the upper, middle and lower reaches
of the River Stour with its tributaries

'The Lord is my shepherd, I shall not be in want.
He makes me lie down in green pastures,
He leads me beside quiet waters,
He restores my soul.'

Psalm 23 v1-3a
(The Bible, New International Version)

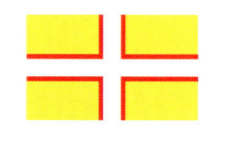

Chapter 33

RIVER STOUR

The River Stour derives its name from the Old English word *steu* or *stauro*, which means 'firm' or 'strong'. It is a strong-flowing river.

The Stour begins its course in the Stourhead estate in Wiltshire, which is owned by the National Trust. The Stour winds through the Wiltshire and Dorset countryside while being joined by other rivers, including the Cale and Lydden near Marnhull and the River Allen in Wimborne. Smaller tributaries flow into the Stour along the way. The River Stour converges with the River Avon near Christchurch Harbour.

In its upper and middle reaches the Stour courses through the chalk hills of the Dorset Downs and through the clay of Blackmore Vale (once a medieval hunting forest) until it comes to Blandford Forum. The landscape is a picturesque patchwork of agricultural fields and beautiful trees.

After Blandford Forum the countryside becomes heathland before the River Stour passes through clay once more as it approaches Christchurch Harbour. The clay often causes the river to flood, creating fertile flood plains on the meadows around the river.

Designated footpath, the Stour Valley Way, follows the Stour for most of its course. The walk is marked by a kingfisher symbol.

AT A GLANCE

SOURCE
St Peter's Pump, Stourhead estate in Wiltshire, near Mere.

MOUTH / OUTLET
Christchurch Harbour, after confluencing with the River Avon and flowing into the English Channel. The final few miles are tidal.

LENGTH
About 97km (60.5 miles)

River Stour and Tributaries – River Stour

VILLAGES AND TOWNS IN DORSET AND THE ORIGINS OF THEIR NAMES
(from source to mouth of the river)

The Stour Valley Way near Sturminster Marshall

BOURTON
1212 Bureton
Old English:
burgh – a fortified place
tun – a farm or estate
'a farm or estate situated near a fort'

Dam burst and hand grenades
During the First World War men, women and children made hand grenades, known as Mills bombs, at the Bourton Foundry. The men there were too old to enlist, while the women replaced the younger men who were away fighting. Children divided their week between school and working in the foundry. On 29th June 1917, a fierce storm washed away the dam of the lake in Gasper Lane. Water surged through Bourton Foundry and swept away countless hand grenade cases. Local children spent many happy hours 'treasure hunting' – some were found in flooded fields as far downstream as Blandford.

New Lake Reservoir in Gasper Street

157

The ancient oak tree where Judge Wyndham used to sit, a tangible connection to Dorset's history.

SILTON
1086 (Domesday Book) Seltone
Old English:
sealh – a willow tree
tun – a farm or estate
'a farm or estate where willow trees grow'

Judge Wyndham's oak tree
Oliver Cromwell appointed Sir Hugh Wyndham (1602-1683) a judge in the Court Of Common Pleas. After the monarchy was restored, Sir Hugh was regarded with suspicion and spent a short term of imprisonment in the Tower of London until he was pardoned by King Charles II. After the Great Fire of London in 1666, Sir Hugh and his brother Sir Wadham served at the Fire Court along with 20 other judges. They heard cases concerning loss of property in the fire and decided who should pay for homes to be rebuilt. The verdict was usually given within 24 hours to avoid delay. The judges served without pay and, in recognition of their dedication, John Michael Wright was commissioned to paint their portraits. The portrait of Sir Hugh, dressed in the robes of a Fire Court judge, hangs in the Guildhall Art Gallery, London.

When Sir Hugh returned to his home in Silton he enjoyed relaxing under his favourite oak tree where he could look across the Forest of Gillingham. The tree is a pedunculate oak and is more than 1,000 years old.

There is a memorial to Sir Hugh, sculpted by Jan van Nost, in St Nicholas Church.

MILTON ON STOUR
1086 (Domesday Book) Mideltone
1397 Milton on Stoure
Old English:
middel – middle
tun – a farm or estate
'the middle farm on the River Stour'

River Stour near Milton Farm Caravan Site

GILLINGHAM

Early 11th century Gillinga ham
1086 (Domesday Book) Gelingeham
Old English:
Gylla – personal name
ing – associated with
ham – a homestead
'a homestead associated with a man named Gylla'.

EAST AND WEST STOUR

1086 (Domesday Book) Sture
1268 Sturewestouere
1371 Stoure Estouere
Old English:
ofer – a river bank
estouere – east bank
westouere – west bank
'a settlement on the east and west banks of the River Stour'
In medieval times these villages were known as Stour Cosin and Stour Wake. Cosin and Wake were the names of families who owned the land.

Henry Fielding (1707-1754)
The author of Tom Jones lived in East Stour when he was a child. In 1734 he returned for a couple of years to live in the rectory, which has since been demolished.

STOUR PROVOST

1086 (Domesday Book) Stur
1270 Stur Preauus
1549 Stowr Provost
Preauus – the abbey in Preaux, Normandy, owned the manor in the 12th and 13th centuries.
Provost – Edward IV (1442-1483) gave the manor to the provost (an administrative office) of King's College, Cambridge
'a settlement owned by the provost (of King's College) on the River Stour'

FIFEHEAD MAGDALEN

1086 (Domesday Book) Fifhide
1388 Fifyde Maudeleyne
Old English:
fif – five
hid – a hide
'an estate of five hides with a church dedicated to Mary Magdalen'
A hide, as assessed in the Domesday Book, was a measurement of productivity of land that was deemed able to support one family (including dependants) for one year. It averaged about 30 acres, depending on fertility of the land and size of family.

MARNHULL

1267 Marnhulle
Old English:
mearn – marl (marl was originally the word for a soft stone consisting of a mixture of clay and calcium carbonate formed under freshwater conditions)
or Mearna – personal name
hyll – a hill
'a settlement on a hill where marl could be found' or *'a settlement owned by a family named Mearna'*

Tess Of The D'Urbervilles
In Thomas Hardy's novel Tess Of The D'Urbervilles, Marnhull was called Marlott and was the birthplace of Tess. The Crown Inn was renamed by Hardy as the Pure Drop Inn.

Hinton St Mary

944 Hamtune
1086 (Domesday Book) Hainetone
1627 Hinton Marye.

Old English:
heah – high
tun – a farm or estate
'a farm or estate on high ground owned by the abbey of St Mary (in Shaftesbury)'

Roman mosaic
In 1963, while the local blacksmith was digging a post hole, he unearthed part of a Roman mosaic floor detailing the head of Christ. The mosaic is now in the British Museum, London.

Sturminster Newton

968 Nywetone at Stoure
1291 Sturminstr Nyweton

Old English:
mynster – a church
niwe – new
tun – a farm or estate
'a new farm or estate with a church on the River Stour'

Sturminster Newton Mill
The mill (below) is mentioned in the Domesday Book (1086). It was rebuilt in 1566. The mill is still in use grinding grain into flour in the traditional way.

In the distance is the ancient Town Bridge that straddles the River Stour taking traffic on the B3092 to Sturminster Newton

When Ryan and I visited the mill in early August 2020, it was closed because of the coronavirus pandemic. However, it is a beautiful place to visit and has picnic areas and car parking. We look forward to a return visit once the mill and museum reopen to the public.

Sticky sign
Glue Hill can be found on the outskirts of Sturminster Newton. As you turn into Glue Hill there is a sign requesting pedestrians 'stick to the pavement'.

Fiddleford

1244 Fitelford

Old English:
Fitela – personal name
ford – a ford
'a ford owned by a man named Fitela'

Fiddleford Manor,
Owned by English Heritage, Fiddleford Manor is one of the oldest medieval buildings in Dorset. In the late 14th century it was the home of William Latimer, sheriff of Somerset and Dorset. The great hall and solar have beautiful 600-year-old timber roofs (see also Darknoll Brook in the chapter on smaller Stour tributaries).

The old Fiddleford Mill…

… and the new

Fiddleford Mill

Near Fiddleford Manor lies Fiddleford Mill, which was used during the late 19th century to store contraband. Brandy, silk and wine were smuggled from France and taken upriver to the mill before being distributed further afield.

Archimedes' screw

Before steam engines were invented the main source of power was from rivers. Flowing water was used to turn waterwheels, which rotated millstones that ground corn to flour. Today, many flour mills are redundant and the waterwheels motionless. However, at Fiddleford Mill the power of water is being harnessed. It flows down the weir over an Archimedes' screw that rotates, driving a generator and producing electricity.

HAMMOON

1086 (Domesday Book) Hame
1280 Hamme Moun

Old English:
hamm – a river meadow or enclosure

Norman:
Moion – personal name
'an enclosure or river meadow owned by the Moion family'

CHILD OKEFORD

1086 (Domesday Book) Acford
1227 Childacford

Old English:
cild – a young nobleman
or cielde – a spring
ac – an oak tree
ford – a ford or river crossing
'a ford with an oak tree owned by a young nobleman'
or *'a ford near a spring'*

SHILLINGSTONE

1444 Shillyngeston

Old English:
Schelin – personal name
tun – a farm or estate
'a farm or estate owned by a man named Schelin'

HANFORD
(AND LITTLE HANFORD)

1086 (Domesday Book) Hanford

Old English:
han – stone
ford – a ford or river crossing
Probably *'a ford by the stone'*

Downstream Dorset – River Tales and Local History

May 2011 Prince Charles and Camilla, Duchess of Cornwall, visited the pub to congratulate the owners on their initiative.

DURWESTON
1086 (Domesday Book) Derwinestone
Old English:
Deorwine – personal name
tun – a farm or estate
'a farm or estate owned by a man named Deorwine'

STOURPAINE
1086 (Domesday Book) Sture
1280 Sture Payn
In the 13th and 14th centuries the land was owned by the Payn family.
'a settlement owned by the Payn family on the River Stour'

Pub is the Hub
In 2010 the village post office and shop closed. In 2011 it reopened inside The White Horse pub *(above)*. This was part of 'The Pub is the Hub' scheme introduced by Prince Charles to preserve rural ways of life. A letter from the Prince of Wales' office is displayed on the wall of the shop and in

BRYANSTON
1086 (Domesday Book) Blaneford
1268 Blaneford Brian
1292 Brianeston
In the 13th century during King John's reign, Brian de Insula from Breton was a feudal baron.
Old English:
tun – a farm or estate
'a farm or estate owned by a man named Brian'

Bryanston School
Bryanston School was built in 1894 as a country house for Viscount Portman. The building was bought by Australian schoolmaster JG Jeffreys in 1928 and it has been a co-educational

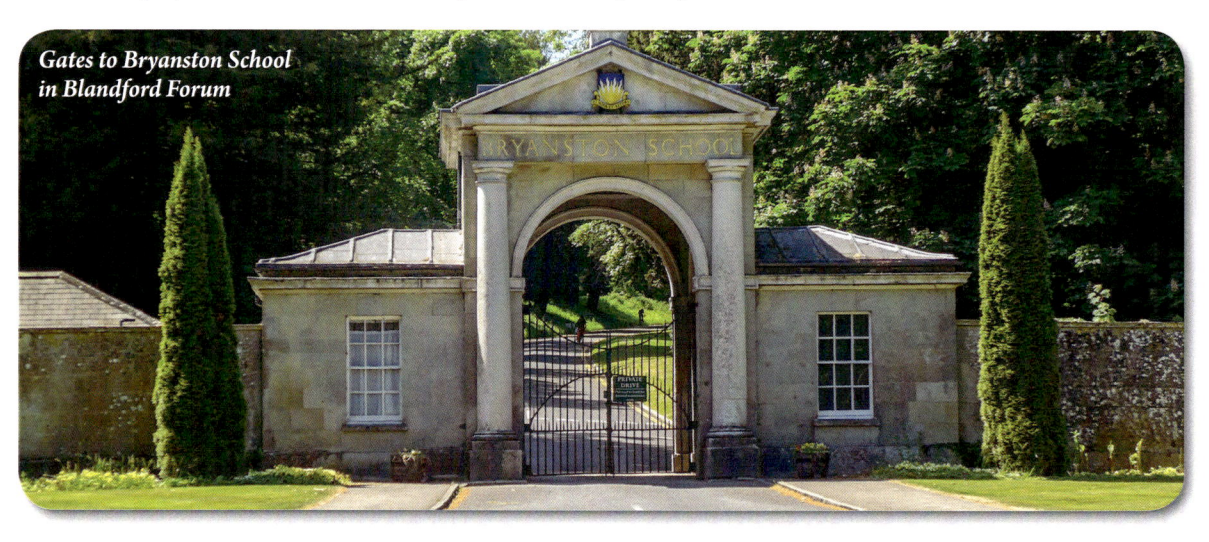

Gates to Bryanston School in Blandford Forum

independent school for day pupils and boarders since. Set in more than 162 hectares (400 acres) of land, some of it woodland, it boasts the tallest plane tree in Europe standing at 49m (160ft).

BLANDFORD FORUM
1086 (Domesday Book) Bleaneford
1297 Blaneford Forum

Old English:
blaegna – gudgeon
ford – a ford or river crossing

Latin:
forum – a market

'a settlement with a market and a ford where gudgeon swim'

Fire of Blandford 1731
In front of the town hall is a paving stone with an inscription written by the Blandford Poetry Society as part of the Millennium Project.

The plaque commemorates victims of the Fire of Blandford in 1731, when 14 people died and about 450 homes were destroyed.

Recipe for regeneration take one careless tallow chandler and two ingenious Bastards

After the fire, local architects John and William Bastard rebuilt the town in the elegant Georgian style. John Bastard designed a monument, Bastard's Pump, erected outside the church of St Peter & St Paul to provide water to tackle any future fires. The Kings Arms pub now sits on the site of the tallow chandler's (candle-maker's) shop where the fire started.

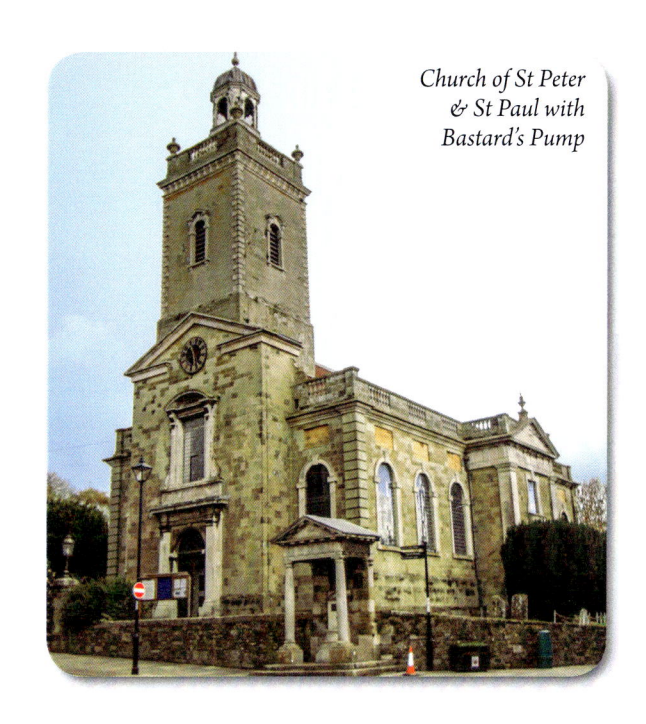

Church of St Peter & St Paul with Bastard's Pump

LANGTON LONG BLANDFORD
1086 (Domesday Book) Bleneford
1280 Blaneford Langeton

Old English:
lang – long
tun – a farm or estate
blaegna – gudgeon
ford – a ford or river crossing

'a long farm or estate near the ford where gudgeon swim'

CHARLTON MARSHALL
1086 (Domesday Book) Cerletone
1288 Cherleton Marescal

Old English:
ceorl – peasants
tun – a farm or estate
13th century Marshall – the Mareschal family became the landowners and later became the earls of Pembroke (see also Sturminster Marshall).

'a farm or estate owned by the peasants, later owned by the Mareschal family'

Sturminster Marshall Bridge

STURMINSTER MARSHALL

9th century Sture minster
1268 Sturministre Marescal

Old English:

mynster – a church
13th century Marshall – the Mareschal family were the landowners and later became the earls of Pembroke (see also Charlton Marshall).
'a settlement on the River Stour with a church, owned by the Mareschal family'

The White Mill

Owned by the National Trust, this 18th century corn mill *(below)* still contains original wooden machinery. Inside you can find information about the millers and their families who have lived and worked there for generations.

Nearby is a magnificent eight-arched bridge, which has spanned the Stour since 1175. It is 64m (210ft) long and only 3.5m (12ft) wide. Probably the oldest bridge in Dorset, it has been repaired several times but has never been widened. At road level there are pedestrian refuges between each arch.

Sturminster Marshall bridge is a 'transportation bridge' featuring a notice that warns would-be vandals the penalty for damaging the bridge is a long stay in Australia. This statute was repealed in 1857 and there are no records showing this penalty was ever enforced.

The Knowlton Bell

Legend has it a church bell lies at the bottom of the river. The tale says the bell was hidden there by thieves from Sturminster Marshall who had stolen it from the ruined church at Knowlton. When they went to retrieve it, the bell kept slipping from their grasp and remains in the river to this day.

Traditional folk song:
Knowlton bell is stole
And thrown into White Mill Hole
Where all the devils in hell
Could never pull up the Knowlton bell

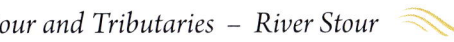

SPETISBURY
1086 (Domesday Book) Spesteberie
Old English:
speoht – a green woodpecker
burh – a fortified place
'a fortified place where the green woodpecker can be seen'

Iron Age skeletons
Spetisbury Rings is an Iron Age hill fort that overlooks the village. In 1857, while the railway was being built, almost 100 skeletons were unearthed. Archaeologists deemed they were defenders of the fort killed in battle with the Roman invaders.

SHAPWICK
1086 (Domesday Book) Scapeuuic
Old English:
sceap – sheep
wic – a specialised farm or a dwelling place
'a settlement with a sheep farm'

Floating coffin
In 1870 the village flooded and a coffin floated from the church, down the river, never to be seen again. It was thought the coffin washed out to sea.

Badbury Rings
Owned and managed by the National Trust, Badbury Rings is an ancient Iron Age fort almost 2,500 years old (550 BC). Among the Celtic tribes who lived within the three rings were the Durotriges. The name Badbury Rings derives from an Anglo Saxon name Badda and the word for a fortification, burh.

In the 4th century its name was Vindocladia, meaning 'white ditches'. The Celtic words *uindo* (white) and *clado* (ditches) probably refer to the chalk before the grass covered the ditches and ramparts.

A flint tool was discovered nearby during an archaeological dig. It is estimated to have been made between 12,000 and 40,000 years ago (see also River Tarrant).

COWGROVE
1288 Cugrave
Old English:
cu – a cow
graf – a grove
'a grove where cows graze'

Cowgrove, Eye Bridge

Kingston Lacy, Pamphill

PAMPHILL
1168 Pamphilla
Old English:
Pampa – personal name
hyll – a hill
'a settlement on a hill owned by a man named Pampa'

Pamphill Dairy
Pamphill Dairy is always worth a visit with tearooms, a butcher, delicatessen and gift shops. There is plenty of outside seating with grassy banks and trees and is very relaxing.

Kingston Lacy house and estate
The estate was originally a royal estate with a hunting lodge. It was leased to the De Lacy family, who fought for William the Conqueror, and later in the 15th century to the Beaufort family. Margaret Beaufort, mother of Henry VII, was born and grew up on the estate.

In 1603 the estate was sold to John Bankes, attorney general to King Charles I. John and Mary Bankes also owned Corfe Castle and 8,000 acres of surrounding countryside (see the chapter on Corfe River for the heroism of Dame Mary).

In 1663 Sir Ralph Bankes commenced building the present Kingston Lacy house and gardens.

In the 19th century William John Bankes commissioned Charles Barry to remodel the house. He created an extensive collection of art and antiquities from his travels abroad, including the Philae obelisk from Ancient Egypt, which can be seen in the photo.

However, in 1841 William Bankes was arrested and was under threat of execution for being involved in homosexual acts. William fled to Italy, abandoning all his priceless possessions. It is believed he never returned to see the completion of his home. However, the Bankes family owned land as far as Studland Bay so it is possible he made clandestine visits to Kingston Lacy, landing in Studland and travelling cross-country.

In 1981 the house and estate were bequeathed to the National Trust, including Corfe Castle and 12 working farms.

Beech Avenue
William John Bankes planted this magnificent avenue of trees *(below)* in 1835 as a gift to his mother, Frances. The 365 trees on one side and 366 trees on the other lined the road to Blandford, a turnpike road from which the Bankes family earned significant revenue. It is thought French prisoners from the Napoleonic Wars undertook the physical work of planting the trees. Today the National Trust is replacing any dying beech trees with hornbeam, a variety more resistant to disease and the effects of traffic.

River Stour near Wimborne

WIMBORNE MINSTER
1086 (Domesday Book) Winburne
1236 Wymburneminstre
Old English:
winn – a meadow
burna – a stream
mynster – a church
'a meadow stream with a church'

Jack the Ripper suspect
In 1888 Montague John Druitt, a barrister, teacher and sportsman, drowned in the River Thames and was buried in his home town at Wimborne cemetery. Druitt was thought by many to be the notorious Jack the Ripper because the brutal killing of prostitutes in London's East End ceased after his death. However, there are many other theories and no proof.

Some believe Druitt's death to have been suicide while others think he was murdered. Druitt worked as a part-time assistant schoolmaster to supplement his living as a barrister. He was dismissed by the school in November 1888 because of a 'very serious

Wimborne cemetery

matter', which was never revealed. A note written by Druitt was found among his possessions saying he feared becoming like his mother who had been committed to an asylum.

Montague Druitt's father was a respected surgeon in Wimborne until his death in 1885. It seems his son was a troubled man with little help available to him.

Canford Magna suspension bridge

MERLEY
Myrle (unsure of date first recorded)
Old French:
myrle – a blackbird
Or possibly the same derivation as Marley Wood, near Winfrith Newburgh.
Old English:
myrge – pleasant
leah – a wood or clearing
'a settlement where blackbirds sing'
or *'a settlement near a wood in pleasant surroundings'*

Castleman Trailway
The Castleman Trailway, which extends from Ringwood to Upton Country Park, passes close to Merley. The trailway is 26.5km (16.5 miles) of disused railway and is very popular with walkers, cyclists and horse riders.

Wimborne solicitor Charles Castleman was responsible for building the railway line that connected Dorset to the national rail network. The railway was closed in 1964, along with many other rural branch lines deemed unprofitable by the chairman of British Railways, Dr Beeching.

CANFORD MAGNA
1086 (Domesday Book) Cheneford
1612 Canford
Old English:
Cana – personal name
ford – a ford crossing
Latin:
magna – great
'a ford crossing the river on land owned by a man named Cana'
Magna distinguishes the village from Little Canford on the east bank of the River Stour.

Gates to Canford School

Canford Manor, from John of Gaunt to Canford School

In the 14th century Canford Manor was the main residence of John of Gaunt, the first Duke of Lancaster and son of King Edward III. His heirs included Henry IV, Henry V and Henry VI, all from the House of Lancaster. In the 19th century the 6,880 hectare (17,000 acre) Canford Estate was owned by the Guest family. In 1868 Sir Ivor Guest married Lady Cornelia Spencer-Churchill, the aunt of Sir Winston Churchill.

Sir Ivor and Lady Cornelia held the titles Lord and Lady Wimborne. Between 1867 and 1904 they built more than 100 homes for families who worked on the estate. These houses have a distinctive style and are known as Lady Wimborne Cottages.

Lord Wimborne gave some land to create a 'people's park'. Today it is known as Poole Park and is enjoyed by families for picnics and boating on the lake.

In 1923 the Manor House and its 120 hectares (300 acres) of grounds were sold and became Canford School, a co-educational independent secondary school for day and boarding pupils.

Priceless work of art discovered

The Guest family may have been unaware of the value of an ancient Assyrian relief mounted on the wall of the school tuck shop. The school auctioned it for £7.7 million.

Protecting the heathland

Canford Heath, once part of Canford Estate, is now owned by the Borough of Poole, while Dorset Wildlife Trust acquired Upton Heath. Both heaths are nature reserves with many rare species of plant, insect, bird and reptile, including the sand lizard and Dartford warbler.

River Stour near Canford Magna suspension bridge

River Stour viewed from Longham Bridge

HAMPRESTON
1086 (Domesday Book) Hame
1244 Hamme Preston
Old English:
hamm – an enclosure or river meadow
preost – a priest
tun – a farm or estate
'a farm or estate with a river meadow, possibly owned by Wimborne Minster'

FERNDOWN
1321 Fyrne
Old English:
fergen – a hill with a wood
The later addition of down could be from the Old English dun – hill
'a settlement on a wooded hill'

KNIGHTON
1288 Knyghteton
Old English:
cniht – a knight
tun – a farm or estate
'a farm or estate owned by a knight'

DUDSBURY
1086 (Domesday Book) Dodesberie
Old English:
Dudd – personal name
burh – a fort
'a fort owned by a man named Dudd'

LONGHAM
1541 Longeham
Old English:
lang – long
hamm – an enclosure or river meadow
'a settlement with a long enclosure or river meadow'

BEARWOOD
1840 Bearwood
Old English:
bearu – a wood
'a settlement near a wood'

KINSON
1086 (Domesday Book) Chinestanestone
1231 Kynestanton
Old English:
Cynestan – personal name
tun – a farm or estate
a farm or estate owned by a man named Cynestan'

Smuggler 'barbarously murdered'
Robert Trotman was shot on 24th March 1765 during a skirmish between a group of smugglers unloading tea on Sandbanks beach and a team of customs officers. It wasn't clear who fired the fatal shot but the inquest declared the smuggler's death was a 'wilful murder by person unknown'. However, the jury was thought to have included several of the smugglers.

Trotman is buried in St Andrew's churchyard. The inscription on his headstone is mostly illegible but read:

> "To the Memory of ROBERT TROTMAN
> Late of Rond in the County of Wilts
> Who was barbarously Murder'd
> On the shore near Poole the 24 March 1765.
> A little Tea one leaf I did not steal
> For Guiltless Blood shed I to GOD appeal
> Put Tea in one scale human Blood in tother
> And think what tis to slay thy harmles Brother."

St Andrew's church, Kinson

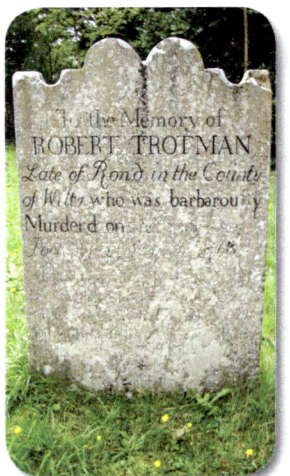

The Shapwick Express, Olympic champion
Charles Bennett was Britain's first Olympic athlete to win a gold medal. He triumphed in the Olympic Games held in Paris in 1900, where he won two gold medals and one silver. He is buried alongside his wife Sarah in St Andrew's churchyard.

WEST PARLEY
1086 (Domesday Book) Perlai
1305 Westperele
Old English:
peru – a pear tree
leah – a wood or clearing
'a settlement near a wood or in a clearing where pear trees grow'
West distinguishes the village from East Parley, which is closer to Bournemouth International airport.

ENSBURY
(Kinson) 1463 Eynesburgh
Old English:
Aegen – personal name
burh – a fortified place
'a fortified place owned by a man named Aegen'

Above: Downstream by the bridge over the weir at Throop Mill
Right: Upstream of the same bridge
Below: Throop Mill itself

THROOP
(Bournemouth) 12th century la Throup
Old English:
throp – an outlying farm
'a settlement with an outlying farm'

Throop Mill
A mill at Throop was mentioned in the Domesday Book (1086). The present flour mill has been derelict since 1974 but, thanks to local initiatives, there is a plan to restore the mill to working order and create a visitors' centre.

It's sad to see it so neglected but there are beautiful walks along the millstream and the River Stour

HOLDENHURST
1086 (Domesday Book) Holehest
1397 Holnhurst
Old English:
holegn – a holly tree
hyrst – a wooded hill
'a settlement on a hill where holly trees grow'

BLACKWATER
(near Hurn)
As the name suggests, in the 18th century the water was black or dark-coloured.
'a settlement where the river is dark, not clear water'

JUMPERS COMMON
16th century from the family name, Jumper
'common land lived on by a family named Jumper'

LITTLEDOWN
13th century Le Lytildoune
Old English:
dun – a hill or down
'a settlement on or near a small hill'

IFORD
12th century Huver
Old English:
yfer – a slope
'a settlement on a slope'

TUCKTON
1248 Tuketon
Old English:
Tucca – personal name
tun – a farm or estate
'a farm or estate owned by a man named Tucca'

Tolstoy in print

In 1897 the Tuckton waterworks were converted to printing works. Several Russian exiles were living in the area, one of whom, Count Vladimir Tchertkov, was a friend of Leo Tolstoy. Tolstoy's writings had been banned in Russia so they were printed in Tuckton. The building (*below*) is now residential with gardens overlooking the river.

While visiting the old waterworks I met a group of coronavirus coffee friends sitting outside their homes in Iford Close. Despite social distancing they were having a lively chat and showed great interest in my research. During our travels and explorations I am always impressed by the friendliness of Dorset folk.

Small scale

Tucktonia was a model village consisting of more than 200 famous British landmarks in miniature, including Buckingham Palace and Stonehenge. It was created by Formula 3 racing champion Harry Stiller.

There were also fairground rides, go-karting and a 'haunted house' on the site. A model railway took passengers for a half-mile ride through the attractions.

Tucktonia was officially opened in May 1976 by comedian Arthur Askey. Other famous people to visit include Tommy Cooper and Jon Pertwee, in the guise of Worzel Gummidge.

Sadly the number of visitors declined and Tucktonia closed in 1986. The model buildings were dismantled and stored in a warehouse in Verwood. They were all destroyed in a fire in 1990 except Buckingham Palace, which found a temporary home in Wimborne Model Town & Gardens. The steam engine, Tinkerbell, moved to Moors Valley Country Park, where it is still enjoyed today.

Christchurch Priory

WICK
12th century la Wych
1263 Wyke
Old English:
wic – a dwelling place
'a dwelling place'

CHRISTCHURCH
10th century Tweoxneam
934 Twynham
1086 (Domesday Book) Thuinam
1318 Cristeschirche of Twynham
Old English:
betweoxn – between or betwixt
ea – a stream
'a settlement between two streams' (River Stour and River Avon)

By 1318 it was known as 'the church of Christ between two streams' later shortened to 'Christchurch'.

Miracle of Christchurch Priory
The priory was built in the 11th and 12th centuries and its nave is said to be the longest in the country at 95m (311 feet). During its construction a wooden beam was cut and hoisted into place but was found to be slightly under length. As it was evening, the tired workmen decided to rectify the problem the following day. Returning the next morning they discovered the beam had suddenly become the correct length. Many believed that there had been a miracle. Jesus, carpenter by trade, had visited the site and lengthened the beam. As a result, the name of the

Christchurch Norman House

Christchurch Great Castle Tower

town was changed from Thuinam to Christchurch out of respect for Christ's intervention.

Christchurch Castle Great Tower

Christchurch Castle Great Tower, also known as the Keep, was built on the castle mound, north of the priory. Originally the fortified Saxon settlement was called Twyneham, meaning 'between two rivers'.

In the 12th century the earlier wooden buildings were rebuilt in stone by Richard, 2nd Earl of Devon, creating the Norman castle. The Great Tower was used by the landowner as a refuge when under attack. The Norman House was also built in the 12th century. It was the luxurious home of the earl and his family. In later years it was the residence of the constable of the castle, who was responsible for its security.

PUREWELL

1300 Perewell

Old English:

peru – a pear tree
wella – a spring
'a settlement with a spring by a pear tree'

HENGISTBURY HEAD

12th century Hedenesburia
19th century Hengistbury Head

Old English:

Heddin – personal name
burh – a fortified place
head – a headland
'a fortified place on a headland owned by a man named Heddin'

175

Chapter 34

RIVER CALE, FILLEY BROOK AND BOW BROOK

The River Cale rises in Somerset, near Nyland in Dorset. The Cale is joined by two tributaries, on its western side by Bow Brook and on its eastern side by Filley Brook. The river flows under the A30 to confluence with the River Stour west of Marnhull.

RIVER CALE

VILLAGES AND TOWNS IN DORSET AND THE ORIGINS OF THEIR NAMES
(from entering Dorset to confluence with the River Stour)

BUCKHORN WESTON
see Filley Brook opposite

KINGTON MAGNA
see Filley Brook opposite

HIGHER AND LOWER NYLAND
see Nyland, Filley Brook opposite

FIFEHEAD MAGDALEN
1086 (Domesday Book) Fifhide
1388 Fifyde Maudeleyne

Old English:
fif – five
hid – a hide
'an estate of five hides with a church dedicated to Mary Magdalen'
A hide, as assessed in the Domesday Book, was a measurement of productivity of land that was deemed able to support one family (including dependants) for one year. It averaged about 30 acres, depending on the fertility of the land and size of the family.

MARNHULL
1267 Marnhulle
Old English:
Mearna – personal name
hyll – a hill
'a settlement on a hill owned by a man named Mearna'

FILLEY BROOK
VILLAGES AND TOWNS AND THE ORIGINS OF THEIR NAMES
(from source to confluence with the River Cale)

FILLEY BROOK
Old English:
filethe – hay
'a brook along which hay is harvested'

QUARR
The name is probably taken from a quarry in the area.

BUCKHORN WESTON
1086 (Domesday Book) Westone
1275 Boukeresweston
Middle English:
bouker – a bleacher of cloth
Old English:
west – west
tun – a farm or estate
'a farm or estate to the west of Gillingham where a bleacher of cloth lives'

Captain Hugh Stapleton
The wrought-iron gates to the church of St John the Baptist *(right)* were installed in memory of Captain Hugh Stapleton. He was born in Buckhorn Weston in 1863 and had a distinguished naval career. Starting as a cadet aged 13, by the time he was 22 he had been promoted through the ranks to lieutenant. He served on HMS Seagull, HMS Agincourt and HMS Benbow, attaining the rank of commander before he resigned his commission in 1895, aged 32. At the outbreak of the First World War in 1914, Commander Hugh Stapleton rejoined the navy and served with HM Coastguard. He was awarded three medals and the rank of captain in 'recognition of his services during the war'.

NYLAND
1086 (Domesday Book) Iland
1581 Nilonde
Old English:
ieg-land – an area of dry land in a marsh
'a settlement on an island of dry ground within marsh land'

KINGTON MAGNA
1086 (Domesday Book) Chintone
1243 Magna Kington
1290 Great Kington
Old English:
cyne – a king
tun – a farm or estate
Latin:
magna – great
'a royal estate of greater importance or size than Little Kington, near West Stour'

BOW BROOK
possibly from **Old English:**
bula – bulls
'a brook where bulls come to drink'

Chapter 35

BIBBERN BROOK

AT A GLANCE

SOURCE
Rises from springs near Stourton Caundle, Purse Caundle and Stalbridge.

MOUTH / OUTLET
Confluences with the River Stour north of Kings Mill Bridge.

LENGTH
About 7.7km (4.8 miles)

Bibbern Brook derives its name from the Old English words *byden* meaning a 'hollow', and *burna* meaning a 'stream', so it is a stream flowing along a hollow or depression in the landscape. The brook rises in Blackmore Vale. A footpath follows its flow to Poolestown, joining with the River Stour north of Kings Mill Bridge.

VILLAGES AND TOWNS IN DORSET AND THE ORIGINS OF THEIR NAMES
(from source to confluence with the River Stour)

STOURTON CAUNDLE
1086 (Domesday Book) Candel
1275 Caundelhaddon
1709 Stourton Candel
Haddon – family name of the owners since 1202
Stourton – family name of the owners since 15th century
'a settlement near Caundle Brook originally owned by the Haddon family, later by Lord Stourton and his descendants'

PURSE CAUNDLE
1241 Purscaundel
Purse – possibly the family name of the owner
'a settlement near the Caundle Brook possibly owned by the Purse family'

COCKHILL FARM
1332 Cukhull
Old English:
cocc – a cock or male bird
hyll – a hill
possibly *'a hill where woodcocks (wuducocc) are found'*

STALBRIDGE
860 Stapulbrige
1086 (Domesday Book) Staplebrige
Old English:
stapol – a post or a pile
Brycg – a bridge
'a bridge supported by posts or piles'

POOLESTOWN
possibly *'a settlement where the water (from Bibbern Brook) pools'*

A delicious surprise!
As we were driving along Cook's Lane to join the A357 to Poolestown and Stalbridge, we noticed a sign pointing to a cafe. Turning off the main road we found ourselves in a farmyard containing several enterprising businesses. Among them was Thyme After Time, Café and Catering. We were expecting a roadside caff but were invited instead into a friendly, attractive tearoom serving delicious home-made food. Steve, who owns the cafe with Margot, told us we were eating in the milking parlour, while the tables behind us were in the piggery!

Steve and Margot paid for the site of the signage we had spied in a hedgerow by giving the farmer and all the farmhands a free full English breakfast.

STALBRIDGE WESTON
1086 (Domesday Book) Westone
Old English:
west – west
tun – a farm or estate
'a farm or estate to the west'
Stalbridge is the name of the parish

Chapter 36

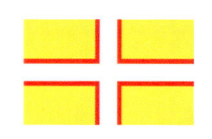

RIVER LYDDEN

AT A GLANCE

SOURCE
Chalk escarpment south of Buckland Newton, near the Church of the Holy Rood

MOUTH / OUTLET
Confluences with the River Stour downstream from Kings Mill Bridge, near Marnhull

LENGTH
About 25km (15 miles)

TRIBUTARIES
- Caundle Brook, confluences with the River Lydden near Lydlinch
- Wonston Brook, confluences with the River Lydden south of Lydden House, east of Woodbridge and Kingston in the parish of Hazelbury Bryan
- Several smaller tributaries

The River Lydden, a tributary of the River Stour, flows through Blackmore Vale. The Celts named the river, meaning the 'wide or broad one'. The Lydden flows over Oxford clay so is prone to flooding, perhaps giving rise to its name. There are few settlements along its banks as most of the villages, churches and manor houses have been built away from the flood plain.

The River Lydden as it leaves the hills and starts its journey, passing under the road in Buckland Newton

River Stour and Tributaries – River Lydden

VILLAGES AND TOWNS AND THE ORIGINS OF THEIR NAMES
(from source to its confluence with the River Stour)

Church of the Holy Rood, showing the window of the priests' room above the porch

BUCKLAND NEWTON
854 Bocland
1576 Newton Buckland
Old English:
bocland – land given by charter
tun – a farm or estate
Newton was probably taken from Sturminster Newton
'a farm or estate on land given by charter'

Bocland and Focland
Bocland was land owned by individuals with rights given under charter in perpetuity, passing on to the next generation. The owners of Bocland gave their residents the right to pay rent for their homes and grow food on the land.

Focland was common land with rights granted by the king to the people who lived there, mainly for foraging and grazing.

Brothers' bed and breakfast
When they visited Buckland Newton to preach, monks from Glastonbury Abbey or Milton Abbey probably rested in the small room with a fireplace above the porch of Holy Rood Church.

DUNTISH
1268 Donetys
Old English:
dun – a hill
etisc – a pasture
'a settlement on hill pastures'

BEAULIEU WOOD
1288 Beleye
Old English:
beo – bees
leah – a wood, a clearing in a wood
'a settlement in a wood where there are swarms of bees'

PULHAM
1086 (Domesday Book) Poleham
Old English:
pol, pull – a pool
ham – an enclosure or homestead
'a homestead or enclosure beside a pool'

KING'S STAG (KINGSTAG)
1337 Kingestake
Old English:
cyning – a king
staca – a stake or post, indicating a boundary
'a settlement on the boundary of the king's land'
Today, three civil parish boundaries come together on the bridge that crosses the River Lydden – Pulham CP, Lydlinch CP and Hazelbury Bryan CP.

Royal protection
There is a legend that when King Henry III was hunting in this area, he spared the life of a magnificent white stag. To the king's fury the

181

bailiff of Blackmore Vale killed the stag, possibly to please his majesty. The bailiff was imprisoned and all the inhabitants of Blackmore Vale fined.

You have been warned!

Outside the village of King's Stag the smallest bridge in Dorset crosses the River Lydden and displays a 'transportation' sign. It warns against vandalism. The punishment for transgression was transportation to Australia for life.

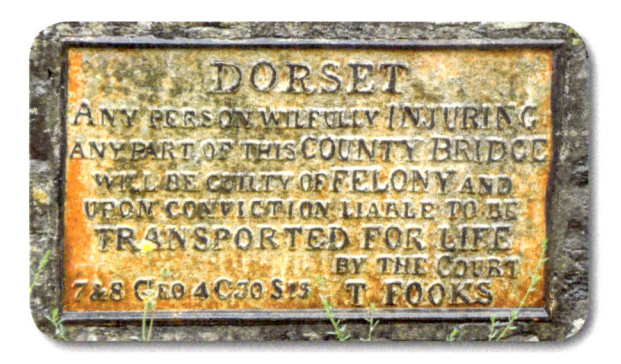

LYDLINCH
see also Caundle Brook
1285 Lidelinch
Old English:
Lide – refers to the River Lydden
hlinc – a slope
'a settlement on a slope near the River Lydden'
or *'on the banks of the River Lydden'*

Haven for butterflies and moths

Lydlinch Common is an area of scrubland, grassland and woods. Many species of butterflies and moths thrive in this area thanks to the tireless work of the Butterfly Conservation Dorset Branch. Its volunteers have created a habitat for these beautiful creatures to breed, including the marsh fritillary, marbled white, white admiral and purple hairstreak.

The nightingale can be heard singing in its favourite habitat, blackthorn scrub, which has been maintained and preserved. Lydlinch Common is privately owned but offers access to the public. It is a Site of Special Scientific Interest and receives funding from Natural England towards its preservation.

BAGBER
1201 Bakeberge
Old English:
Bacca – personal name
beorg – a hill
bearu – a grove
'a settlement on a hill, or in a grove, owned by a man named Bacca'

STALBRIDGE
860 Stapulbrige
1086 (Domesday Book) Staplebrige
Old English:
stapol – a pillar or post
brycg – a bridge
'a settlement by a bridge built on pillars or piles

Stalbridge Park gate columns

Looking from Kings Mill Bridge, the River Lydden joins the River Stour

Boyle's Law
The 17th century scientist Robert Boyle lived for six years in his Elizabethan house at Stalbridge Park, which no longer exists. The only remnants of the estate are the gate columns featuring heraldic beasts and a portion of the wall.

Boyles Law is well known by schoolchildren studying physics and chemistry… the volume of a gas varies inversely with pressure.

After he moved to Oxford, Boyle worked on his inventions and discoveries around compressed air, including the pneumatic tyre.

MARNHULL
1267 Marnhulle
Old English:
Mearna – personal name
hyll – a hill
'a settlement on a hill owned by a man named Mearna'

Bull baiting
Until 1763, bull baiting was a very popular sport in Marnhull. The rivalry between the supporters could be so intense it often led to outbreaks of great violence, eventually resulting in its ban.

What is life?
In the church there was once a memorial dedicated to the parish clerk, John Warren, who died in 1752 aged 94. The wording has been recorded as saying:

Here under this stone lie Ruth and old John
Who smoked all his life and so did his wife,
And now there's no doubt
But their pipes are both out,
Be it said without joke
That life is but smoke
Though you live to fourscore,
'tis a wiff and no more

183

Chapter 37

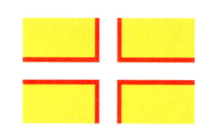

CAUNDLE BROOK WITH RIVER CAM

AT A GLANCE

SOURCE
Rises close to Clinger Farm at the foot of Dogbury Hill, near Cosmore

MOUTH / OUTLET
Confluences with the River Lydden near Lydlinch

LENGTH
21.7km (13.5 miles)

TRIBUTARIES
The Cam and smaller tributaries that drain Caundle Marsh

Caundle Brook is a tributary of the River Lydden and for a short distance they flow almost parallel. The brook then flows in a northerly direction through Blackmore Vale and eastward under Cornford Bridge, Caundle Bridge and Warr Bridge, until it reaches its confluence with the River Lydden.

The name Caundle has been used for centuries but its meaning is uncertain. One possibility is the Caundle villages lie on an outcrop of cornbrash. Cornbrash is a type of limestone containing fossils from the Jurassic period. It made good soil for growing corn but was also used in local buildings and stone walls, often combined with forest marble.

Round Chimneys Farm, August 2019, a holiday cottage on a working farm. The annexe to the right used to house the kitchen

VILLAGES AND TOWNS AND THE ORIGINS OF THEIR NAMES
(from source to confluence with the River Lydden)

TILEY
1299 Tyleye
Old English:
tigel – tiles
leah – a wood
'a settlement near a wood where tiles were made'

MIDDLEMARSH
1277 Middelmersh
Old English:
middle – middle
mersc – a marsh
'a settlement surrounded by marshland'

GLANVILLES WOOTTON
1086 (Domesday Book) Widetone
1288 Wotton Glaunuill
Old English:
Glaunuill – personal name
wudu – a wood
tun – a farm or estate
'a farm or estate near a wood owned by the Glanville family'

Churchill roots
Round Chimneys Farm lies to the north of the village of Glanvilles Wootton. John Churchill, son of the first Sir Winston, was born at Round Chimneys Farm in 1650. He later became the first Duke of Marlborough.

In 1685, John Churchill fought at the Battle of Sedgemoor alongside the Bishop of Winchester (see the Cavalier Bishop – Purse Caundle). The battle resulted in the execution of the Duke of Monmouth who was leading a rebellion against King James II.

In 1704 Churchill won a major victory at the Battle of Blenheim and was rewarded with the Woodstock estate in Oxfordshire, where he built the magnificent Blenheim Palace.

Sir John was married to Sarah Churchill (nee Jennings), keeper of the privy purse to Queen Anne and the queen's confidante until political intrigue brought an end to their friendship.

Highwayman, lawyer and physician
John Clavell lived at Round Chimneys Farm for a while in the early 17th century. The son of an impoverished aristocratic family, he was sent down from Oxford University after stealing silver plate. Clavell then chose to embark on a career as a highwayman.

After his arrest and being sentenced to death by hanging, he received a pardon from King Charles I in 1627. Soon after he wrote a poetic literary work entitled A Recantation Of An Ill Led Life. Clavell was an educated man. Despite his expulsion from Oxford University he worked as a lawyer and physician, recording cures for various illnesses.

John Clavell's uncle, Sir William Clavell, was the owner of Smedmore House and estate in Kimmeridge but disinherited his nephew, possibly because of the ill-repute he had brought to the family name.

BOYS HILL
1582 Boies Hill
Old English:
hyll – a hill
Norman:
De Boys – personal name
'a hill owned by William de Boys'

SANDHILLS
13th century Sandhulle
Old English:
sand – sand
hyll – a hill
'a settlement on or near a sandy hill'

HOLWELL
1188 Holewala
Old English:
hol – a hollow
walu – a bank or ridge
'a settlement by the banks of Caundle Brook'

UK's oldest pillar box
Barnes Cross, which lies to the west of the village of Holwell, is the site of the oldest pillar box still in use in the UK. Made in the 1850s, it has an unusual octagonal shape with a vertical slit for posting letters and is shorter than modern pillar boxes.

BISHOP'S CAUNDLE
1086 (Domesday Book) Candel
1294 Caundel Bishops
'a settlement owned by the Bishop of Salisbury near Caundle Brook'

An alternative meaning
In 1983 Douglas Adams, author of The Hitchhiker's Guide to the Galaxy trilogy, published tongue-in-cheek dictionary The Meaning Of Liff. Bishop's Caundle is defined as: "An opening gambit before a game of chess whereby the missing pieces are replaced by small ornaments from the mantelpiece."

Victory celebrations
On 18th June 1815, Napoleon Bonaparte was defeated at the Battle of Waterloo. This hard-fought British victory was celebrated in towns and villages throughout the country. The Rev William Barnes contributed to these celebrations by writing a lengthy poem in the Dorset dialect entitled Bishop's Caundle. In it he describes feasting and dancing on the village green, with musicians playing on a farm wagon painted in bright colours for the occasion.

The following is an extract:

'At Peace day, who but we should goo
To Caundle for an hour or two:
As gay a day as ever broke
Above the heads of Caundle volk …
… in Caundle, vor a day at least
You woudden vind a scowlen feace
Or dumpy heart in al the pleace'

PURSE CAUNDLE
1241 Purscaundel
Purse – possibly a personal name
'a settlement near the Caundle Brook possibly owned by the Purse family'

River Stour and Tributaries — Caundle Brook with River Cam

The Cavalier bishop

Peter Mews (1619-1706) was born in the Manor House, Purse Caundle *(above)*, during the English Civil War. Mews joined the army and fought on the side of King Charles I as a Cavalier soldier. He was courageous in battle, receiving more than 30 wounds and eventually being taken prisoner. Later portraits of Bishop Mews show a black patch on his cheek covering a scar from a battle wound.

Captain Mews also spent time in Holland as a Royalist spy and messenger. He was skilled at inventing disguises that helped him escape the hangman's noose.

In 1684, aged 66, Peter Mews was installed as Bishop of Winchester but soon returned to battle when the Duke of Monmouth attempted to seize the throne from James II. The Cavalier Bishop fought at the Battle of Sedgemoor in Somerset where the King's army was victorious. Bishop Mews pleaded for mercy for the Duke of Monmouth but to no avail, he was executed on Tower Hill, London, in 1685.

CAUNDLE WAKE

1288 Caundelwake
Wake – personal name
'a settlement near the Caundle Brook owned by the Wake family'

STOURTON CAUNDLE

1086 (Domesday Book) Candel
1275 Caundelhaddon
1709 Stourton Candel
Haddon – family name of the owners since 1202
Stourton – family name of the owners since 15th century
'a settlement near Caundle Brook originally owned by the Haddon family, later by Lord Stourton and his descendants'

Enid Blyton (1897-1968)

The much-loved children's author lived with her husband at the 16th century Manor Farm *(below)* in Stourton Caundle in the 1950s. It is thought she based the story of Five On Finniston Farm on her time at Manor Farm.

WOODBRIDGE
1194 Wudebrige
Old English:
wudu – wood
brycg – a bridge
'a settlement near a wooden bridge across Caundle Brook'
Lydlinch
see also River Lydden
1285 Lidelinch
Old English:
Lide – refers to the River Lydden
hlinc – a slope
'a settlement on a slope near the River Lydden'
or *'on the banks of the River Lydden'*

Lydlinch Common
The Dorset branch of Butterfly Conservation has devoted many years to clearing scrubland to create a conservation site for butterflies and moths. Multiple species of butterfly live and breed on the common, including the white admiral, marsh fritillary and purple hairstreak.

(For more information, see the chapter on the River Lydden.)

Lydlinch Common

RIVER CAM
(tributary)
Cam is an Old Celtic word meaning 'winding' or 'crooked'.

HERMITAGE
1309 the hermitage of Blakemore
1389 Ermytage
'a place where a religious person, probably a monk, lives separately from the rest of the community'

HOLNEST
1185 Holeherst
Old English:
holegn – holly
hyrst – a wooded hill
'a wooded hill where holly trees grow'

LONGBURTON
1244 Burton
1460 Lange Bourton
Old English:
lang – long
burh – a fortified place
tun – a farm or estate
'a long or spread-out fortified farm or estate'

Twisted Cider
Driving along Bradford Lane we came across Spring Farm Cider Barn. Sam, the father of Ben who owns the business, Twisted Cider, told us the variety of orchards on the farm provide the apples for pulping and pressing to make craft cider. We tasted several flavours and while chatting to Sam we learned that not only had the business suffered because of coronavirus, it had also experienced a devastating fire. The flames destroyed the barn that housed the presses and their trailer for selling produce at fairs and markets. At the time we visited they were using a temporary set-up in another barn while a new barn was being built in a nearby field. If you like cider we would recommend you call in at Spring Farm. They also sell chilli sauce and honey.

FOLKE
1244 Folk
Old English:
folc – the people or folk
'common land owned by the people who lived in the area'

Chapter 38

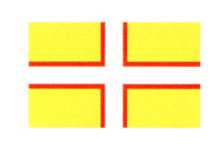

RIVER DIVELISH

AT A GLANCE

SOURCE
Springs north of Bulbarrow Hill near Hazelbury Bryan, Stoke Wake, Ibberton and Woolland

MOUTH / OUTLET
Confluences with River Stour upstream from Sturminster Newton

LENGTH
About 11km (6.8 miles)

Several streams flow together near Fifehead St Quentin to form the River Divelish.

VILLAGES AND TOWNS AND THE ORIGINS OF THEIR NAMES
(from source to confluence with the River Stour)

HAZELBURY BRYAN
1237 Haselber
1547 Hasilbere Bryan
Old English:
haesel – a hazel tree
bearu – a wood
Norman Bryene – from Brienne in France
'a settlement where hazel trees grow, owned by a family from Brienne'

STOKE WAKE
1086 (Domesday Book) Stoche
1285 Stoke Wake
Old English:
stoc – a secondary farm
Wake – personal name
'a secondary farm owned by a man named Wake'

190

WOOLLAND
833 Wennland
1212 Wuland
Old English:
wynn – a meadow
land – tilled land or an estate
'meadowland as part of an estate where some of the land is cultivated'

IBBERTON
1086 (Domesday Book) Abistetone
1212 Hedbredinton
1288 Edbrightinton
Old English:
Eadbeorht – personal name
ing – associated with or belonging to
tun – a farm or estate
'a farm or estate owned by a man named Eadbeorht'

KITFORD
Possibly from **Old English:**
cyta – a kite
ford – a ford or river crossing
'a ford where kites are seen to fly or nest'

FIFEHEAD ST QUINTIN
1086 (Domesday Book) Fifhide
1268 Fifhide Quintyn
Old English:
fif – five
hid – a hide
Quintyn – personal name from de Sancto Quintino
'an area of land measuring five hides owned by a family named St Quintin'

FIFEHEAD NEVILLE
1086 (Domesday Book) Fifhide
1287 Fyfhud Neuyle
Old English:
fif – five
hid – a hide
Neuyle – personal name from Neuville in France
'Five hides owned by a man named Neville'
One hide is an area of land deemed able to support one family and all dependants.

STURMINSTER NEWTON
968 Nywetone at Stoure
1291 Sturminstr Nyweton
Old English:
mynster – a church
niwe – new
tun – a farm or estate
'a new farm or estate with a church on the River Stour'

Old and new
Rolls Mill Bridge is a double bridge. The older bridge runs parallel with the newer bridge, which takes the traffic along the A357 from Shillingstone to Stalbridge.

Left: Tommy (Jack Russell) crossing the ford in Kitford Lane with Ryan
Right: Arches of the older, non-traffic-bearing bridge

Chapter 39

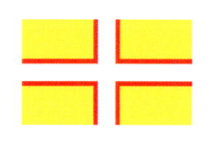

KEY BROOK, STIRCHELL BROOK, TWYFORD BROOK AND MANSTON BROOK

AT A GLANCE

SOURCE
Key Brook rises from several springs in the hills west of Shaftesbury and south of the A30
Stirchell Brook rises from several springs south of Shaftesbury and also around Melbury Abbas
Twyford Brook rises from several springs west of the A350 between West Melbury and Compton Abbas
Manston Brook starts its journey at the confluence between Key Brook and Stirchell Brook in West Orchard

MOUTH / OUTLET
Key Brook and Stirchell Brook confluence at West Orchard
Twyford Brook confluences with Stirchell Brook south of Woodbridge Mill
Manston Brook confluences with the River Stour near the village of Manston

LENGTH
From source of Key Brook to River Stour about 12km (7.5 miles)
From source of Stirchell Brook to River Stour about 10km (6.2 miles)
From source of Twyford Brook to River Stour about 12km (7.5 miles)

River Stour and Tributaries – Key Brook, Stirchell Brook, Twyford Brook and Manston Brook

South of Shaftesbury in the Blackmore Vale two streams, Key Brook and Stirchell Brook, flow together at West Orchard to form Manston Brook, a tributary of the River Stour. Twyford Brook is a tributary that joins Stirchell Brook just south of Woodbridge Mill. Manston Brook travels southward past Manston House to its confluence with the River Stour. Another minor tributary flows into Manston Brook near Manston.

KEY BROOK

I could find no history on the naming of Key Brook. It may have the meaning of 'fundamental' in reference to Key Brook being the source of Manston Brook.

STIRCHELL BROOK

Stir is probably derived from Stur – an older name for the River Stour.

Old English:
ceole – a gorge
or cealc – chalk
'a stream associated with the River Stour flowing through a gorge'
or *'a chalk stream associated with the River Stour'*

TWYFORD BROOK

The name is taken from Twyford village (see below) where there are two fords that cross streams.

MANSTON BROOK

The name is taken from Manston village (see below) where the settlement was fortified and owned by an Anglo Saxon named Mann.

Schematic diagram of Key Brook, Stirchell Brook, Twyford Brook, Manston Brook and the River Stour

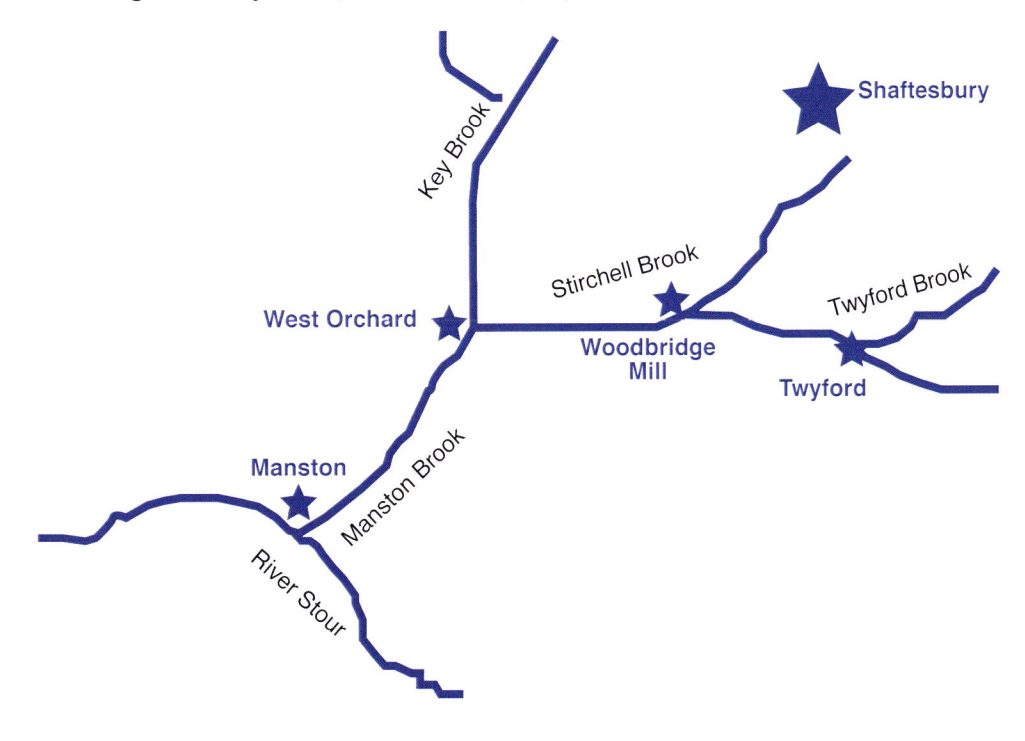

Villages and Towns and the Origins of their Names
(from source to mouth of brooks)

Gold Hill, Shaftesbury

SHAFTESBURY
877 Sceaftesburi
1086 (Domesday Book) Sceftesberie
Old English:
Sceaft – personal name
burh – a fortified place
'a fortified settlement owned by a man named Sceaft'

Shaftesbury
This ancient Saxon market town is the only notable settlement on top of a hill in Dorset being about 215m (700ft) above sea level. It has wonderful views across the Blackmore Vale and is on the edge of Cranborne Chase, a former royal hunting ground that stretches into Wiltshire.

Gold Hill is a steep, cobbled road made famous by an advertisement for Hovis bread. It is a favourite site for photographers, both amateur and professional.

Shaftesbury Abbey
The abbey was founded by King Alfred in 888 AD and he appointed his daughter as abbess. In the following century King Athelstan founded two royal mints at the abbey so it became the wealthiest Benedictine nunnery in the country.

In the 10th century the remains of King Edward the Martyr were moved from Wareham to Shaftesbury Abbey (for more information about his death see the chapter on Corfe Rivers). It became a place of pilgrimage where people came to pray for healing. During the reign of King Henry VIII the abbey was almost destroyed as part of the Dissolution of the Monasteries (1536-1540).

The foundations are now part of tranquil gardens that feature a museum displaying archaeological discoveries from the once wealthy and powerful abbey.

ALCESTER
1433 Alcestre
'land owned by Alcester Abbey, Wiltshire'

DUNCLIFFE HILL
1247 Dunclive
Old English:
dunn – brown or dark
clif – a steep slope or long cliff
'a dark, steep slope or cliff'

WOODVILLE
1444 Wodefeld
Old English:
wudu – a wood
feld – a field
'a wooded field'

CANN
12th century Canna
Old English:
canne – a cup or crater
'a settlement in a deep valley'

River Stour and Tributaries – Key Brook, Stirchell Brook, Twyford Brook and Manston Brook

MELBURY ABBAS
1086 (Domesday Book) Meleberie
1291 Melbury Abbatisse
Old English:
mele – a bowl or basin
or maele – multi-coloured
burh – a fortified place
Latin:
abbatissa – an abbess
'a fortified settlement in a hollow between hills'
or
'a fortified settlement in an area that is multi-coloured, possibly from surrounding fields, soil and woodland'
By the 13th century Melbury Abbas was owned by Sherborne Abbey

Melbury Hill and Melbury Beacon
At the summit of Melbury Hill lies the remains of Melbury Beacon and a circular enclosure. It was one of a chain of beacons that stretched from London to Plymouth. Fire from lit beacons at night would warn of impending invasion, while smoke would be used during the day.

The National Trust acquired Melbury Hill, also known as Melbury Down, to commemorate Dorset novelist and poet Thomas Hardy. Many of Hardy's novels were set in Blackmore Vale.

GUYS MARSH
1401 Gyesmersch
Old English:
Gyes – personal name
mersc – marshland
'marshland owned by a man named Guy'

Guys Marsh Prison
The prison was originally a US military hospital but became a borstal for young offenders in the 1960s. After refurbishment in the 1980s it was renamed a young offenders' institution until a decade later, when it became the adult prison it remains today.

TWYFORD
1395 Tweyford
Old English:
twi – two
ford – a ford
'a settlement where there are two fords, one crossing Twyford Brook the other crossing a small, unnamed tributary'

WOODBRIDGE
932 wde bricge
1395 Wodebrygge
Old English:
wudu – wood
bricg – a bridge
'a settlement by a wooden bridge'
Woodbridge Mill is a private residence.

Driveway leading to Woodbridge Mill with Twyford Brook flowing towards its confluence with Stirchell Brook

HARTGROVE
12th century Haregrave
Old English:
hara – hares
graf – a grove
'a grove where many hares live'

WOODVILLE
1244 Wodelande
Old English:
wudu – a wood
land – cultivated land
'an area of cultivated land within a wood'

MARGARET MARSH
1395 Margaretysmerschchurche
1575 Margaret Marshe
Old English:
Margaret – personal name, probably an abbess from Shaftesbury Abbey
mersc – marshland
'marshland owned by Abbess Margaret'

EAST ORCHARD
939 Archet
1330 Orchet

WEST ORCHARD
1427 West Orchard
1527 Estorchard
Celtic:
ar – alongside or opposite
ced – a wood
'a settlement alongside a wood'

BEDCHESTER
12th century Bedeshurste
1576 Bedcester
Old English:
Bedi – personal name
hyrst – a small wooded hill
'a small wooded hill owned by a man named Bedi'

MANSTON
1086 (Domesday Book) Manestone
Old English:
Mann – personal name
tun – a farm or estate
'a farm or estate owned by someone named Mann'

The first cremation in Victorian Britain

The original Manston House, which dated to the 17th century, was destroyed by fire in 1857. It was rebuilt by owner Thomas Hanham as a Victorian mansion. Hanham was a justice of the peace, Freemason and deputy-lieutenant of Dorset. He was widowed several times while his only child, Maud, died in 1869. At this time Thomas and his third wife, Edith, discovered the church vault – where the body of his second wife Josephine lay – had flooded. That led Thomas and Edith to promise each other they would be cremated.

Cremation was illegal at that time so, when Edith died in 1876, Thomas had to challenge the law for six years. He had a mausoleum built to house his wife's body until he could arrange her cremation. In 1882 a crematorium was built in the grounds of Manston House, where Hanham held services of cremation for Edith and his mother, who had died during his lengthy battle to change the law. The crematorium is now used for storage but the mausoleum has been maintained in good condition despite the lead from its roof being stolen in the 1960s.

River Stour and Tributaries – Key Brook, Stirchell Brook, Twyford Brook and Manston Brook

Manston Brook near its confluence with the River Stour

Chapter 40

FONTMELL BROOK

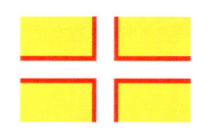

AT A GLANCE

SOURCE
Collyer's Brook rises from springs around Springhead Farm. A longer tributary rises from springs south of Compton Abbas.

MOUTH / OUTLET
Confluences with the River Stour to the west of Fontmell Parva House.

LENGTH
About 12km (7.5 miles)

The site of the Fontmell Magna village sheep wash until 1930

A tributary of the River Stour, Fontmell Brook travels southward through Spear Copse and past Manor Farm. At Fontmell Magna it is joined by the small Collyer's Brook. Fontmell Brook continues in a westward direction for a short distance until turning south again at Piper's Mill. The stream flows in a south-westward direction until it joins the waters of the River Stour to the west of Fontmell Parva House (privately owned).

Dorset Wildlife Trust has played a vital role in conserving Fontmell Down and Collyer's Brook. The Trust has created nature reserves in both areas protecting rare wildlife and enabling visitors to enjoy this beautiful part of the Dorset countryside. On Fontmell Down there are expanses of ancient chalk grassland, which support many varieties of orchids and endangered wild flowers. According to the Trust's website, only 20% of Britain's chalk grassland has survived during the past 70 years, a disturbing fact.

The Collyer's Brook nature reserve boasts a former fish pond that was used to breed brown trout and rainbow trout during the Middle Ages.

River Stour and Tributaries – Fontmell Brook

VILLAGES AND TOWNS AND THE ORIGINS OF THEIR NAMES
(from source to mouth)

COMPTON ABBAS

956 Comtune
1086 (Domesday Book) Cuntone
1293 Cumpton Abbatisse

Old English:
cumb – a valley
tun – a farm or estate
abbatissa – abbess
'a farm or estate in a valley, owned by Sherborne Abbey'

FONTMELL MAGNA

877 Funtemel
1086 (Domesday Book) Fontemaale
1391 Magnam Funtemell

Celtic:
funton – a spring or stream
mailo – a bare hill

Latin:
magna – great
'a bigger or more important settlement (compared with Fontmell Parva) by a stream near a bare hill'

Collyer's Brook in Mill Street, Fontmell Magna

SUTTON WALDRON

932 Suttune
1086 (Domesday Book) Sudtone
1297 Sutton Walerand

Old English:
suth – south
tun – a farm or estate
Waleran – personal name
'a farm or estate to the south (probably of Fontmell Magna) owned by a man named Waleran'

Philanthropist, pioneer, agriculturalist and rector

In the 19th century, Canon Anthony Huxtable paid for a church to be built. It was dedicated to St Bartholomew in 1847. Sir John Betjeman, a 20th century Poet Laureate and champion of Victorian buildings, described the church as: "One of the best and most lovely examples of Victorian architecture."

Canon Huxtable was an agricultural pioneer and probably the first farm owner to use liquid manure on his fields. His aim was to make farming more cost-effective, enabling him to employ more parishioners to work on the land and so lessen their poverty.

FONTMELL PARVA

1360 Parva Funtemel

Celtic:
funton – a spring or stream
mailo – a bare hill

Latin:
parva – little
'a smaller or less important settlement (compared with Fontmell Magna) by a stream near a bare hill'

Chapter 41

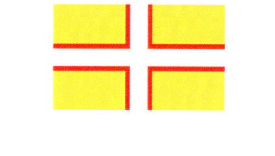

RIVER IWERNE

The waters of the River Iwerne, a chalk stream in the Blackmore Vale, empty into the River Stour near Blandford Forum. Iwerne is a Celtic word that probably means 'yew river'. It dates to before the 10th century.

AT A GLANCE

SOURCE
Within the village of Iwerne Minster

MOUTH / OUTLET
Confluences with the River Stour north of Blandford Forum

LENGTH
About 5km (3 miles)

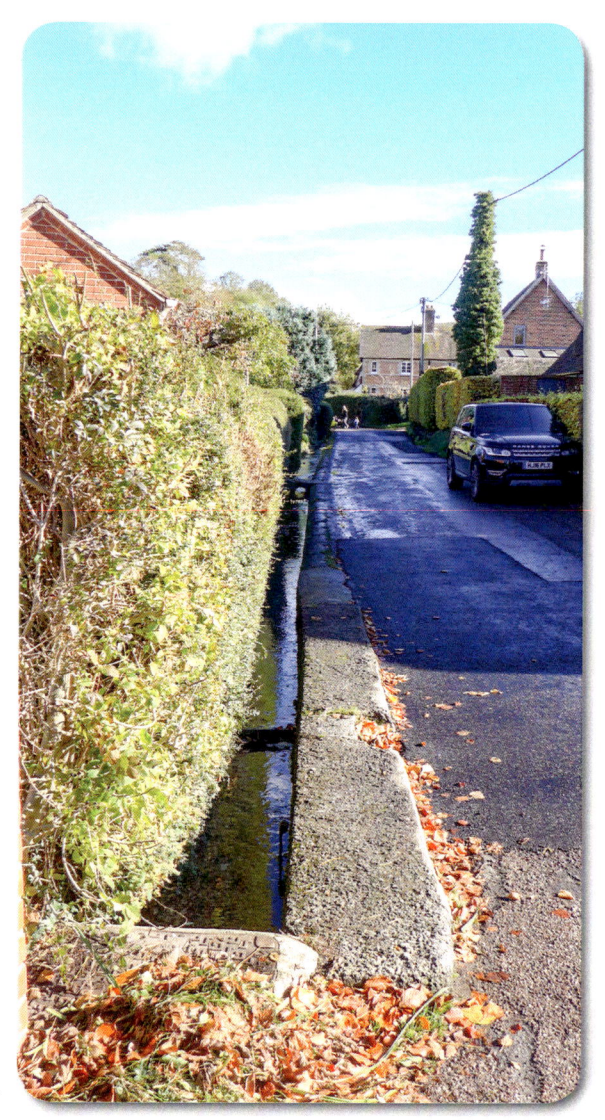

River Iwerne channelled through the village of Iwerne Minster

Villages and towns and the origins of their names
(from source to confluence with the River Stour)

Iwerne Minster
877 Ywern
1086 (Domesday Book) Evneminstre
Old Celtic:
Ywern – yew trees
Old English:
mynstre – a large church
'a settlement by a river with yew trees and a large church'

Titanic connection
In 1908 James Ismay acquired the Iwerne estate from Baron Wolverton. Ismay was a director of the White Star Line shipping company, which owned the Titanic. At the time of its tragic maiden voyage he lay seriously ill, otherwise he would have been on board and probably perished along with so many other passengers.

Benevolent lord of the manor
James Ismay, lord of the manor, repaired houses and provided health care and agricultural work. During the First World War he was too old to enlist so undertook to write to every villager fighting for his country, giving news of village life, family and friends. He built a brick and stone structure near the village pump to display news of the war for villagers. This structure was nicknamed the 'War Office' and is still known by that name.

Village pump with the 'War Office' in the background

Shroton (Iwerne Courtney)
1086 (Domesday Book) Werne
1244 Yuern Curtenay
1337 Schyreuetone
Old English:
scir-refa – a sheriff
tun – a farm or estate
Curtenay – personal name
The Courtenays were the Earls of Devon dating from the 13th century.
'a settlement by the River Iwerne owned by the Courtenay family'
and *'a farm or estate belonging to the Sheriff of Devon'*

Hod Hill ramparts

STEEPLETON IWERNE
1086 (Domesday Book) Werne
1234 Stepleton
1346 Iwernestapleton
Old English:
stiepel – a steeple
tun – a farm or estate
'a farm or estate on the River Iwerne featuring a church with a steeple'

HOD HILL
1270 Hod
The word Hill was added in the 18th century.
Old English:
hod – a hood
possibly *'a hill in the shape of a hood'*
or *'a hill with shelter at the summit (the fort)'*

Largest hill fort in Dorset
Hod Hill is the largest hill fort in Dorset but not the highest, nearby Hambledon Hill is 200ft

higher. Hod Hill, owned by the National Trust, has an area of 22 hectares (54 acres) at its summit. The earthworks of the original Iron Age fort and later Roman fort can still be seen. Excavations revealed there were 250 roundhouses in the Iron Age fort.

The Roman fort, established after Emperor Vespasian's invasion in 43-44 AD, would have accommodated 600 foot soldiers and 200 cavalry.

It is thought Hod Hill is probably the site of the ancient city of Dunium (Celtic *duno* meaning fort). 2nd century Greek geographer and astrologer Ptolemy (Claudius Ptolemaeus) included Dunium in his list of places in Roman Britain. However, he may have been referring to Maiden Castle near Dorchester.

ASH
1086 (Domesday Book) Aisse
1280 Assche
Old English:
aesc – an ash tree
'a settlement with ash trees'

STOURPAINE
1086 (Domesday Book) Sture
1280 Sture Payn
Old English:
sture – strong, powerful
Payn – personal name
'a settlement on the River Stour owned by a family named Payn'

DURWESTON
1086 (Domesday Book) Derwinestone
Old English:
Deorwine – personal name
tun – a farm or estate
'a farm or estate owned by a man named Deorwine'

Discovering the River Iwerne
One windy October day Ryan and I visited Iwerne Minster in the hope of locating the source of the Iwerne. Despite looking at maps, asking a couple of friendly dog walkers and following the stream through the village, we failed in our endeavours. We concluded the spring was situated in Claysmore School's grounds and therefore inaccessible to tourists.

Our next objective was to explore the Hod Hill forts and we set off with an information sheet from the National Trust website.

From the bottom of Hod Hill we could see what looked like a bull watching us from the top. We found a couple of sticks suitable for walking – and possibly for defence! We were mistaken, the cattle showed no sign of resenting our intrusion.

What a wonderful view awaited us and how awesome to imagine the physical work required to build the ramparts.

On our return to Iwerne Minster we enjoyed locally sourced, home-made food at The Talbot hotel.

Chapter 42

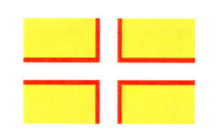

RIVER TARRANT

AT A GLANCE

SOURCE
A spring in Stubhampton Bottom near Tarrant Gunville

MOUTH / OUTLET
Confluences with the River Stour near Tarrant Crawford and Spetisbury

LENGTH
About 12km (7.5 miles)

The River Tarrant is a tributary of the River Stour and flows through the Tarrant Valley in the chalk hills of Cranborne Chase. Its name comes from *tarente*, the old Celtic word for 'trespasser', referring to its tendency to flood.

Eight of the villages along its course are named after the river, with the addition of the landowners' names.

By the 9th century the Saxons had moved into the Tarrant valley and by the 11th century all the settlements along the river were sufficiently established to merit an entry in the Domesday Book. At that time there were six mills being worked along the river but sadly none have survived the passing of the centuries.

The upper reaches of the river are winterbourne, they tend to dry out during the summer months. South of Tarrant Monkton the waters flow freely all year, although in recent years the lower reaches have reduced in volume, possibly due to the pumping station at Shapwick.

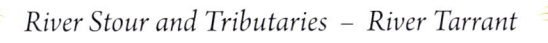

VILLAGES AND TOWNS AND THE ORIGINS OF THEIR NAMES
(from source to mouth of the river)

STUBHAMPTON
1086 (Domesday Book) Stibemetune
1262 Stubhamtune
Old English:
stybb – tree stumps
hamm – an enclosed settlement
tun – a farm or estate
'an enclosed farm on land with many tree stumps'

TARRANT GUNVILLE
1086 (Domesday Book) Tarente
1233 Tarente Gundevill
Old Celtic:
tarente – a trespasser
Gundevill – personal name, probably of Norman origin
'a settlement on the River Tarrant owned by a family named Gundevill'

Dry riverbed at Tarrant Gunville

A dandy's extravagance

Eastbury House was the dream of George Dodington, Lord of the Admiralty. He commissioned architect Sir John Vanbrugh to draw up plans in 1718. Vanbrugh was the architect for Blenheim Palace and Castle Howard. However, Dodington died without offspring so in 1720 his nephew, George Bubb, son of a Weymouth apothecary, inherited his estate and vast fortune.

After almost 20 years the completed mansion was one of the largest in Dorset. George Bubb took his uncle's name, became the 1st Baron Melcombe and Member of Parliament for Weymouth and then Melcombe Regis.

Dodington has been described as a Georgian dandy. He socialised with the monarchy and philosophers such as Voltaire, dressed in the latest fashions of lace and brocade, and lived a lifestyle only a fortune could buy. His political enemies taunted him with his original name Bubb. When King George II refused to give Dodington the honour of the Order of the Bath, it was said of him: "For the King would not dub so low-born a scrub, nor the Order disgrace with a fellow like Bubb."

After Dodington's death in 1762 the mansion was demolished because his heirs could not afford its upkeep. The last owner offered to pay £200 per annum to anyone who would live in Eastbury Park and maintain the property – there were no takers. Today only the impressive gateway and stable block remain, they can be seen as you drive through the village. The stables have been converted into a private residence.

Gates to Eastbury Estate, the driveway in front of the gates passes over the River Tarrant

The beginnings of photography

Thomas Wedgwood lived at Eastbury House from 1800 to 1805. He was a pioneer of photography and he discovered that an image could be made on paper using silver nitrate and sunlight. His problem was he couldn't make the image permanent. He died without discovering the answer – fixing agent hyposulphite of soda.

TARRANT HINTON

877 Terente
1086 (Domesday Book) Tarente Hyneton
Old Celtic:
tarente – a trespasser
Old English:
hiwan – a religious community (genitive tense higna)
tun – a farm or estate
'a farm or estate on the River Tarrant owned by a religious community, probably Shaftesbury Abbey'

Roman villa

The parish church of St Mary dates to the 13th century but excavations in the parish, near Barton Hill Dairy, uncovered remains of a much earlier settlement, a Roman villa. There is also evidence of an Iron Age settlement on Tarrant Hinton Down.

TARRANT LAUNCESTON

1086 (Domesday Book) Tarente
1280 Tarente Loueweniston
Old Celtic:
tarente – a trespasser
Old English:
tun – a farm or estate
Leofwine or Lowin – personal name
'a farm or estate on the River Tarrant owned by a family with the name Leofwine or Lowin'

TARRANT MONKTON

1086 (Domesday Book) Tarente
12th century Tarenta Monachorum
1280 Tarent Moneketon

Old Celtic:
tarente – a trespasser
Latin monachorum – of the monks

Old English:
munuc – monks
tun – a farm or estate

'a farm or estate on the River Tarrant owned by the Abbey of Tewkesbury and Cranborne Priory'

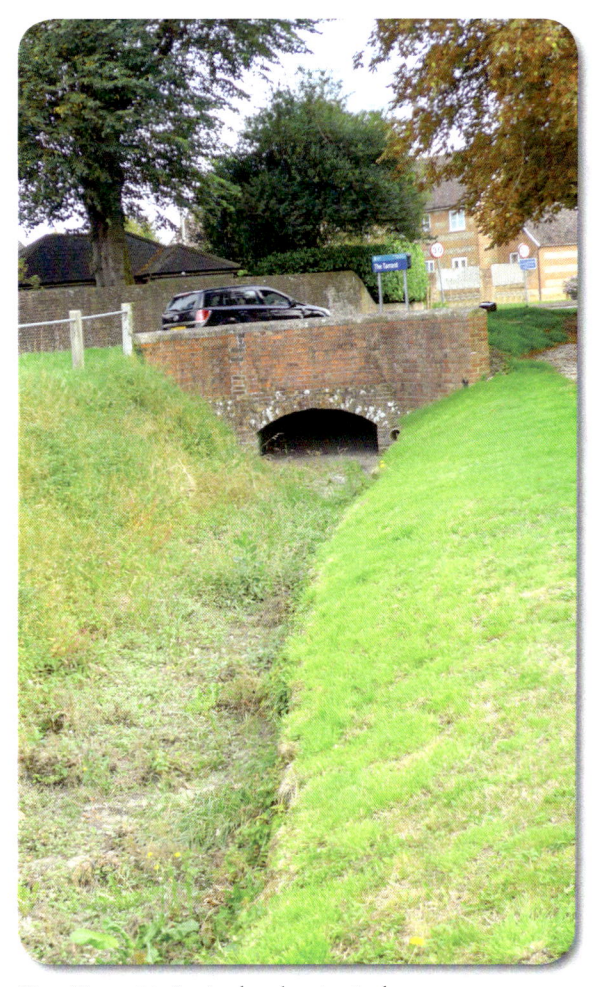

A splash and a bridge
As the road from Tarrant Launceston enters Tarrant Monkton there is a ford, known as the Splash. An old packhorse bridge, one of only three remaining in Dorset, dates to medieval times (the other packhorse bridges are in Rampisham and Fifehead Neville).

That rings a bell
The Church of All Saints contains the original three bells cast in the 17th century. Each has an inscription 'Feare the Lord', 'Prayse the Lord', and 'Thomas Isaack', who was churchwarden in 1694. A wheel on the wall of the church tower was used for swinging the earliest bell.

River Tarrant in September showing its dry season

Tarrant Monkton Splash and packhorse bridge

TARRANT RAWSTON

1086 (Domesday Book) Tarente
1288 Tarente Antyoche
1535 Tarrant Rawston alias Antyocke

Old Celtic:
tarente – a trespasser
Antyoche – personal name (Antioch)
Raw – personal name (possibly Ralph)

Old English:
tun – a farm or estate

'a farm or estate on the River Tarrant originally owned by a family named Antioch until the early 16th century, then owned by a man named Ralph'

Confluence of the River Tarrant with the River Stour

TARRANT RUSHTON

1086 (Domesday Book) Tarente
1307 Tarente Russcheweston

Old Celtic:

tarente – a trespasser

Old English:

tun – a farm or estate
Russchewes – personal name (de Rusceaus)
'a farm or estate on the River Tarrant owned by a family named de Rusceaus'

Tarrant Rushton airfield

Tarrant Rushton airfield, built in 1942 during the Second World War, played a vital role in the D-Day landings. Halifax bombers towed Horsa gliders filled with British troops – the first of the Allied forces to land in Normandy. These men captured two strategic bridges, one over the River Orne and another crossing the Caen Canal – later known as the Pegasus and Horsa bridges. Aircraft from Tarrant Rushton continued to fly from the airfield throughout the war, dropping supplies to the French Resistance who were hampering German plans and assisting Allied troops as they pushed the enemy forces back.

After the war, the airfield became the home of aerospace company Flight Refuelling for 30 years until it relocated to Hurn. The company developed a method of fuelling aircraft in flight.

The airfield officially closed in September 1980. Today the land is used for farming – but some hangars can still be seen.

TARRANT KEYNESTON

1086 (Domesday Book) Tarente
1225 Tarente Kahaines
1303 Tarente Keyneston

Old English:

tun – a farm or estate
Kahaines – personal name (Cahaignes)
'a farm or estate on the River Tarrant owned by a family named Cahaignes'

(Photograph reproduced with kind permission of Emily van Coller)

Badbury Rings

Badbury Rings is an Iron Age fort only a five-minute drive from Tarrant Keyneston. It has a National Trust car park and is a great place for a walk or picnic. Dogs are welcome when on a lead, the views are spectacular, and there is freedom for children to run and explore. See also River Stour.

TARRANT CRAWFORD

1086 (Domesday Book) Tarente
1795 Tarrant Crawford

Old Celtic:

tarente – a trespasser

Old English:

crawe – a crow
ford – a ford
'a farm or estate on the River Tarrant where there is a ford crossing the river and many crows'

Tarrant Crawford gives its name to the bridge over the River Stour slightly further south, see Spetisbury in the chapter on the River Stour.

Crawford Bridge

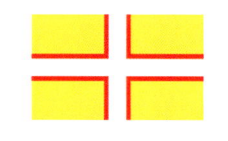

Chapter 43

RIVER WINTERBORNE

AT A GLANCE

SOURCE
Springs at Winterborne Houghton

MOUTH / OUTLET
Confluences with the River Stour at Sturminster Marshall

LENGTH
About 24km (15 miles)

The River Winterborne, also spelled Winterbourne and known as the Winterborne North, flows through settlements named after the river. It often dries up during the summer months but is prone to flooding in wet weather, being the reason for its name in Old English, *wyntre burna*, which means 'winter stream'.

Winterborne is the name of one other river in Dorset, the South Winterborne River, which is further west and confluences with the River Frome (see separate chapters).

Both rivers pass over chalk, which is porous. The strength of flow depends on the height of the water table and volume of water in the underground aquifers.

Winterborne Stickland stream

WINTERBORNE HOUGHTON

1086 (Domesday Book) Wintreburne
1288 Wynterburn Hugheton

Old English:

wyntre – winter

burna – a stream

Hugh – personal name (Norman)

tun – a farm or estate

'a farm or estate owned by Hugh de Boscherbert near the River Winterborne'

Mistaken identity

Villagers were once known as 'Houghton Owls' because a local resident mistook the sound of owls for people calling out to him when he was lost in the woods.

WINTERBORNE STICKLAND

1086 (Domesday Book) Winterburne
1203 Winterburn Stikellane

Old English:

wyntre – winter

burna – a stream

sticol – steep

lane – a lane

'estate situated on the River Winterborne with a steep lane'

Dorset dialect

Stickle is still used as the word for steep.

The Repair Shop

The river passes through the village green as a pretty stream. The village sign, carved in wood, has the ancient name for the village on one side and its present name on the reverse.

The villagers of Winterborne Stickland approached BBC programme The Repair Shop to have the sign restored. The restoration has been carried out with skill and craftsmanship, and the finished piece is beautiful.

Winterborne Stickland sign

WINTERBORNE CLENSTON

1086 (Domesday Book) Wintreburne
1243 Winterborn Clench
1303 Wynterburn Clencheston

Old English:

wyntre – winter
burna – a stream
Clench – personal name
tun – a farm or estate

'a farm or estate situated on the River Winterborne owned by the Clench family'

WHATCOMBE, HIGHER AND LOWER

1288 Whatecumbe

Old English:

waet – wet
or hwaete – wheat
cumb – a valley

'a wet valley (possibly prone to flooding)'
or *'a valley where wheat is grown'*

WINTERBORNE WHITECHURCH

1086 (Domesday Book) Wintreburne
1212 Winterburn Blancmustier
1268 Wynterborn Wytecherch

Old English:

wyntre – winter
burna – a stream
hwit – white
cirice – a church

Old French:

blanc – white
moustier – a monastery/minster

'estate situated on the River Winterborne having a white church'

So named because St Mary's church was built of stone instead of wood.

Young war hero

Sydney Ware was born in nearby Whatcombe. The son of a dairyman, he was a war hero awarded the Victoria Cross in 1916. Although wounded while fighting the enemy in Mesopotamia, he carried many soldiers to safety before dying ten days later aged 24. He is buried in Amara War Cemetery in modern day Iraq.

Winterborne Whitechurch

WINTERBORNE KINGSTON
1086 (Domesday Book) Wintreburne
1194 Kingeswinterburn
Old English:
wyntre – winter
burna – a stream
tun – a farm or estate
'a farm or estate situated on the River Winterborne owned by the king'
King John owned the estate in 1194. He reigned from 1167 to 1216.

Dorset buttons
Buttony was an important craft in the 17th and 18th centuries. Although nearby Blandford Forum was the centre for marketing, many of the women of Winterborne Kingston were button-makers. The buttons were made from ram's horn wrapped with yarn in different patterns.

The Industrial Revolution brought an end to the home crafters as machine-made buttons were manufactured in their thousands in factories. Today, original Dorset buttons are highly sought by collectors.

WINTERBORNE MUSTON also named (WINTERBORNE TURBERVILLE)
1086 (Domesday Book) Wintreburne
1242 Winterborn Turbervill
1310 Winterborne Mousterston
Old English:
wyntre – winter
burna – a stream
tun – a farm or estate
de Musters – personal name
Turberville – personal name
'a farm or estate situated on the River Winterborne owned by the de Musters family and the Turberville family'

ANDERSON
1086 (Domesday Book) Wintreburne
1268 Wynterborn Fifasse
1331 Andreweston
Old English:
wyntre – winter
burna – a stream
fif – five
aesc – an ash tree
tun – a farm or estate
originally *'a farm or estate situated on the River Winterborne with five ash trees'*
later *'a farm or estate with the church of St Andrew'*

The Court Leet
Introduced by the Normans in 1066, the Court Leet was still operating in 1905. The town crier paraded through the village to announce the court would sit on November 11th, Martinmass. The Court Leet was presided over by the lord of the manor at his home, Anderson Manor. After the court session he would visit all the cottages to check if they required repairs.

Anderson Manor was owned by the Tregonwell family until 1910. During the Second World War it was used as the headquarters and training ground for 55 members of the Small Scale Raiding Force – 62 Commando. The driveway became an assault course, built among the trees and across the river.

Anderson Manor sign and driveway

Winterborne Tomson church

WINTERBORNE TOMSON

942 Winterburne
1280 Wynterbourn Thomaston

Old English:

wyntre – winter
burna – a stream
tun – a farm or estate

'a farm or estate situated on the River Winterborne owned by a man named Thomas'

En route to deportation

A signpost *(below)* to the south of the village was painted red to show illiterate prison guards the way to Botany Bay Barn in Bloxworth (turn right at the signpost). Bloxworth was the first overnight stay for prisoners being taken from Dorchester to Portsmouth before transportation to Australia.

Thomas Hardy saves St Andrew's Church

This tiny single-cell church dedicated to St Andrew is almost unchanged since it was built by the Normans. It was made from flint and stone with lime-washed walls and flagstones.

The oak fittings date from the 18th century, donated by Archbishop of Canterbury William Wake, whose family lived locally.

In 1931 this gem of a church was saved from the ravages of time when the Society for the Protection of Ancient Buildings sold some of Thomas Hardy's architectural manuscripts to pay for repairs.

This seems fitting as Hardy was an architect's apprentice in this part of Dorset and was very fond of St Andrew's. The boxed pews, pulpit and font cover were included in the refurbishment. St Andrew's is now cared for by the Church Conservation Trust.

Far From The Madding Crowd

When visiting Winterborne Tomson, Ryan and I were delighted to meet Karen *(top right)* who lives in a thatched cottage next to St Andrew's Church. She was in her garden with her dog and told us she hailed from Oxfordshire. When she was a child

214

her father had supplied horses and carriages for the original film of Far From The Madding Crowd (1967) starring Julie Christie and Alan Bates. To add to the story, the parents of her friend Bec, who lives on a farm near Winterborne Tomson, stabled the horses during filming. Many years later Karen and Bec met, became good friends and discovered the connection between their parents. What an unexpected story and how surprising life can be. Thank you Karen!

Historical haven

I fell in love with this ancient church when I was quite young and on holiday in Dorset. For me it was a haven of peace amid the storms of teenage angst. As I walked through the doorway I felt I was breathing in the history of the people who had worshipped there for centuries. I wonder if others experience the same?

WINTERBORNE ZELSTON

1086 (Domesday Book) Wintreburne
1350 Wynterbourn Selyston
Old English:
wyntre – winter
burna – a stream
tun – a farm or estate
de Seles – personal name
'a farm or estate situated on the River Winterborne owned by the de Seles family'

ALMER

943 Elmere
1212 Almere
Old English:
ael – an eel
mere – a pool
'place with a pool of eels'

STURMINSTER MARSHALL

1086 (Domesday Book) Sturminstre
(See also River Stour)
1268 Sturministre Marescal
Old English:
steu or stauro – firm or strong
mynster – a church or minster
Mareschal – personal name
'place with a church on the River Stour owned by a family named Mareschal who were the earls of Pembroke (later the spelling changed to Marshall)'

Cheese and Lord Haw-Haw

Founded in 1888, Bailey Gate in Sturminster Marshall was home to the largest cheese-making factory in Europe. Between the 1950s and its closure in 1978, the factory processed 52,000 gallons of milk every day, transporting some to London by rail and turning the remainder into cheese.

During the Second World War, American-born fascist William Joyce broadcast Nazi propaganda from Germany and was nicknamed Lord Haw-Haw. On two occasions he falsely announced the factory had been bombed, such was the importance credited to Bailey Gate Dairy.

Chapter 44

THE RIVER ALLEN WITH GUSSAGE BROOK AND CRICHEL STREAM

AT A GLANCE

SOURCE
Several springs around Wyke Farm near Monkton Up Wimborne

MOUTH / OUTLET
Confluences with the River Stour, south of Wimborne Minster near Canford Bridge (circa 1813)

LENGTH
About 21km (13 miles)

TRIBUTARIES
Several tributaries including:
- Crichel Stream rises north of the A354 near Thickthorn Wood and flows through Crichel House estate where it fills Crichel Lake, confluences with the River Allen near New Town.
- Gussage Brook rises near Farnham north of Gussage St Andrew, flows through the Gussage villages, confluences south of Wimborne St Giles.
- Divisions of the river in the town of Wimborne Minster create a long, narrow island. Once an island of water meadows known as Mill Mead, it has now been developed with housing.

River Stour and Tributaries – The River Allen with Gussage Brook and Crichel Stream

River Allen flowing into the River Stour (between the trees on the far bank). Taken from the footbridge at Canford Bridge

The River Allen is a tributary of the River Stour, the two rivers confluence just south of the old town of Wimborne Minster.

Originally known as the Winburna Stream, its name was changed to Allen. A man named Aldewyne or Ealdwine owned a bridge over the river. Today, Canford Bridge straddles the river at the same site.

The River Allen is a winterbourne stream in its upper reaches, meaning it can be dry during the summer months. Downstream, it becomes a permanent, flowing chalk stream.

From Monkton Up Wimborne, the River Allen can be followed through Wimborne St Giles and joins with two tributaries north of Witchampton. A further two tributaries confluence north of Wimborne Minster.

Walford Bridge (16th century) a Grade ll-listed structure near Walford Mill

Villages and Towns and the Origins of Their Names
(from source to confluence with the River Stour)

Monkton Up Wimborne
1086 (Domesday Book) Winburne
1504 Wymborne Monkton
Old English:
munuc – a monk
tun – a farm or estate
winn – a meadow
burna – a stream
up – higher up the river
'a farm or estate owned by the monks higher up the Winburna Stream'

Village stocks at Wimborne St Giles

Wimborne St Giles
1086 (Domesday Book) Winburne
1268 Vpwymburn Sancti Egidij
1399 Upwymbourne St Giles
Old English:
winn – a meadow
burna – a stream
Latin:
Sancti Egidius – Saint Giles
'a settlement on the Winburna Stream with a church dedicated to St Giles'

Farming skills at school
Shortly after the end of the Second World War, the local headmaster and his wife decided to run the village school as a working farm. They taught the children farming skills, including rearing livestock, growing vegetables, spinning and dyeing. Maths and English were learned through budgeting, balancing accounts and administrative tasks. They recognised that the village children would earn their living from the land rather than in factories and offices.

Wimborne St Giles village school

GUSSAGE BROOK (TRIBUTARY)

FARNHAM
1086 (Domesday Book) Ferneham
1199 Farnham
Old English:
fearn – ferns
ham – a homestead
'a homestead where ferns grow'

Ancient well
Opposite the entrance to the church there is a shelter *(right)*, similar to a lych gate, which houses the ancient village well. The opening to the well is boarded over for safety.

MINCHINGTON
1307 Munecheneton
Old English:
mynecena – of the nuns
tun – a farm or estate
'a farm belonging to the nuns (of Shaftesbury Benedictine nunnery)'

CASHMOOR
possibly there were watercress beds along the Gussage Brook, which gave their name to Cashmoor
Old English:
caerse – watercress
mor – moorland
'a settlement on moorland where watercress is grown'

GUSSAGE ALL SAINTS GUSSAGE ST ANDREW AND GUSSAGE ST MICHAEL
10th century Gyssic
1155 Gersich Omnium Sanctorum
1258 Gissick St Andrews
1280 Gyssiche Sancti Michaelis
Old English:
gysic – a gushing stream
Latin:
omnium sanctorum – all saints
Sancti Michaelis – Saint Michael
'a settlement near a strongly flowing stream with a church dedicated to All Saints, St Michael or St Andrew'

Chariot factory
Gussage All Saints was built on the site of an Iron Age chariot factory, which was abandoned around 80 AD.

Westminster Abbey organ
The 18th century organ in the church at Gussage All Saints once stood in Westminster Abbey, where it was used during choir practice.

AMEN CORNER
1869 Amen Corner
(in Gussage All Saints)
Said to be the site of a chapel.

King Henry III
The medieval monarch visited the chapel at Amen Corner on 1st July 1245 and granted land to the abbess of Tarrant Keyneston.

Knowlton Church and earthworks

Knowlton Church memorial

GUSSAGE BROOK THEN CONFLUENCES WITH THE RIVER ALLEN

KNOWLTON
1086 (Domesday Book) Cheneltune
1212 Cnolton
Old English:
cnoll – a hillock
tun – a farm or estate
'a farm or estate near a small hill (Knowle Hill)'
(see also River Stour chapter)

Church Henge
The ruins of the Norman church at Knowlton stand in the centre of Neolithic ceremonial earthworks (henge). Owned by English Heritage, it marks the transition from Paganism to Christianity and is now known as Church Henge. One of the greatest concentrations of round barrows in Dorset lies nearby.

On the edge of the ramparts are trees and shrubs festooned with brightly coloured ribbons. A poster indicates this is a memorial to loved ones who have died, perhaps in the pagan or new age tradition.

LONG CRICHEL AND MOOR CRICHEL
1086 (Domesday Book) Circel
1208 Langecrechel
1212 Mor Kerchel
Celtic:
crug – a mound or hill
Old English:
hyll – a hill
lange – long
mor – marshy ground
'a long settlement on or near a hill'
and
'a settlement with marshy ground on or near a hill'
(the hill is Crichel Down, Old English dun – hill or down)

Lord of the manor relocates village
In the 18th century, people living in Moor Crichel were moved a mile further south so the original village could be flooded to create a picturesque lake for the Crichel House estate. Some villagers were rehoused in New Town on the outskirts of Witchampton, with others relocated to the present Moor Crichel.

Beautiful avenue of beech trees leading to Moor Crichel

Thatched cottages in Manswood. The local post-lady kindly allowed me to include her in the photo

NEW TOWN
A village built in the late 18th century specifically to rehouse some of the residents of Moor Crichel.

CRICHEL STREAM THEN CONFLUENCES WITH THE RIVER ALLEN

MANSWOOD
1774 Mangewood
Possibly from mange which is a parasitical skin disease affecting animals
'a wood where mange disease is evident'

Record holders
Manswood can claim to have the longest stretch of thatch in the country – 110m (120 yards) covering 11 cottages and a former post office. Residents have chosen some imaginative names for their cottages, including Penny Black, Hen's Teeth and Goosedown.

KNOB'S CROOK
Middle English:
knob – a knoll
crok – a bend
possibly *'a grassy mound with a sharp ridge'*

WITCHAMPTON
1086 (Domesday Book) Wichemetune
1216 Wichamton
Old English
wic – a dwelling place
ham – an enclosure or homestead
tun – a farm or estate
Possibly *'a dwelling place with a farm in an enclosure'*

Ancient chess pieces discovered
11th-century chess pieces made of whalebone were found in the parish of Witchampton. They are said to be some of the best-surviving early English chess pieces and can now be seen in the British Museum.

St Kenelm's Church, Hinton Parva

Wimborne Minster

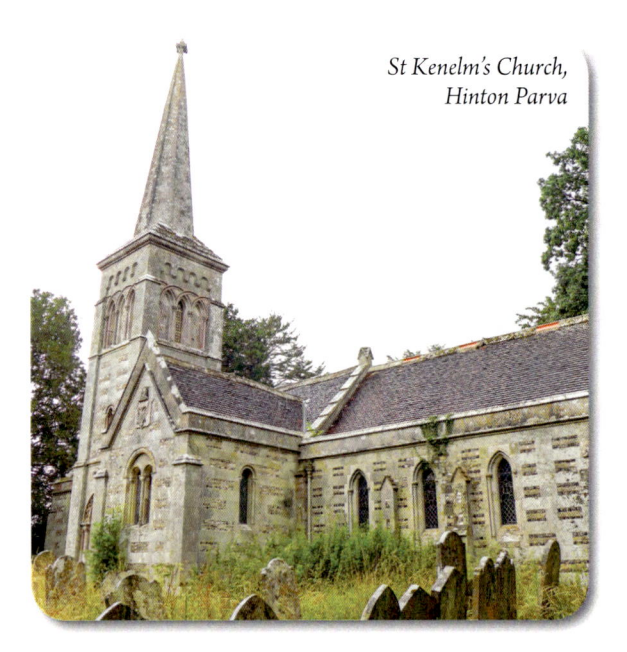

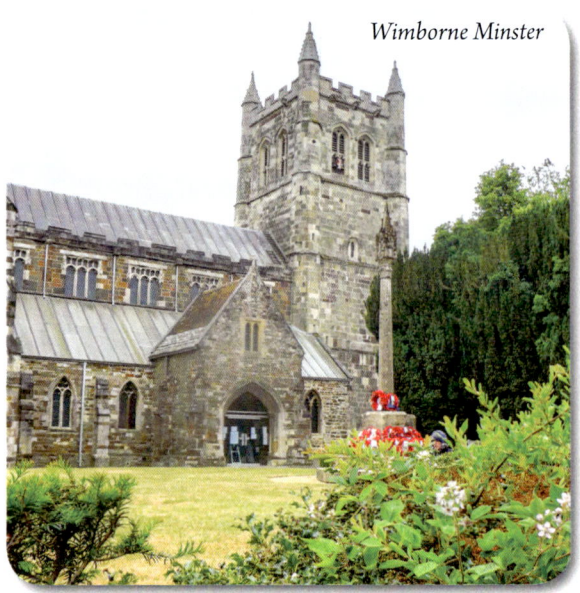

Hinton Parva

1285 Parva Hyneton

Latin:
parva – little

Old English
hean – poor or humble
or hiwan – monks
tun – a farm or estate
'a small farm or estate of poor productivity'
or *'a small farm or estate owned by monks, probably of Wimborne Minster'*

Fratricide

The church is dedicated to St Kenelm, who was a young prince and heir to the throne of Mercia. When his father, Coenwulf, died in 819 AD his sister, Quendryda, arranged for Kenelm to be murdered so she could become queen. Kenelm was seven years old.

There are only eight churches in the country dedicated to St Kenelm. This one is sadly locked and redundant. St Kenelm was mentioned in the Canterbury Tales.

Stanbridge

1230 Stanbrig

Old English:
stan – a stone
brycg – a bridge or causeway
'a settlement near a stone bridge or causeway'

Wimborne Minster

9th century Winburnan
1236 Wymburneminstre

Old English:
winn – a meadow
burna – a stream
mynstre – a minster, the church of a monastery
'a settlement by a meadow stream with a minster'

Wimborne Minster

The minster was dedicated to St Cuthburga in 705 AD and it has been the dominant building in the town for about 1,300 years.

It was originally a Benedictine nunnery and has been a place of prayer, worship, pilgrimage and mission since.

Tivoli Theatre

A spire was added in the 12th century. It survived 450 years until it collapsed and was never replaced.

The astronomical clock hanging in the baptistry dates to around the 13th century. It features wonderful blue-and-gold colours and shows the sun orbiting the earth, a 24-hour dial, and the phases and positions of the moon.

A Grenadier Guardsman quarter jack *(above)* strikes the bells from the outside of the bell tower.

In the minster lies the tomb of Margaret Beaufort, mother of King Henry VII. She established a chapel with a resident priest whose duties included teaching English grammar to 'all comers'.

This eventually led to the founding of Queen Elizabeth Grammar School whose name is now Queen Elizabeth's School, known as QE.

Priests at the minster used to live in the building that is now the Priests' House Museum, a small museum displaying artefacts from Victorian life.

The Tivoli Theatre
This wonderful little theatre was originally a Georgian townhouse but was converted into a cinema in 1936.

The cinema closed in 1980 and the building remained unused until volunteers formed the Friends Of Tivoli. These dedicated volunteers restored the building to its present 1930s Art Deco style and reopened it in 1993.

Since then the Tivoli has been used for films and live performances, with audiences coming from miles around to enjoy an evening's entertainment.

Beautiful art deco doors to The Tivoli Theatre

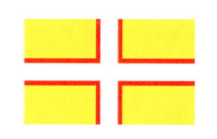

Chapter 45

UDDENS WATER

AT A GLANCE

SOURCE
Uddens Water rises from springs around Gaunt's Common, Chalbury Common and Woodlands Park.

MOUTH / OUTLET
Confluences with the Moors River near Trickett's Cross.

LENGTH
About 18km (11 miles)

TRIBUTARIES
Mannington Brook rises south of Woodlands and Holt, passing through Mannington, Crooked Withies and Lower Mannington. It confluences with Uddens Water between Ameysford and West Moors, about 250m west of Station Road bridge.

Uddens Water is a tributary of the Moors River (River Crane in the upper reaches – see separate chapter), which itself is a tributary of the River Stour.

An Anglo Saxon man named Udd may have owned property near the river, which then became known as Udden's Water. There used to be Uddens House in Holt, built in about 1747 for Nathaniel Gundry who was a High Court judge.

The Castleman Trailway follows the route of Uddens Water as it passes through Uddens Plantation, near Ameysford. It is popular with walkers and cyclists.

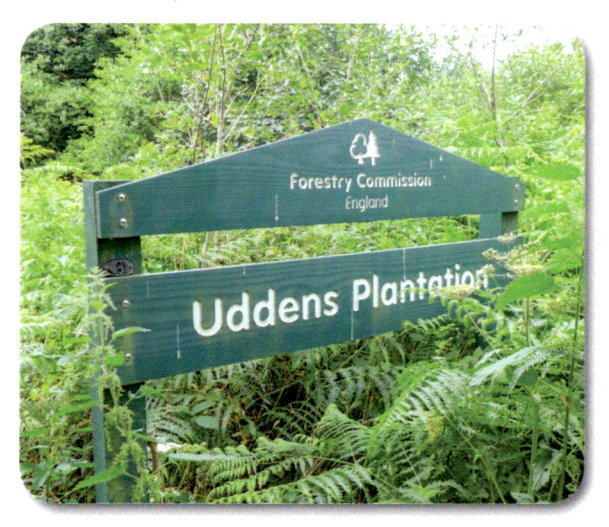

River Stour and Tributaries – Uddens Water

VILLAGES AND TOWNS WITH THE ORIGINS OF THEIR NAMES
(from source to mouth of the river)

WOODLANDS
1244 Wodelande
Old English:
wudu – a wood
land – cultivated land
'cultivated land near or within a wood'

Duke of Monmouth
James Scott, Duke of Monmouth, was the eldest illegitimate son of Charles II. After his father's death in 1685, his uncle acceded to the throne as James II. Monmouth was in Holland but headed back to England to assert his own claim to the throne. He landed at Lyme with a small number of supporters. More men rallied to his cause but Monmouth was defeated at the Battle of Sedgemoor in Somerset.

He fled into Dorset where an elderly woman, Amy Farrant living in Woodlands, recognised Monmouth and reported him to soldiers looking for the duke. Monmouth, disguised as a shepherd, was found hiding in a ditch below an ash tree. He was arrested and, after a brief visit to the magistrate at Holt Lodge, was taken to London for execution.

Not far from Woodlands, close to the hamlet of Mannington is Monmouth Ash Farm. Nearby, in the small town of Verwood, you can enjoy a drink and a good meal at The Monmouth Ash pub *(above)*.

HAYTHORNE
1551 Heythorne
Old English:
haeg-thorn – hawthorn
'a settlement where many hawthorn trees grow'

Horton Tower viewed from the outskirts of Hinton Martell

Chalbury Rectory, now Chalbury Hill House, protects its privacy with mature trees and beautiful lawns

HORTON
1033 Hortun
Old English:
horu – muddy or dirty
tun – a farm or estate
'a muddy or dirty farm'

Horton Tower
Horton Tower can be seen for miles. It is one of the tallest follies at 43m (140ft). Sir Humphrey Sturt, Lord of Horton Manor, Dorset MP and architect, had it built so he could enjoy an uninterrupted view of the hunt. He also enjoyed stargazing.

Today it is in a state of disrepair but a mobile phone company has carried out renovations after receiving planning permission to secure signal masts to the top of the tower.

Sir Humphrey also owned Crichel House at Moor Crichel and was responsible for the creation of the lake after flooding the site where the original village stood (see chapter on River Allen).

CHALBURY
946 Cheoles Burge
Old English:
burh – a fortified place
Ceol – personal name
'a fortified place owned by a man named Ceol'

Author and journalist
Miss Mary Frances Billington was born in Chalbury Rectory in 1862, the daughter of Rev George Henry Billington. She worked as a journalist at several London newspapers, travelling extensively in India, Nepal, Canada and Russia. She was the author of several books including Women In India and The Red Cross In Wartime, which she wrote during the First World War.

After a long career as the leading female journalist of her time Mary retired to her home village of Chalbury, where she focused her energy on parish affairs and played the organ during church services. She is buried alongside her family in the churchyard.

Hinton Martell
1086 (Domesday Book) Hinetone
1226 Hineton Martel
Old English:
hiwan – members of a religious community or house
tun – a farm or estate
Martel – personal name
'a farm or estate belonging to a religious community (possibly Wimborne Minster), later owned by a family named Martel'

Uppington
1838 Uppington
Old English:
upp – above or higher
ing – a water meadow, or belonging to
tun – a farm or estate
'a farm or estate on higher ground, also having a water meadow'
or *'land on higher ground belonging to a farm or estate'*

Gaunt's Common
1535 The Great Gawntz
1646 Gantts farme
'an area of land or farm owned by John of Gaunt, Duke of Lancaster (1340-1399)'

Holt
1185 Winburneholt
1372 Holte
Old English:
holt – a thicket
Winburne – Wimborne Minster
'a settlement with a thicket near, or owned by, Wimborne Minster'

Holt Forest is an ancient Dorset woodland harbouring rare species of wildlife, including the Dartford warbler and sand lizard. In 1985 the forest was designated a national nature reserve.

God's Blessing Green
1694 Godsblessing
Probably named out of gratitude to God for blessing the owners of the land with good productivity.

Wigbeth
First recorded in the 19th century
Unknown origin

Knob's Crook
Middle English:
knob – a knoll
crok – a bend
possibly *'a grassy mound with a sharp ridge'*

Crooked Withies
no known origin
Old English:
withig – a willow tree
The branches of a willow tree are strong and flexible and used for making baskets and thatching. Perhaps the willows that grew in this area weren't considered to be of good enough quality to be useful?

Mannington
1086 (Domesday Book) Manitone
Old English:
Manna or Mann – personal name
ing – associated with
tun – a farm or estate
'a farm or estate associated with, or named after, a person named Mann'

Three Legged Cross
First recorded in the 16th century, the name probably refers to a three-ways crossing at this junction where the village now stands.

Ameysford

1791 Ameysford
Old English:
Amey – personal name
ford – a ford or river crossing
'land with a ford (across Uddens Water) owned by a family named Amey'

West Moors

1310 La More
1591 West Moors
Old English:
mor – marshy ground
West – probably in relation to East Moors Farm
'a settlement built on marshy ground (to the west of East Moors Farm)'

Ferndown

1321 Fyrne
Old English:
fergen – a wooded hill
dun – a hill
'a settlement on a wooded hill'

Trickett's Cross

1871 census George Trickett 1834 -1905
1901 census Trickett's Cross
'land with a crossing of the ways near the residence of a man named George Trickett'

George Trickett, a labourer at a nursery, was living at 1 Branch Road at the time of the 1871 census. Branch Road is now known as Wimborne Road East. It is believed this area was named after George and his family.

Tributary of Uddens Water near the police headquarters in Ameysford

River Stour and Tributaries – Uddens Water

Sunlight reflects on muddy Uddens Water in West Moors

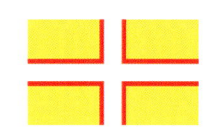

Downstream Dorset – River Tales and Local History

Chapter 46

RIVER CRANE – MOORS RIVER

The River Crane changes its name to the Moors River halfway along its course. It rises in north-east Dorset as a winterbourne stream but below Cranborne it is augmented by more springs. The river takes its name from Cranborne until it reaches Moors Valley Country Park with all its popular attractions. It then becomes the Moors River which meanders southwards, often out of sight.

The lower reaches of the Moors River skirt Bournemouth Airport, pass through the water meadows at Blackwater near Hurn and confluence with the River Stour. Together they flow into the English Channel at Christchurch harbour.

AT A GLANCE

SOURCE
Springs north of Cranborne

MOUTH / OUTLET
Confluences with the River Stour near Hurn

LENGTH
32.2km (20 miles)

TRIBUTARIES
Uddens Water and other tributaries confluence near the site where the River Crane changes its name to Moors River

Dragonfly at the entrance to Moors Valley Country Park

River Stour and Tributaries – River Crane-Moors River

VILLAGES AND TOWNS AND THE ORIGINS OF THEIR NAMES
(from source to mouth of the river)

Fleur de Lys, Cranborne

CRANBORNE
1086 (Domesday Book) Creneburne
Old English:
cran – a crane or heron
burna – a stream
'a settlement near a stream where cranes or herons can be seen'

Revenge served cold
Algar, a Saxon lord of the manor in the West Country, had a son named Britic. According to legend, Britic rejected the love of Princess Matilda of Flanders. Later, Matilda married the sixth Duke of Normandy, known as William the Bastard. In 1066 William invaded England and became King William I (William the Conqueror). Queen Matilda exacted retribution for her earlier spurned love. She confiscated all the lands Britic owned, including Cranborne, and had him thrown into prison, where he died.

Disappointed expectations
First World War poet Rupert Brooke was passing through Cranborne on a walking tour with his friend Dudley Ward. They had chosen to stay at the Fleur de Lys but arrived late into the evening and were unable to find the inn. During an uncomfortable night at the Victoria Inn, Brooke wrote a poem praising all the comforts he imagined had been waiting for them at the Fleur de Lys.

Ode to the Fleur de Lys Inn

In Cranborne town two inns there are,
And one the Fleur-de-Lys is hight, (named)
And one, the inn Victoria,
Where, for it was alone in sight,
We turned in tired and tearful plight
Seeking for warmth, and company,
And food, and beds so soft and white
These things are at the Fleur-de-Lys.
Where is the ointment for the scar?
Slippers? and table deftly dight? (prepared)
Sofas? tobacco? soap? and ah!
Hot water for a weary wight? (person)
Where is the food, in toil's despite?
The golden eggs? the toast? the tea?
The maid so pretty and polite?
These things are at the Fleur-de-Lys.
Oh, we have wandered far and far,
We are fordone and wearied quite.
No lamp is lit; there is no star.
Only we know that in the night
We somewhere missed the faces bright,
The lips and eyes we longed to see;
And Love, and Laughter, and Delight.
These things are at the Fleur-de-Lys.
Prince, it is dark to left and right.
Waits there an inn for you and me?
Fine noppy ale and red firelight?
These things are at the Fleur-de-Lys.

EDMONDSHAM
1086 (Domesday Book) Amedesham
1195 Edmundesham
Old English:
Eadmund – personal name
ham – a homestead
'a homestead owned by a man named Edmund'

ROMFORD
1268 Runford
Old English:
hrung – a pole
ford – a ford
'a settlement with a ford across the river which is marked by a pole'

EBBLAKE
1280 Abbelake
Old English:
Abba – personal name
lacu – a stream, pond, lake
probably 'a pond or stream owned by a man named Abba'

WOOLSBRIDGE
1618 Woolles bridge
(or Wools Bridge)
Old English:
wella – a stream
'a settlement with a bridge over the stream'

WEST MOORS
1310 La More
1591 West Moors
Old English:
mor – marshy ground
'a settlement near or on marshland west of the river'

SOPLEY COMMON

1086 (Domesday Book) Sopelie
Old English:
Soppa – personal name
leah – a wood or clearing in a wood
'a settlement in a wood or clearing owned by a man named Soppa'

Radar station
The Ground Controlled Interception (GCI) radar station was set up outside the village of Sopley in 1943. Its purpose was to detect and track enemy aircraft, defending Britain against attack.

RAF Sopley
Built in the early 1950s, RAF Sopley was used by the Ministry of Defence until 1974. After that it accommodated refugees from Vietnam. The site is now known as Merryfield Park.

Stop the train!
Avon Lodge Station was a private halt. The occupiers of Avon Cottage, later known as Avon Castle, had the right to stop the train at the platform by waving a red flag in daytime or a red lamp at night. This arrangement came to an end with the arrival of express trains.

HURN

1242 Hurne
Old English:
hyrne – a corner or angle
Probably *'a settlement near the corner of land where the Moors River joins the River Stour'*
The confluence takes place about 1km (1,100 yards) from the village.

From railway station to hotel
From 1863 until 1935, the railway passed through Herne Bridge Station enabling Hurn villagers to travel to Ringwood and London or Christchurch and Bournemouth.

Herne Bridge Station's buildings and platform now form part of the Avon Causeway Hotel (*above*). The hotel's owners have also purchased a Pullman passenger carriage and shunter locomotive, which are used as restaurants.

Hurn airport
Bournemouth airport was originally RAF Station Hurn. It opened in 1941 and was used by the Royal Air Force and United States Army Air Force during the Second World War, primarily as a transport and fighter airfield. In 1969 it was renamed Bournemouth airport but older residents still affectionately call it Hurn airport.

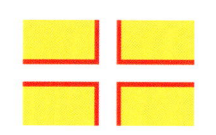

Chapter 47

RIVER AVON

AT A GLANCE

SOURCE
Wiltshire, in the Vale of Pewsey

OUTLET / MOUTH
Joins the waters of the River Stour in Clay Pool, Christchurch, and empties into the English Channel through Christchurch Harbour

LENGTH
About 77km (48 miles)

TRIBUTARIES
Tributary within Dorset – Sleep Brook

The River Avon rises in Wiltshire and flows through Hampshire until it confluences with King Stream, east of Ashley Heath. From there it follows the border between Dorset and Hampshire until joining the waters of the River Stour south of Christchurch Priory in Dorset. The mouth of the two rivers is in front of Christchurch Sailing Club, an area of water known as Clay Pool.

A small tributary, Sleep Brook, passes through north Dorset, rising from springs south of Cripplestyle and Alderholt.

Avon is from the Celtic name *afon* meaning 'river'.

River Avon flowing downstream under the Christchurch Bypass (A35) to Purewell. Part of the Avon Valley Path

River Stour and Tributaries – River Avon

Villages and towns and the origins of their names
(from entering Dorset to the mouth of the river)

Ashley
1280 Aisshele
Old English:
aesc – an ash tree
leah – a wood or clearing
'an ash tree wood'

Week Common
1327 Wike
1759 Week
Old English:
wic – a dwelling place or specialised farm, often dairy
'a dwelling place or dairy farm on common land'

Sopley Common
1086 (Domesday Book) Sopelie
Old English:
Soppa – personal name
leah – a wood or clearing in a wood
'common land with a wood or clearing lived on by a man named Soppa'

Hurn
1242 Hurne
Old English:
hyrne – a corner or angle
Probably *'a settlement near the corner of land where the Moors River joins the River Stour'*
The rivers confluence about 1km (1,100 yards) from the village. For more information, see the River Crane – Moors River.

Dudmoor Farm
1269 Duddemore
Old English:
Dudda – personal name
mor – marshland
'marshland owned by a man named Dudda'

Dudmoor Farm
Our granddaughter, Ellie, had lessons at Dudmoor Farm Riding School while Ryan's daughter, who has special needs, enjoyed supervised time grooming one of the horses and cleaning out the stables.

In August 2020 the stables were permanently closed because of loss of business during the coronavirus pandemic. Thank you for the good times we had. We miss you.

Dudmoor Farm

An example of a bowl barrow, St Catherine's Hill

ST CATHERINE'S HILL
14th century Catelineford
Old French:
Cateline – personal name, Catherine
Old English:
ford – a ford or river crossing
'a hill near a ford owned by a person named Cateline (Saint is a later addition)'

Big hill, little hill
The hill was originally called Richedon, probably meaning 'great hill'. Across the River Stour there is an area named Littledown, meaning 'small hill'. In 1331 a chapel at the summit of Richedon was dedicated to St Catherine and the hill eventually became known as St Catherine's Hill.

St Catherine's Hill Nature Reserve
St Catherine's Hill Nature Reserve is an area of 35 hectares (8.5 acres) of heathland and coniferous forest. Rare species such as the Dartford warbler and sand lizard live there and the reserve is jointly managed for nature conservation by the council, the RSPB (Royal Society for the Protection of Birds), Dorset Wildlife Trust and The Amphibian and Reptile Conservation Trust.

Barrows and earthworks
At 53m (163ft) above sea level, St Catherine's Hill is the highest area of Christchurch and offers spectacular views. It has been used as a look-out and beacon since prehistoric times. There are Bronze Age bowl barrows and the earthworks of a Roman camp.

Training for war
St Catherine's Hill was used as an army training ground for trench warfare and to practise throwing hand grenades during the First and Second World Wars. The Royal Horse Artillery and Dragoons from Christchurch Barracks also exercised there.

WINKTON
1086 (Domesday Book) Weringeton
1236 Wineketon
Old English:
Wineca – personal name
ton – a farm or estate
'a farm or estate belonging to a man named Wineca'

RAF Winkton
RAF Winkton was created towards the end of the Second World War. Its runway construction was the prototype for the temporary Advanced Landing Grounds, essential to the progression of allied forces through France and Germany after the D-Day landings. In July 1944 the runway was taken up to be used in France. Today the land has returned to its original agricultural use.

River Stour and Tributaries – River Avon

Eastern part of Christchurch Priory

River Avon in the background, flowing towards the waters of the River Stour in Christchurch

BURTON
1100 Bureton
Old English:
burh – a fortified place
ton – a farm or estate
'a fortified farm or estate'

JUMPERS COMMON
16th century from the family name, Jumper
'Common land lived on by a family named Jumper'

PUREWELL
1300 Perewull
Old English:
peru – a pear
wella – a spring
'a settlement near a spring where pear trees grow'

CHRISTCHURCH
10th century Tweoxneam
934 Twynham
1086 (Domesday Book) Thuinam
1318 Cristeschirche of Twynham
Old English:
betweoxn – between or betwixt
ea – a stream
'a settlement between two streams (River Stour and River Avon)'
By 1318 it was known as 'the church of Christ between two streams', later shortened to 'Christchurch'.
For more information, see the River Stour.

SLEEP BROOK
(tributary)
The name has uncertain origins

CRIPPLESTYLE
Old English:
crypel – a narrow pass
or creopan – to crawl or creep
stigel – a style
'a settlement by a narrow pass with a style over a fence'
or *'a settlement with a style that could be crept through – possibly by sheep?'*

ALDERHOLT
1285 Alreholt
Old English:
alor – an alder tree
holt – a wood or copse
'a settlement with a copse of alder trees'

237

Chapter 48

RIVER STOUR'S SHORTER TRIBUTARIES

SHREEN WATER

Shreen Water rises in Wiltshire north of Mere, crossing the county border into Dorset at Huntingford. It runs parallel with the B3092 en route to its confluence with the River Stour in Gillingham.

HUNTINGFORD

1258 Hunteneford
Old English:
huntena – of the hunter
ford – a ford or river crossing
'a ford belonging to, or used by, huntsmen'

King's deer
Huntingford was once on the edge of the Royal Forest of Gillingham where the king's deer were kept. The forest and its hunting lodge were visited by King Henry I, Henry II, John and Henry III. The lodge was eventually destroyed by fire.

Along a lane in Huntingford, Ryan and I met Bill, a villager walking his dog, Lark. He shared with us many stories about the local history, including...

- Hinckes Mill was a major employer as a silk mill from 1830 until forced to close because of financial difficulties in 1894.
- A non-conformist chapel was opened in the 19th century where many of the mill workers would congregate to worship. The Duchy of Cornwall is the landowner around Mere and Huntingford so the chapel, not being part of the established Church of England, was built just outside its domain.
- The volume of Shreen Water has reduced considerably over several decades causing great concern and affecting agriculture and market gardens. Questions have been asked of the water board about the amount of water abstraction.

MILTON ON STOUR

1086 (Domesday Book) Mideltone
1397 Milton on Stoure
Old English:
middle – middle
tun – a farm or estate
'a middle farm or estate on the River Stour'

Shreen Water

COLESBROOK
Old English:
col – charcoal
'a brook where charcoal was burnt nearby'

PEACEMARSH
1535 Pesemershe
Old English:
pise – peas
mersc – a marsh
'a settlement where peas are grown on marsh land'

GILLINGHAM
early 11th century Gillinga ham
Old English:
Gylla – personal name
ing – associated with, belonging to
ham – a homestead
'a homestead associated with a man named Gylla'

RIVER LODDEN

The River Lodden rises in Wiltshire and crosses the county border into Dorset north east of Gillingham. There are tributaries rising around Motcombe, west of Shaftesbury, joining the waters of the River Lodden near Ham Common in Gillingham. The main tributary is Fern Brook.

The River Lodden flows past the site of King's Court Palace and Ham Common until it reaches its confluence with the River Stour south of Gillingham.

Lodden probably has the same Celtic derivation as the River Lydden, which means 'broad' or 'wide'.

MOTCOMBE
1244 Motcumbe
Old English:
mot – a meeting
cumb – a valley
'a valley where meetings were held'

ECCLIFFE
1292 Eggcliue
Old English:
Ecga – personal name
clif – a riverbank
'a settlement on a river bank owned by a man named Ecga'

MADJESTON
1205 Malgereston
Old English:
Malger – personal name
tun – a farm or estate
'a farm or estate owned by a man named Malger'

STOCK WATER

Stock Water rises in Somerset and runs parallel with the B3081 to Gillingham. It flows beneath the railway line to join the River Stour just south of the viaduct near Kine Bush Lane.

BAINLY FARM
1609 Binley
Old English:
bean – bean
leah – a clearing in a wood
'a clearing in a wood where beans are grown'

WYKE
1244 Wyke
Old English:
wic – a dwelling place or dairy farm
'a dwelling place, possibly with a dairy'

Stock Water flows under a bridge in Culver Lane, Wyke

THORNGROVE
1292 Thorngraue
Old English:
thorn – a thorn tree
graf – a copse
'a settlement near a copse where thorn trees grow'

Employ My Ability
Employ My Ability is an organisation that supports young people with learning disabilities and special needs. It recently acquired Thorngrove Garden Centre, where it offers vocational training in horticulture, retail and in the Secret Garden Cafe. It is a great place to visit for plants and gardening supplies, as well as a relaxing cup of coffee.

WEST BROOK
West Brook rises near Langham, flows south to pass under the railway and arrives at its confluence with the Stour near Walnut Tree Farm.

LANGHAM
1156 Langeham
Old English:
lang – long
hamm – a river meadow
'a settlement near a long river meadow'

BUGLEY
1275 Bogeley
Old English:
Bucge – personal name
leah – a wood or clearing in a wood
'a clearing in a wood owned by a woman named Bucge'

DARKNOLL BROOK
Darknoll Brook rises in the steep hills near Hibbett Bottom, flows past Okeford Fitzpaine and under the A357, then reaches its confluence with the River Stour at Fiddleford Mill.

OKEFORD FITZPAINE
10th century Acford
1321 Fitz Payn
Old English:
ac – an oak tree
ford – a ford
Fitz Payn – personal name
'a settlement by a ford where an oak tree grows, owned by a family named Fitz Payn'

FIDDLEFORD
1244 Fitelford
Old English:
Fitela – personal name
ford – a ford
'a ford owned by a man named Fitela'

Fiddleford Manor expertly preserved by English Heritage

Fiddleford manor roof beams

COOKWELL BROOK

The brook emerges from Cookwell Spring near Okeford Fitzpaine, flows west towards Shillingstone, and under the A357 to its confluence with the River Stour close to Hayward Bridge.

SHILLINGSTONE

1220 Akeford Skelling
1444 Shillyngeston
Originally included the same name as Child Okeford and Okeford Fitzpaine – see Darknoll Brook above.
Old English:
Schelin – personal name
tun – a farm or estate
'a farm or estate owned by a man named Schelin'

Cookwell Brook on the North Dorset Trailway near Shillingstone

CHIVRICK'S BROOK

Chivrick's Brook rises near Marnhull and Todber, passes Hinton St Mary to the west, and flows under the B3091 to join the River Stour north of Fiddleford.

TODBER

1086 (Domesday Book) Todeberie
Old English:
Tota – personal name
bearu – a grove
'a settlement near a wooded grove owned by a man named Tota'

MARNHULL

1267 Marnhulle
Old English:
Mearna – personal name
hyll – a hill
'a settlement on a hill owned by a man named Mearna'

HINTON ST MARY

944 Hamtune
1086 (Domesday Book) Hainetone
1627 Hinton Marye
Old English:
hean – high
tun – a farm or estate
'a farm or estate on high ground owned by the abbey of St Mary (in Shaftesbury)'

FIDDLEFORD

1244 Fitelford
Old English:
Fitela – personal name
ford – a ford
'a ford owned by a man named Fitela'

Weir at Fiddleford Mill

PIMPERNE BROOK

Pimperne Brook rises south of the village of Pimperne. It travels southward and turns towards the old town of Blandford Forum before reaching Black Lane, which leads to Blandford Camp military base. Pimperne Brook then passes through Blandford Forum and confluences with the River Stour near the southern border of the town.

PIMPERNE

935 Pimpern
The derivation of Pimperne is uncertain, possibly
Old English:
pimp – a hill
aen – a dwelling
'a dwelling on a hill'

Beheaded, survived
Henry VIII granted the Manor of Pimperne to his ill-fated fifth wife Katherine Howard. After her execution the king bestowed the manor on Katherine's successor, Catherine Parr, who managed to outlive her notorious husband.

Ho!
Charles Kingsley, author of The Water Babies and Westward Ho!, was a young curate at St Peter's Church in the 1840s. He went on to develop a career as a historian, university professor and social reformer.

BLANDFORD FORUM

1086 (Domesday Book) Bleaneford
1297 Blaneford Forum
Old English:
blaegna – a gudgeon
Latin:
forum – a market
'a settlement with a ford where gudgeon swim and a market'

Castleman Trailway

BLACKWATER STREAM

The Blackwater Stream rises from several sources around Broadstone. When the railway was built through Broadstone in 1872 part of the stream was channelled underground – but it still flows alongside a section of the Castleman Trailway between Broadstone and Wimborne, passing Broadstone golf course.

Blackwater Stream then turns eastward through Delph Woods and Arrowsmith Coppice and north-eastwards to join the River Stour east of Canford Magna.

BROADSTONE

The name was first recorded in 1795. Before then it was simply known as West Heath. The name Broadstone probably derives from the three broad stepping stones laid to cross the Blackwater Stream near Brookdale Farm. Two of the original stones have been preserved by Broadstone United Reformed Church in Higher Blandford Road and can be seen outside the building.

DELPH WOODS

Old English:
delf – excavation, quarry, digging
The ponds in Delph Woods were probably former gravel pits. Gravel would have been used for building projects in the area.

Ancient oak
An ancient oak tree stands in Delph Woods. It is 200 years old, 24.3m (80ft) tall and has a circumference of 4m (13ft). In summer the dense foliage prevents plants from growing in its shade.

Pansy's Bathing Place

ARROWSMITH COPPICE
The name probably derives from coppice wood used in the manufacture of arrows. The Dorset Wildlife Trust and The Amphibian and Reptile Conservation Trust manage the coppice and surrounding nature reserves.

CANFORD MAGNA
1086 (Domesday Book) Cheneford
1195 Kaneford
1612 Canford
Old English:
Cana – personal name
ford – a ford crossing a river
Latin:
magna – great
'a ford crossing the river on land owned by a man named Cana'

LEADEN STOUR
Leaden Stour is a stream that joins the River Stour at both ends. It divides from the Stour north of Throop Mill and rejoins it just over a mile downstream.

THROOP (BOURNEMOUTH)
12th century la Throup
Old English:
throp – an outlying farm
'land or settlement with an outlying farm'

Pansy's Bathing Place
A wide ford that crosses Leaden Stour became known as Pansy's Bathing Place after Pansy, a golden retriever. The dog was owned by Dr and Mrs James Fisher of Throop and loved swimming there.

EAST DORSET

Following the rivers and streams that flow through East Dorset

'This fashionable watering-place, with its eastern and its western stations, its piers, its groves of pines, its promenades, and its covered gardens, was, to Angel Clare, like a fairy place suddenly created by the stroke of a wand, and allowed to get a little dusty.'

**Tess of the D'Urbevilles describing Bournemouth (Sandbourne)
by Thomas Hardy**

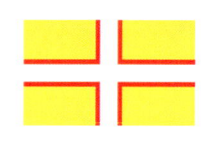

Chapter 49

BRANKSOME CHINE STREAM

AT A GLANCE

SOURCE
Emerges from beneath Lindsay Road, near Penn Hill Corner, Branksome

MOUTH / OUTLET
Branksome Chine beach

LENGTH
About 3.2km (2 miles)

Branksome Chine Stream surfaces in the Penn Hill area and flows through Branksome Chine Gardens to the beach. The water enters the sea through a 50m (55 yard) culvert pipe buried beneath the sand. A walk through the gardens is a peaceful experience surrounded as you are by woodland trees and mature shrubs, and accompanied by the sound of the stream flowing over small waterfalls.

There is plenty of space for walking dogs and for children to play hide-and-seek in the rhododendrons. My son Ian used to love hiding from me with his Dalmatian, Lottie!

A small waterfall where Branksome Chine Stream flows from below a stone footbridge

East Dorset – Branksome Chine Stream

VILLAGES AND TOWNS AND THE ORIGINS OF THEIR NAMES
(from source to mouth of the river)

PENN HILL

Celtic:
penn – a hill
or **Old English:**
penn – an enclosure for animals
probably *'a settlement on a hill'*
or *'an enclosure for animals'*

Studio stars
Arny's Shack *(below)* was a recording studio in Penn Hill, now known as Active Music Studios. It was opened in 1973 by late-owner Tony Arnold. Many well-known musicians have recorded there including Robert Fripp (guitarist in King Crimson), Andy Summers (guitarist in The Police), The Troggs, Eurythmics and Max Bygraves. It is now owned by Martin Condon. Clients who have recorded at Active Music include Mungo Jerry, Zoot Money, The Script, Paul Weller and Steve Marriott.

BRANKSOME CHINE

The name Branksome was taken from a poem by Sir Walter Scott, The Lay Of The Last Minstrel. The setting for this lengthy poem is Branksome Hall. The poem was published in 1805 to much popular acclaim.

Old English:
cinu – a narrow gorge cut through cliffs by a river leading to the sea
'a deep ravine leading to the sea, named Branksome'

Branksome Park – from smugglers to millionaires
In the 18th century Branksome Chine was used by smugglers to transport contraband from their boats inland to Kinson for distribution – see chapter on River Stour.

Branksome Estate was originally owned by the Bruce family from Scotland. There were 300 hectares (745 acres) of wild heathland so the Bruces planted many of the Scots pines for

The Avenue, looking towards Westbourne

249

Branksome Chine Stream approaching the culvert under the road and beach to empty into the sea. In the distance is the restaurant that was once a solarium

Branksome Chine stream

which Branksome Park is renowned. In 1851, MP for South Leicestershire Charles Packe acquired Branksome Estate from the Bruce family for £12,000. On cliffs above the beach he built Branksome Tower, a magnificent Tudor-style stone mansion. Packe built a high wall around his estate for privacy, including huge wrought-iron gates at the entrance to the driveway.

Part of the original wall still exists in Poole Road, between Branksome railway station and Frizzell House, which is now the head office of Liverpool Victoria Insurance.

The driveway has become The Avenue, a wide road lined with pine trees that leads from Westbourne to Branksome Chine beach.

Henry Bury bought the estate, moved into Branksome Tower in 1869 and created Branksome Park. He removed most of the wall and the gates. He ensured every house had one acre of land so the area would attract wealthy and

East Dorset – Branksome Chine Stream

upper class residents. In the 1890s Branksome Tower became a hotel until it was demolished in 1973.

Today the area features apartment blocks and houses, keeping the name Branksome Tower and retaining wonderful views across Poole Bay.

Public gardens

Branksome Chine Gardens were preserved by Henry Bury and were opened to the public by Poole Council in 1930. The gardens are a haven for birds and plants including magnificent azaleas and rhododendrons.

Restorative waters

There is a story that smugglers hid barrels of brandy in a well near Branksome Chine while being pursued by customs officers. Water from the well became popular with local residents as it was said to have special attributes. No doubt many of the barrels shattered when they were dumped in the well and the brandy enhanced the quality of the water!

First solarium

The UK's first solarium (*above*) was opened at Branksome Chine beach in 1932. The floor was covered with sand, while ultraviolet lights created enough warmth for sunbathing. Deckchairs and refreshments were provided and the windows offered sea views.

However, the solarium proved unsuccessful so the art deco building was converted into a cafe and restaurant, which remain popular today.

The original plaque of Poole Pottery tiles portrays a lady in a swimsuit standing in the sea and calling to others to join her.

251

Chapter 50

Alum Chine Stream

The stream that flows through Alum Chine, near Bournemouth, surfaces in Westbourne close to Alum Chine Road and joins the sea in Poole Bay almost 2km (1.2 miles) west of Bournemouth Pier. It is channelled underground for the final part of its journey to the sea. Alum Chine is a lovely woodland walk to the sandy beach, about 1km (0.6 miles) long. There are tropical gardens behind the children's play area.

AT A GLANCE

SOURCE
Emerges in Westbourne, near Alum Chine Road

MOUTH / OUTLET
Poole Bay, between Sandbanks and Bournemouth

LENGTH
About 1km (0.6 miles)

Westbourne, R L Stevenson Gardens, lighthouse and below Skerryvore notice

ORIGINS OF PLACE NAMES
(from source to mouth of the river)

ALUM CHINE
alum – alum was mined in this region in the 16th century

Old English:
cinu – a narrow gorge cut through cliffs by a river, leading to the sea
'a deep ravine where alum was mined'

Young Winston's close call
In his 1930 memoir My Early Life, Sir Winston Churchill recollected that in his youth: "My aunt, Lady Wimborne, had lent us her comfortable estate at Bournemouth for the winter." During a game of chase through Alum Chine with his brother and cousin he fell 29ft (almost 9m) from a bridge straddling the chine. Winston lay unconscious for several days and was close to dying. There is a difference of opinion over whether this bridge was across Alum Chine or Branksome Dene Chine. Whichever is the correct location, what would life have been like today if he had not recovered to lead this country through the Second World War?

WESTBOURNE
The name describes its position in relation to Bournemouth.

Lighthouse honours famous author
Robert Louis Stevenson, the 19th century Scottish author of books such as Treasure Island, Kidnapped and The Strange Case Of Dr Jekyll And Mr Hyde, spent many summer months in Westbourne and lived there from 1885 to 1887. His uncle owned a house, 'Seaview'. Stevenson later changed the name to 'Skerryvore' after a lighthouse of the same name built by the Stevenson family in Argyll, Scotland. Skerryvore, the house, was where Stevenson recovered from tuberculosis, although a bomb destroyed the building during the Second World War. There is now a small, tranquil, wooded garden on the site to commemorate him. A stone lighthouse stands at its centre.

Smallest cinema
Westbourne Arcade *(left)* is a Grade II-listed building containing many independent shops and the smallest cinema in the country. The arcade was built in 1885 by Henry Joy and is described as Gothic in style. The arcade has a high, glazed roof so it is full of light and the contrast between the brickwork and wrought iron is very effective.

End of the line
Bournemouth West station was opened by the Poole & Bournemouth Railway on 15th June 1874. The station was initially a terminus for trains from Poole but, by 1886, the railway continued to Bournemouth Central Station in Holdenhurst Road, now known simply as Bournemouth Station.

The Somerset & Dorset Joint Railway made Bournemouth West its terminus until the line closed temporarily in 1965 while the line from Waterloo was electrified. It was found Bournemouth Central Station could cope with the number of passengers so Bournemouth West station was closed. Its former site in Queens Road is now a car park and part of the A338 Wessex Way.

Chapter 51

RIVER BOURNE

The River Bourne, or Bourne Stream as it is often known, flows through the urban areas of Bournemouth and Poole with almost half its length hidden in culverts.

At the head of the river, four of these culverts come together, emerging from beneath Ringwood Road not far from the Mountbatten Arms pub restaurant. One culvert flows from the waterworks in Francis Avenue, one drains Canford Heath and the other two culverts are fed by surface water from the roads.

After winding through Talbot Heath and Bourne Valley Nature Reserve the stream disappears under the railway line, emerging into daylight once more in the picturesque gardens at Coy Pond – a favourite place for wedding photographs.

From Coy Pond it flows through the Upper and Central Gardens in Bournemouth. It is channelled back underground again at The Square, a pedestrianised shopping and entertainment area, until it reaches the Lower Gardens heading for the sea. At Bournemouth Pier it travels under the beach, which hides its outlet into Poole Bay and the English Channel.

AT A GLANCE

SOURCE
Many springs around Canford Heath, as well as surface water

MOUTH / OUTLET
Bourne Stream flows into Poole Bay

LENGTH
About 8km (5 miles) above ground

Bourne Stream near Coy Pond

East Dorset – River Bourne

PLACE NAMES OF AREAS AROUND THE COURSE OF THE BOURNE STREAM

WALLISDOWN
Originally Wallis Down

CANFORD HEATH
– part of the Canford Estate
1086 (Domesday Book) Cheneford
1195 Kaneford

Old English:
Cana – personal name
ford – a ford
'a ford owned by a man named Cana'
In 1938 most of the heathland was destroyed by fire. Since then there have been many fires, always a threat to wildlife and sometimes to homes.

During the Second World War, Canford Heath was used for munitions storage.

TURBARY COMMON
A district of Bournemouth, named after the right of turbary, the legal right to cut turf or peat on common ground or a landowner's ground.

Old French:
tourbe – turf
'common land with the right for commoners to cut turf for fuel'

COY POND
This was originally a decoy pond, used to lure ducks and other wildfowl where they could be trapped and used for food and for their feathers. Coy Pond (below) was recreated in 1888 as gardens with willow and alder trees, which now attracts ducks, coots and moorhen in a much safer atmosphere.

BRANKSOME
A district in Poole named after a 19th century house, Branksome Tower in the Avenue. The name of the house was taken from a Sir Walter Scott novel, Lay Of The Last Minstrel – see Branksome Chine Stream for more information.

255

Gasworks bombed

Until the 1970s, Bourne Valley gasworks in Branksome was close to the magnificent viaduct carrying the railway track between Weymouth and London. The viaducts were the target of a German bomber on 27th March 1941. Two bombs were released as the low-flying aircraft passed over the gasworks.

One bomb struck the staff canteen during lunchtime with 32 men and a 14-year-old boy killed. The viaducts escaped damage except for a few machine-gun bullet holes.

The site of the canteen is now part of Branksome Business Park. The gasworks no longer exist and an estate of bungalows has been built on the grounds. In 2020 the gas holders were dismantled, the surrounding area has always been a haven for birds and other wildlife.

Branksome Recreation Ground

Bourne Valley gasworks had its own football team with the pitch now Branksome Recreation Ground, owned and managed by Bournemouth, Christchurch and Poole Council.

A local football club hoped to develop part of the land for its own use, with floodlights, parking etc. The perseverance of local residents saved the 'Rec' so it can still be used by families, joggers and dog walkers. Local football and cricket teams of all ages use the grounds for training and matches, while a circus and fair visit the Rec every year. The community centre hosts a variety of clubs and groups, as well as serving refreshments to people and dogs alike!

George enjoying Branksome Rec

East Dorset – River Bourne

Bourne Stream flowing through Bournemouth Upper Gardens

TALBOT HEATH AND TALBOT VILLAGE
Districts of Bournemouth named after landowners the Talbot sisters in 1860.

POOLE
1183 Pole
1347 La Poule
Old English:
pol – a pool or creek
'a settlement by a pool or creek, referring to Poole Harbour'

BOURNEMOUTH
1406 La Bournemowthe
Old English:
burna – a stream
mutha – a mouth
'settlement at the mouth of a stream '

Bournemouth's founders
A sculpture of modern Bournemouth's founders *(right)* can be seen outside the Bournemouth International Centre. The seaside humour of the sculptor, Jonathan Sells, is displayed by a smiling Lewis Tregonwell facing in one direction holding a bucket and spade hidden behind his back. Facing the opposite direction is C.C. Creeke, looking thoughtful and sitting on a toilet seat.

Tregonwell built the first houses while Christopher Crabbe Creeke, as town surveyor and inspector of nuisances, was responsible for sewerage and roads.

The sculpture also includes Bournemouth Town Hall, a symbol of respectability, with a disreputable smugglers' boat at the rear. A couple of running squirrels may represent the many that can be seen in Bournemouth Gardens – but they could also be 'squirrelling away' the contraband?!

The town of Bournemouth had a poignant beginning. Lewis Tregonwell's wife, Henrietta, became depressed while grieving the death of their young son, Grosvenor. Lewis brought her to stay in Mudeford, near Christchurch. Henrietta found some comfort while visiting Bourne Heath with its sea views and sandy beach. So Lewis bought some land (now Bournemouth town centre) and in 1810 built her a house as a summer retreat. Soon friends and family moved to live nearby and a community was founded. Their original house is now part of the Royal Exeter Hotel.

Invalids and gentlemanly sunsets

During his adolescent years the poet Rupert Brooke often stayed with his grandfather and two 'faded but religious' aunts (Brooke's words) in Bournemouth. During those visits he read the poems of Robert Browning and was inspired to write poetry.

His grandfather's house was named Grantchester Dene *(above)* and is still standing in Dean Park Road, Bournemouth. It's interesting that his lodgings, while at Cambridge University, were in a village that also bears the name Grantchester.

By the time he was in his late teens, Brooke was growing a little tired of Bournemouth. He wrote to a school friend: "I have been in this quiet place of invalids and gentlemanly sunsets for about a hundred years, ever since yesterday week."

While exploring the Isle of Purbeck, Brooke fell in love with the village of Lulworth and its beautiful cove overlooked by the Purbeck Hills. He rented rooms above the village post office.

So many stories could be told about Bournemouth and Poole, ranging from smuggling to heroism and from wars to tourism. Poole is steeped in history whereas Bournemouth is a comparatively new town, flourishing with holidaymakers, commerce and the constantly developing university.

The two towns and villages between them have been joined by in-building and road networks. It is now said to be the largest urban conurbation in the country.

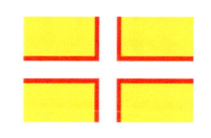

Chapter 52

RIVER MUDE

AT A GLANCE

SOURCE
Springs in the New Forest near Bransgore

MOUTH / OUTLET
Mudeford, Christchurch Harbour flowing into the English Channel

LENGTH
About 10km (6 miles)

The River Mude flows along the county border between Dorset and Hampshire. Travelling past the three Bockhampton villages, the Mude continues under the railway line before emptying into Christchurch Harbour at Mudeford.

Looking towards Hengistbury Head from Mudeford Quay

VILLAGES AND TOWNS WITHIN DORSET AND THE ORIGINS OF THEIR NAMES
(from source to mouth of the river)

BOCKHAMPTON
1199 Bachamton
(North, Middle and South)
Old English:
boc – a beech tree
ham – a homestead
tun – a farm or estate
'a homestead where beech trees grow'

SOMERFORD
12th century Sumerford
Old English:
sumor – summer
ford – a ford, river crossing
'a settlement with a ford during the summer months'

STANPIT
1086 (Domesday Book) Stanpeta
Old English:
stan – a stone
pytt – a pit
'a stone pit'

Selfridge's marsh
Stanpit Marsh is a nature reserve consisting of salt marsh, reed beds, freshwater marsh and sandy scrub. American-born Harry Gordon Selfridge, founder of London department store Selfridges, once owned the marsh. He also owned the land at Hengistbury Head and lived for a while at Highcliffe Castle.

Harry Gordon Selfridge and his family are buried in St Mark's churchyard in Highcliffe.

MUDEFORD
13th century Modeford
Middle English:
mode – mud
Old English:
ford – a ford
'a settlement with a muddy ford'

1784 the Battle of Mudeford
The historic Haven House Inn at Mudeford Quay has a past associated with smuggling. The landlady, Hannah 'Mother' Sillar, stored the contraband at the site and gave the smugglers safe haven.

In 1784 the violent Battle of Mudeford was instigated by three customs ships converging at the entrance to the harbour as smugglers were unloading tea and spirits.

Seeing two rowing boats approaching from the naval ships, the smugglers gathered on Mudeford Quay firing their muskets and killing customs officer Captain William Allen. The smugglers were defeated and one was subsequently hanged and his body chained to Haven House Inn.

A creek flowing through Stanpit Marsh was named after Hannah Sillar and is still known as Mother Sillar's Channel.

Haven House Inn at Mudeford Quay

Chapter 53

BURE BROOK

Bure Brook rises in Lakewood, a little north of Nea Meadows in Highcliffe. It passes under Smugglers Lane South, alongside Hoburne Holiday Park, then travels through Friars Cliff and runs parallel with Bure Lane until it reaches the sea in Christchurch Harbour.

AT A GLANCE

SOURCE
Bure Brook rises in Lakewood, north of Nea Meadows in Highcliffe

MOUTH / OUTLET
Near the car park at Mudeford Quay, Christchurch Harbour flowing into the English Channel

LENGTH
About 1.5km (1 mile)

Bure Brook emptying into the sea near the car park at Mudeford Quay

Nea Meadow Lake

VILLAGES AND TOWNS AND THE ORIGINS OF THEIR NAMES
(from source to mouth of the river)

LAKEWOOD AND NEA MEADOWS

Lakewood pond is surrounded by a housing estate in Highcliffe. It is the source of Bure Brook, which flows south underground to Nea Meadows Nature Reserve.

The larger lake in Nea Meadows was created in 1988 as a flood defence for Bure Brook and is now part of a nature reserve and recreation area.

Nea in Greek means 'new'.

HIGHCLIFFE

1610 Black Cliffe
1759 High Clift
'a settlement on a high cliff'

Steamer Point

Lord Stuart de Rothesay had a paddle steamer pulled up on to the beach in 1830 and it was used as a site office while Highcliffe Castle was being built. It was later used as a lodge.

Steamer Point is a 9.7 hectare (24 acre) nature reserve on top of the cliffs between Friars Cliff and Highcliffe Castle.

It features woodland, two ponds and a picnic area with views across the sea to the Isle of Wight and Hengistbury Head.

Friars Cliff

Wondering how Friars Cliff was named, Ryan and I spoke to a couple of elderly local gentlemen who remembered seeing friars walking to the beach and sitting on the cliffs enjoying the views.

A Roman Catholic Claretian seminary once owned Highcliffe Castle and trained priests there from 1953 to 1966.

MUDEFORD

13th century Modeford
Middle English:
mode – mud
Old English:
ford – a ford
'a settlement with a muddy ford'

Famous faces

The Bure Club was a record club in the late 1950s owned by Mrs Clark. Local youngsters could dance to their music and enjoy live bands on Friday and Saturday nights.

One of the first bands to play at the club was The Kapota, whose line-up included Andy Summers. Andy was a local lad who went on to become famous in rock band The Police.

Mrs Clark sold the club to Dave Stickley, who booked many famous bands and singers including Lulu, Joe Brown, The Animals, The Nashville Teens, John Lee Hooker and Chuck Berry. The Bure Club eventually closed for redevelopment and is now The Sandpiper pub.

Highcliffe Castle in July, soon after coronavirus regulations began to ease

Chapter 54

WALKFORD BROOK

Walkford Brook rises in Hampshire but its lower reaches flow along the county line between Dorset and Hampshire, west of Chewton Glen Hotel.

A path from the car park in Wharncliffe Road, overlooking Highcliffe Beach, leads down to the beach and the coastal entrance of Chewton Bunny Nature Reserve.

AT A GLANCE

SOURCE
In the New Forest, Hampshire

MOUTH / OUTLET
From Chewton Bunny Nature Reserve it is culverted under the beach and out to sea

LENGTH
About 8km (5 miles)

WALKFORD

1280 Walkeforde

possibly Old English:
Walca – personal name
forde – a ford
'a settlement with a ford owned by a man named Walca' or *'a settlement with a ford that can be walked across'*

CHEWTON BUNNY

12th century Chiventon

Old English:
Cifa – personal name
tun – a farm or estate
bunny – a ravine or chine (local name of unknown origin)
'a farm or estate situated in a chine between cliffs, owned by a man named Cifa'

Smugglers' route

The nature reserve along the Walkford Brook was once a well-used smugglers' path to carry contraband from Highcliffe beach. It only takes about 15 minutes to walk from the beach to Chewton Bunny waterfall, and they would have been almost completely hidden from view as they made their way up the chine.

Run rabbit run

Although 'bunny' means a ravine or chine, it would be easy to believe the reserve was given the name because of the amount of rabbits there. Thousands of bunny droppings cover the grassy slopes leading down to beach level. A woodland walk along the brook in Chewton Bunny Nature Reserve is enjoyed by dogs and their owners.

A collie dog playing in Walkford Brook in Chewton Bunny Nature Reserve

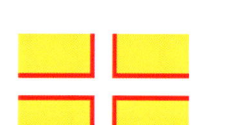

Bibliography

I have made extensive use of:

Place-Names by A.D. Mills

Discover Dorset Series

Dorset Life magazine

Online Parish Clerks Dorset

Other books which have been of invaluable help include:

A User-Friendly Dictionary of Old English by Bill Griffiths

Rivers and Streams by John Wright, Discover Dorset Series

Slow Dorset by Alexandra Richards

A History of Dorset by Cecil N. Cullingford

Domesday Book, Dorset edited by Caroline and Frank Thorn

Dorset Place Names by A. Poulton-Smith

Dorset The Complete Guide by Jo Draper

What's in a Name? Southern Newspapers Publication

Down Your Way Daily Echo (Bournemouth) Publication

Geology for Dummies by Alecia M. Spooner

Thomas Hardy's England by John Fowles and Jo Draper

Ordnance Survey maps covering the county of Dorset

Index

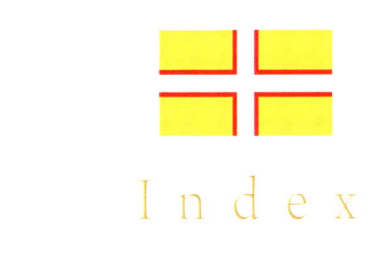

Page numbers in *italics* refer to photographs

A

Abbotsbury 51
Acorn Inn, Evershot 97, *97*
Adams, Douglas 186
Affpuddle 138
Alcester 194
Alderholt 237
Alfred the Great, King of Wessex 108, 194
Alfrida, Queen of England 146
All Saints Church, Gussage All Saints 219
All Saints Church, Nether Cerne 120
All Saints Church, Piddletrenthide 134
All Saints Church, Poyntington 5
All Saints Church, Tarrant Monkton 207
River Allen 217
Aller 141
Allington 35, 39
Almer 215
Alton Pancras 133
Alum Chine 253
Alum Chine Stream 252
Amen Corner 219
Ameysford 228, *228*
Amphibian and Reptile Conservation Trust 236, 245
Amy's Shack (Active Music Studios), Penn Hill 249, *249*
Anderson (Winterborne Anderson) 213, *213*
Ansty 133, 141
Arrowsmith Coppice 245
Ash 203
Ashley 235
River Asker 32, 36, 40, *43*
Askerswell 41
Athelhampton 136
Athelhampton House 136, *136*
Atrim 39
River Avon 234, *234*, 237
Avon Causeway Hotel 233
Avon Lodge Station 233
River Axe 18, *18*, *19*, *20*

B

Badbury Rings 165, 209
Bagber 182
Bailey Gate Dairy, Sturminster Marshall 215
Bainly Farm 240
Bankes Arms 89, *89*
Bankes family at Kingston Lacy 166
Bankes, Mary 86–87
Banksy 23
Barnes, William iii, 17, 124, 186
Bastard, John and William 163
Batcombe 9
Beaminster 33
Bearwood 170
Beaufort, Margaret 223
Beaulieu Wood 181
Bedchester 196
Beer Hackett 13

267

Bennett, Charles (Olympic champion) 171, *171*
Bere Regis *144*, 146, *147*
Bere Stream (tributary of River Piddle) 132, 144
Betjeman, Sir John 199
Bettiscombe 26
Bettiscombe Manor 26–27
Bibbern Brook 178
Billington, Mary Frances 226
Bingham's Melcombe 142
Birdsmoorgate 26
Bishop's Caundle 186
Black Death 60, 69, 114, 133, 150
Blackmore Vale 156, 178, 182, 194
Blackney 28
River Blackwater 18
Blackwater 172
Blackwater Stream 244
Blandford Forum 162, 163, *163*, 243
Bloxworth 149, 150
Blyton, Enid 71, 87, 187, *187*
Bockhampton 261
Bond family and Bond Street, London 80, 85
Bothenhampton 37
River Bourne (Bourne Stream) 254, *254*, 257
Bourne Valley Gasworks 256, *256*
Bournemouth 253, *255*, *257*, 258, *258*, *259*
Bourton 157
Bourton Foundry 157
Bow Brook 177
Bower, William, 'Billy Winspit' 78
Bowleaze Cove 62, 64, 65
Boyle, Robert 183
Boys Hill 185
Bradford Abbas 7, *7*, 13
Bradford Peverell 100
Bradle Farm 85
Bradpole 42
Branksome 255, 256, *256*
Branksome Chine 248–251, *251*
Branksome Chine Stream 248, *248*, 250
Branksome Park 249–251, *249*, *251*

Briantspuddle 138, *138*
River Bride 44
Bridehead House, Little Bredy 45
Bridehead Lake, Little Bredy *44*, 45
Bridport 36, 37, 39, 43
River Brit 32, 35, 36, 38
Broad Bench, Kimmeridge Bay *74*
Broadmayne 127
Broadstone 244
Broadwey 59
Broadwindsor 19
Bronze Age settlements
    Eggardon Hill burial mounds 41
    Five Marys cemetery 131
    Kingston Russell Stone Circle 46
    St Catherine's Hill bowl barrow 236, *236*
Brooke, Rupert 231, 232, 259, *259*
Broomhill Bridge 129
Brother Vincent 9
Brown, Sir Lancelot (Capability) 6, 145
Bryanston 162–163, *162*
Bubb, George 205
Buckham 34
Buckhorn Weston 177, *177*
Buckland Newton 180, 181, *181*
Bugley 241
Bure Brook 262, *262*
Bure Club 263
Burleston 137, 143
Burt, George 93
Burton 121, 237
Burton Bradstock 47
Burton Mere 67
Bury, Henry 250
Byle Brook (East Corfe River) 82, 83, 86

C

Cairn Circle, Poxwell 68, *68*
River Cale 176
River Cam 189
Canford Bridge *217*

Index

Canford Heath 169, 255
Canford Magna 168, *168*, 169, 245
Cann 194
Carey 139
Carpenter, Richard Cromwell 25
Cashmoor 219
Castleman Trailway 168, 224, *244*
Catherston Leweston 29
Cattistock 98, 99, *99*
Caundle Brook 180, 184
Caundle Wake 187
River Cerne 96, 118, *118*
Cerne Abbas 120, *120*
Chalbury 226, *226*
Chaldon Herring 131
Chalmington 98, *98*
Chantmarle 97
Chapman's Pool 76, 77
Chapman's Pool Stream 76, 77
River Char 24, *25*
Charles, Emmanuel 69
Charles II 23, 36, 39, 66, 107, 158, 225
Charlton Marshall 163
Charminster 121, *121*
Charmouth 29
Charmouth beach *28–29*, 29
Chebbard Farm 143
Chedington 14, 19
Cheselbourne 133, 142
Cheselbourne Stream
  (tributary of River Piddle) 132
Chesil Beach *48–49*, 49, 53
Chetnole 10
Chewton Bunny 265, *265*
Chickerell 52, *52*, 53
Chideock 30, *31*
Child Okeford 161
Chivrick's Brook 242
Christchurch 174, 237, *237*
Christchurch Castle 175, *175*
Christchurch Priory 174–175, *174*, 237

Church Henge, Knowlton 220, *220*
Church Knowle 85
Churchill, John, 1st Duke of Marlborough 185
Churchill, Sir Winston 66, 169, 253
Clavell, John 185
Clavell's Tower 75, *75*
Clunes, Martin 34
Cockhill Farm 179
Colesbrook 239
Collyer's Brook 198, *199*
Compton Abbas 199
Coney's Castle 25
Constable, John 69
Cookwell Brook 242, *242*
Cooper, Anthony Ashley, 1st Earl of
  Shaftesbury 107
Corfe Castle 86–87, *87*, 89
Corfe River (River Wych) 82, 88–89, *88*, *89* *see also*
  East Corfe River (Byle Brook);
  West Corfe River (Wicken Stream or
  Steeple Brook)
Coronavirus pandemic 34, 79, *79*, 133, *147*, 160, 173, 235
Court Leet in Anderson 213
Cowards Lake 50
Cowgrove 165
Cox, John 64
Coy Pond, Bournemouth 255
Craig's Farm Dairy, Osmington 68
Cranborne 231, 232
Cranborne Chase 194, 204
River Crane 230
Crawford Bridge, Spetisbury *209*
Creech Barrow hill 80
Creech Grange, Steeple 80, *80*, 84
Creeke, Christopher Crabbe 258
Crichel Stream 216
Cripplestyle 237
Cromwell, Oliver 39, 66, 120, 158
Crooked Withies 227
Cross and Hand, Batcombe 8, 9

269

Cruxton 99
Culverwell 56
Culverwell Stream 54, *54*
Cynewulf, King of Wessex 23

D

Damer, Joseph, Lord Milton 145
Dammer, John 120
Dancing Ledge, Langton Matravers *91*, 93
Daniell, Canon Edward 41
Darknoll Brook 241
Dartford Warbler 126, 169, 227, 236
Davison, Frank and Ann 57
Day-Lewis, Cecil 103
Debenham, Ernest 138, *138*
Delph Woods 244
Devils Brook (tributary of River Piddle) 132, 140, *143*
Dewlish 133, 142–143, *142*
River Divelish 190, *190*
Dodington, George 205
Dorchester 102
Dorset buttons 151, 213
Dorset County Asylum, Forston 121
Dorset Downs 110, 156
Dorset Knobs 99
Dorset Wildlife Trust
    Arrowsmith Coppice 245
    Collyer's Brook 198
    Fontmell Down 198
    St Catherine's Hill 236
    Upton Heath 169
Drimpton 20
Druitt, Montague John 167
Dudmoor Farm 235, *235*
Dudsbury 170
Duncliffe Hill 194
Duntish 181
Durdle Door 73
Durweston 162, 203

E

East Burton *130*, 131
East Corfe River (Byle Brook) 82, 83, 86
East Elworth 51
East Fleet Stream 52
East Holme 107
East Knighton 131
East Orchard 196
East Stoke 107
East Stour 159
Eastbury House, Tarrant Gunville 205–206
Easton 55
Ebblake 232
Eccliffe 240
Edmondsham 232
Edward l 23
Edward ll 21
Edward The Martyr 87, 146, 194
Eggardon Hill Iron Age fort 41
Egliston Gwyle 74
Egliston Stream 74
Egmont Bight 75
Emmetts Hill Memorial 76, 77
Empool Bottom and Heath 127
Encombe Valley Stream 75
English Civil War 33, 102, 107
English Heritage
    Church Henge, Knowlton 220, *220*
    Fiddleford Manor 160, *241*
    Maiden Castle 123, *123*
Ensbury 171
Evershot 97
Eye Bridge *165*
Eype Mouth 66, *67*
Eype Stream 66, *66*

Index

F
Fairfax, General Sir Thomas 33
farming
    Briantspuddle, Ernest Debenham 138
    Canon Anthony Huxton 199
    Kingston Maurward agricultural college 104
    Monkton Wyld Court 25
    Wimborne St Giles village school 218
Farnham 219, *219*
Farrant, Amy 225
Fellowes, Lord Julian and Lady Emma 104–105
Ferndown 170, 228
Fiddleford 160, 161, *161*, 241, *241*, 242, *243*
Fielding, Henry 159
Fifehead Magdalen 159, 176
Fifehead Neville 191
Fifehead St Quintin 191
Filford 39
Filley Brook 177
First World War 5, 106, 151, 157, 201, 231, 236
Fisher, Rev John 69
Fishpond Bottom 25
Five go to Mystery Moor by Enid Blyton 71
Five Marys Bronze Age cemetery 131
Fleet 53
Fleet Lagoon 48–53, *48–49*, *53*
Fleming, Ian 91
Fleur de Lys Inn 231–232, *231*
Folke 189
Fontmell Brook 198
Fontmell Down 198
Fontmell Magna *198*, 199, *199*
Fontmell Parva 199
Forde Abbey 21, *21*
Forston 121
Fort Henry 79, *79*
Fortuneswell 55
Fossil Forest, Lulworth 73
fossil hunting 29, 31, 47
Fox Inn (Hall & Woodhouse), Ansty 141, *141*
Frampton 100, 101
Friars Cliff 263
Frome 99
River Frome 96, 108, *109*, 114, *115*, *130*
Frome St Quintin 98, *110*
Frome Valley Trail 96
Frome Vauchurch 99

G
River Gascoigne 4
Gaunt's Common 227
George III 60–61, 63, *63*
Gillingham 159, 238, 239
Glanvilles Wootton *184*, 185
Godlingston Stream 79
Godmanstone 120
God's Blessing Green 227
Golden Cap 31
Gorges, Ferdinando 127
Gorwell Circle 46
Grey Mare and her Colts, Long Bredy 46
Grey's Bridge, Dorchester 102
Grimstone 100, 117
Guest, Sir Ivor 169
Gulliver, Isaac 47
Gundry, Nathaniel 224
Gussage All Saints 219
Gussage Brook 216
Gussage St Andrew 219
Gussage St Michael 219
Guys Marsh 195

H
Hall & Woodhouse brewers 141
Hammoon 161
Hampreston 170
Hanford 161
Hanham, Thomas 196
Hardy, Florence 102
Hardy, Kate and Mary 135
Hardy, Sir Thomas Masterman 45–46, 50, *50*

271

Hardy, Thomas 68, 97, 102, *102*, 103, *103*, 125, 146, 159, 214, 247
Hardy, Thomas (senior) 136
Hardy's Monument *50*
Harman's Cross 86, 91
Hartgrove 196
Haven House Inn, Mudeford 261, *261*
Haythorne 225
Hayward, Charles 91
Hazelbury Bryan 190
Hengistbury Head 175, *260*
Henry III 181–182, 219
Henry Vlll 21, 34, 50, 194, 243
Herbury 52
Herbury Stream 52
Hermitage 189
Herne Bridge Station 233
Highcliffe 263
Highcliffe Castle *263*
Higher Bockhampton 103, *103*
Higher Kingcombe 113
Higher Waterston 136
Hilfield 9
Hilfield Friary 9
hill forts
    Badbury Rings 165, 209, *209*
    Coney's Castle 25
    Eggardon Hill 41
    Hambledon Hill 202–203
    Hod Hill and ramparts 202–203
    Lambert Castle 25
    Maiden Castle 123, *123*
    Poundbury Camp 101
    Spetisbury Rings 165
Hilton 142, 145
Hinckes Mill 238
Hine, Thomas 33
Hinton Martell 227
Hinton Parva 222
Hinton St Mary 160, 242
Hod Hill 202–203, *202*

Holdenhurst 172
Holditch Court 21
Holme Bridge 107, *107*
Holnest 189
Holt 227
Holt Forset 227
Holton 151
Holton Heath munitions factory 151
Holwell 186, *186*
Holy Rood Church, Buckland Newton *181*
Holy Stream 96
River Hooke 96, 112, *114*
Hooke 113
Hooke Park 113
Horton 226
Horton Tower 226, *226*
Huntingford 238
Hurn 233, 235
Hurn (Bournemouth) Airport 233
Hutchins, Rev John 124
Huxtable, Canon Anthony 199

I
Ibberton 191
Iford 173
Iron Age settlements
    Gussage All Saints chariot factory 219
    Tarrant Hinton Down 206
Isle of Portland 55
Ismay, James 201
River Iwerne 200, *200*, 203
Iwerne Courtney (Shroton) 201
Iwerne Minster 201

J
Jack the Ripper 167
Jenner, Edward 11
Jesty, Benjamin 11, 77, *77*
John of Gaunt 169
River Jordan 62, *62*, 65, *65*
Jumpers Common 172, 237

Index

K

Key Brook 192, 193
Kimmeridge Bay 75
Kimmeridge New Barn Stream 75
Kimmeridge Stream 74
Kimmeridge village 74
King's Arms, Blandford 163
King's Stag 181–182
Kingsley, Charles 243
Kingston 85
Kingston Lacy house and estate 166, *166*
Kingston Maurward 104
Kingston Russell House, Long Bredy 45–46
Kingston Russell Stone Circle, Little Bredy 46
Kington Magna 177
Kinson 171, *171*
Kitford 191
Knighton 13, 170
Knights Hospitaller (Order of Knights of the Hospital of St John of Jerusalem) 113
Knob's Crook 221, 227
Knowlton 220, *220*
Knowlton Bell 164
Knowlton Church and earthworks *220*

L

Lakewood Pond 263
Lambert Castle 25
Langham 241
Langton Herring 52
Langton Long Blandford 163
Langton Matravers 91
Lawrence, Mary 64
Lawrence, Oliver 80, 84
Lawrence, T.E. (Lawrence of Arabia) 106, 139
Leaden Stour 245
Lear, Rosie, *Spare the Rod* 3
Lees, Lord John and Lady Madeline 151
Leigh 10
River Lim (Lyme) 22, *22*
Little Axe (River) 20
Little Bredy (Littlebredy) 45
Little Toller Farm *112*, 113–114
Littledown 173
Littlewindsor 19
Litton Cheney 46
River Lodden 240
Loders 40, 41
Long Bredy 45, 46
Long Crichel 220
Longburton 189
Longham 170, *170*
Loveless, George 137
Lower Bockhampton 103
Lower Kingcombe 113
Lower Waterston 136
Lulworth 259
Lulworth Cove 73
Lulworth Fossil Forest 73
Lulworth Stream 72, 73
Luscombe Valley 152, *153*
Luscombe Valley Stream 152, *153*
Lutton and Lutton Gwyle 84
River Lydden 180, *180*
Lydlinch 182
Lydlinch Common 182, 188, *188*
River Lyme (Lim) 22, *22*
Lyme Regis 23, *23*
Lytchett Minster 150, *151*

M

Madjeston 240
Magiston 117
Maiden Castle Iron Age hill fort 123, *123*
Maiden Newton 99, 114, *114*, 115
Maine, USA 127
Makepeace, John 33
Mangerton 42
Mangerton Brook 40
Mangerton Mill 42, *42*
Mannington 227
Mannington Brook 224

273

Mansell, Juliet, Marcia and Sir Philip 75
Manston 196
Manston Brook 192, 193, *197*
Manston House 196
Manswood 221, *221*
Margaret Green Animal Rescue, Church
    Knowle 85
Margaret Marsh 196
Marley Wood 131
Marnhull 159, 176, 183, 242
Marshalsea 21, 26
Marshwood 21, 26, *26*
Marshwood Vale 27
Maumbury Rings, Dorchester 102, *102*
Medieval settlements
    Crawford Bridge, Spetisbury *209*
    Fiddleford Manor 160
    Holditch Court 21
    Kingston Russell House 45–46
    packhorse bridge at Tarrant Monkton 207, *207*
    Ringstead (village) 69
    Wareham 108
    Whitcombe Church, wall painting 124, *125*
    Winterborne Farringdon (village) 124
    Wolfeton House, Charminster 121
Melbury Abbas 195
Melbury Bubb 10
Melbury Hill (Melbury Down) and Beacon 195
Melcombe Bingham 142
Melcombe Horsey 142
Melcombe Regis 60
Melplash 34
Melplash Manor 34–35
Merley 168
Mews, Peter 187
Middlebere 81
Middlemarsh 185
Milborne St Andrew 146
Mill Stream, Portesham 50
mills
    Fiddleford 161, *161*, 243

Mangerton 42, *42*
Sturminster Newton 160, *160*
Throop 172, *172*
Town Mill, Lyme Regis 23, *23*
White Mill, Sturminster Marshall 164, *164*
Milton Abbas 145
Milton Abbey and House 145, *145*
Milton on Stour 158, 238
Minchington 219
Ministry of Defence land 73
Minterne House 119, *119*
Minterne Magna 119
Minterne Parva 119
Monarch's Way 24, 39, 66
Monkton Up Wimborne 218
Monkton Wyld 25
Monkton Wyld Court 25
Monkton Wyld Stream 24
Monkwood 28
Monmouth, Duke of 23, 185, 187, 225
Monmouth Rebellion 23, 31, 128
Moonfleet Manor Hotel 53
Moor Crichel 220, *221*
Moore, Temple 99
Moore's Biscuits 99
Moors River 230
Moors Valley Country Park *230*
Morcombelake 28, 31
Morden 149
Morden Mill 149
Moreton 106, *106*
Mosterton 14, 19
Motcombe 240
Mowlem, John 93
Muckleford 100
River Mude 260
Mudeford 261, 263
Mudeford Battle 261
Mudeford Quay 260, *262*
Muir, Frank 128

Index

N

Napoleonic Wars 33, 37
Nash, Ogden, *Paradise for Sale* 95
National Trust
    Clouds Hill, Moreton 106
    Coney's Castle 25
    Corfe Castle 86–87
    Eggardon Hill fort 41
    Hardy's Cottage 103, *103*
    Hive Beach to Burton Bradstock cliff walk 47
    Hod Hill fort and ramparts 202–203
    Kingston Lacy house and estate 166
    Lambert Castle 25
    Melbury Hill (Melbury Down) and Beacon 195
    White Mill, Sturminster Marshall 164
nature reserves
    Canford Heath 169
    Chewton Bunny 264–265, *265*
    Collyer's Brook 198
    Fontmell Down 198
    Holt Forest 227
    Kimmeridge Bay marine reserve 74
    Luscombe Valley 152, *152*, *153*
    Nea Meadows *262*, 263
    St Catherine's Hill 236, *236*
    Stanpit Marsh 261
    Steamer Point 263
    Upton Heath 169
Nea Lake *262*
Nea Meadows 263
Neolithic settlements
    Church Henge, Knowlton 220
    Grey Mare and her Colts, long barrow 46
    Knowlton Church and earthworks *220*
    Maumbury Rings 102
    Poundbury Camp 101
Nether Cerne 120
Netherbury 34
New Lake Reservoir, Gasper Street *157*
New Town 221
The Nine Stones, Winterbourne Abbas 123

Norden 81
Norden Station and ticket office *81*
North Bowood 39
North Egliston 73, 84
North River *see* River Piddle (Trent)
Nothe Fort, Weymouth *60*, 61
Nottington 59
Nyland 177

O

The Oak at Dewlish 142–143, *142*
Oathill 20
Oborne 5
Ode to the Fleur de Lys Inn by Rupert Brooke 232
Okeford Fitzpaine 241
Old Harry Rocks 79, *79*
Organford 150
Osmington 63, 68, 69
Osmington Hill 63, *63*
Osmington Stream 68, 69, *69*
Ower 81
Owermoigne 128–129, *129*
Oxbridge 34

P

Packe, Charles 250
Pamphill 166
Pamphill Dairy 166
Pansy's Bathing Place 245
Paradise for Sale by Ogden Nash 95
Parnham House 33
River Parrett 14, *15*
Paye, Harry 79
Peacemarsh 239
Penn Hill 249
Penney, John 26, 27
River Piddle (Trent) 132, *134*, 136
Piddlehinton 134, 135, *135*
Piddletrenthide 134
Pilsdon 27
Pimperne 243

Pimperne Brook 243
Plush 133
Plush Brook (tributary of River Piddle) 132
Poole 258
Poole Harbour 72
Poolestown 179
Portesham 50
Portesham Stream 50
Portland Bill 55, 57, *57*
Portland, Isle of 55
Poundbury 101, *101*
Poundbury Camp 101
Poxwell 68
Poxwell Manor 68
Poyntington 5
Preston 64
Procer's Lake 18
Pucksey Brook 58
Puddletown 136, *136*
Pulham 181
Puncknowle 46, *46*
Purbeck House Hotel, Swanage 93
Purewell 175, 237
Purse Caundle 179, 186, *187*
Pymore 35

Q
Quarr 177

R
Racedown House 26
Radipole 60
RAF Sopley 233
RAF Warmwell 127–128
RAF Winkton 236
railways
    Poole and Bournemouth Railway 253
    Ringwood, Christchurch and Bournemouth Railway 233
    Somerset and Dorset Joint Railway 253
    Southampton and Dorchester Railway 168
    Swanage Heritage Railway 81, *81*, 86
Raleigh, Sir Walter 6
Rampisham 111
Rempstone 81
Ridge 81
Ridge Water 66
Ringstead (medieval village) 69
Ringstead Stream 69
Riviera Hotel, Bowleaze Cove 64, 65
Rodden 52
Rodden Hive 52
Rodden Stream 51
Roman settlements
    aqueduct (Frampton to Dorchester) *100*, 101
    camp, St Catherine's Hill, Christchurch 236
    Hod Hill fort and ramparts 202–203
    Jordan Hill Temple, Bowleaze 64
    mosaic, Hinton St Mary 160
    pavement, Rampisham 111
    villa, Tarrant Hinton 206
Romford 232
Roper Mark 21
Rothesay, Lord Stuart de 263
Royal Society for the Protection of Birds (RSPB) 58, 236
Russell, John, 1st Earl of Bedford 47
Ryall 31
Ryme Intrinseca 10

S
Sadler, John 128
Salwayash 39
San Salvador galleon 60
Sandhills 98, 111, 186
Sandway Bridge (the White Bridge) *100*
Scott, Bessie and John 85
Scott, Sir Walter 249
Seaborough 20
Seacombe Valley Stream 77
Seahorse Trust 69
Seale, John 34

Index

Seatown 31
Second World War 41, 61, 73, 75, 102, 125, 128, 151, 208, 213, 215, 218, 236, 256
Sedgemoor, Battle of 23, 185, 187, 225
Selfridge, Harry Gordon 261
Sells, Jonathan 258
Shaftesbury 194
Shaftesbury Abbey 194
Shapwick 165
Shave Cross 27
Shave Cross Inn 27, *27*
Sherborne 6
Sherborne Abbey 6, *6*
Sherborne Castle (new and old) 6, *6*
Sherford 150
Sherford River 148
Shillingstone 161, 242
Shrapnel, Colonel Henry 46–47
Shreen Water 238, 239
Shroton (Iwerne Courtney) 201
Silkhay 34
Sillar, Hannah 261
Silton 158, *158*
River Simene 32, 38, *38*
Singer, George 104
Sleep Brook 234, 237
Slepe 81, 150
Smedmore House, Kimmeridge 75
Smugglers Inn, Osmington 68–69, *69*
smuggling 31, 47, 68–69, 79, 91, 249, 251, 261, 265
Somerford 261
Sopley Common 233, 235
Sopley radar station 233
South Bowood 39
South Egliston 73
South Perrott 15
South West Coastal Path 66
South Winterborne River 96, 122
Southover 100
Southwell 56
Spanish Armada 60, 129

Spetisbury 165
Spetisbury Rings Iron Age hill fort 165
Sprague, William 59
Spriggs, Robert 117, *117*
St Aldhelm's Head and Chapel 78
St Andrew's Church, Kinson *171*
St Andrew's Church, West Stafford 125
St Andrew's Church, Winterborne Tomson 214, *214*
St Andrew's Church, Yetminster *12*
St Bartholomew's Church, Sutton Waldron 199
St Catherine's Chapel, Abbotsbury 51, *51*
St Catherine's Chapel, Milton Abbas 146, *146*
St Catherine's Hill 236, *236*
St Cuthbert's Church, Oborne 5
St Edwold's Church, Stockwood 10
St Gabriel's Stream 66
St Giles Church, Chideock 31
St John the Baptist, Buckhorn Weston 177, *177*
St Kenelm's Church, Hinton Parva 222, *222*
St Martin's Church, Cheselbourne 133
St Martin's-on-the-Walls Church, Wareham 139, *139*
St Mary the Virgin Church, Piddlehinton 135
St Mary's Church, Charminster 121, *121*
St Mary's Church, Chickerell 52, 53
St Mary's Church, Melbury Bubb 10
St Mary's Church, Winterborne Whitechurch *212*
St Michael and All Angels Church, Askerswell 41
St Michael's Church, Stinsford 103, *103*
St Nicholas' Church, Moreton 106, *106*
St Nicholas Church, Silton 158
St Nicholas Church, Worth Matravers 11, *77*
St Peter & St Paul Church and Bastard's Pump, Blandford Forum *163*
St Peter and St Paul Church, Cattistock 99, *99*
St Peter's Finger pub, Lychett Minster 151, *151*
Stalbridge 179, 182
Stalbridge Park *182*, 183
Stalbridge Weston 179
Stanbridge 222

277

Stanpit 261
Stanpit Marsh 261
Stapleton, Hugh 177
Steamer Point nature reserve 263
Steeple 84
Steeple Brook (West Corfe River or Wicken Stream) 82, 84
Steepleton Iwerne 202
Stevenson, Robert Louis 253
Stinsford 103
Stirchell Brook 192, 193
Stoborough 80, 108
Stock Water 240, *240*
Stockwood 10, *10*
Stoke Abbott 34
Stoke Wake 190
Stoke Water 32
River Stour 156, *158, 160, 167, 168, 169, 170, 172, 197, 208, 217*
Stour Provost 159
Stour Valley Way 156, *157*
Stourpaine 162, 203
Stourton Caundle 179, 187, *187*
Stourton, Charles, 8th Baron 129
Stratton 100
Strode, Lady Anne 33
Stubhampton 205
Studland Stream 79
Sturminster Marshall 164, 215
Sturminster Newton 160, 191
Sturminster Newton Mill 160, *160*
Sturt, Humphrey 226
Sutton Poyntz 64
Sutton Waldron 199
Swanage 93
Swanage Heritage Railway 81, *81*
Swanbrook River 90, *90*
Swyre 47
Swyre Stream 67
Sydling St Nicholas 117
Sydling Water 96, 116

Symondsbury 39
River Synderford 18

T

Tadnoll Brook 96, 126, *127*
Talbot Heath and Talbot Village 258
Talbot Hotel, Iwerne Minster 203
Talbothays Lodge and Cottages 125, *125*
River Tarrant 204, *205, 207, 208*
Tarrant Crawford 209
Tarrant Gunville 205, *205*
Tarrant Hinton 206
Tarrant Keyneston 209
Tarrant Launceston 206
Tarrant Monkton 207, *207*
Tarrant Rawston 207
Tarrant Rushton 208
airfield 208
Temple Brook 18, *20*
Tess of the D'Urbervilles by Thomas Hardy 97, 125, 146, 159, 247
Thorncombe 21
Thornford 7, 13
Thorngrove 241
Thoughts on Beauty and Art by William Barnes iii
Three Legged Cross 227
Throop 138
Throop (Bournemouth) 172, 245
Throop Mill 172, *172*
Tiley 185
Tivoli Theatre, Wimborne 223, *223*
Todber 242
Toller Brook 112
Toller Fratrum 113
Toller Porcorum 113
Toller Whelme 113
Tollerford 114
Tolpuddle 137
Tolpuddle Martyrs 137, *137*
Tolstoy, Leo 173
Town Bridge, Sturminster Newton *160*

Index

transportation bridge 164, *164*, 182
Tregonwell, Lewis 258
River Trent *see* River Piddle (Trent)
Trickett's Cross 228
Trotman, Robert 171, *171*
The Trumpet Major by Thomas Hardy 68
Tuckton 173
Tuckton waterworks 173, *173*
Tucktonia model village 173
Turbary Common 255
Turberville family 146
Turners Puddle 138
Twisted Cider, Longburton 189
Twyford 195
Twyford Brook 192, 193, *195*
Tyneham 73
Tyneham Stream 73, *73*

U

Uddens Plantation, Ameysford *224*
Uddens Water 224, *228*, *229*, 230
Ulwell Stream 78
Up Sydling 117
Upbury Farm, Yetminster *11*
Uploaders 41
Upper Tamarisk 67
Uppington 227
Upton 68, 151
Upton Heath 169
Upwey 59

W

Wake, William, Archbishop of Canterbury 214
Wakeham 55
Walford Bridge, Wimborne *217*
Walford Mill, Wimborne *217*
Walkford 265
Walkford Brook 264, *265*
Wallisdown 255
Walsingham, Francis 117
Ware, Sydney, VC 212

Wareham 108, *108*, 139
Warmwell 127
Warmwell House 128, *129*
Warrand, Major Hugh Munro 5
Washington, George 84
Watch, Bill 127
Watercress Company, Warmwell Mill *128*
Watton 37
Waytown 34
Wedgwood, Thomas 206
Week Common 235
Wellington Clock Tower, Swanage 92, *93*
West Bay 37, *37*
West Bexington 68
West Bexington Stream 67
West Brook 241
West Corfe River (Wicken Stream or Steeple Brook) 82, *84*
West Fleet Stream 52
West Holme 107
West Knighton 127
West Moors 228, 232
West Orchard 196
West Parley 171
West Stafford 104, 125
West Stafford House 104–105, *104*
West Stour 159
Westbourne 253, *253*
Westhay Water 66
Westley, Bartholomew 29
Westley, John 64
Weston 56
River Wey 58, 59
Weymouth 60–61, *61*
Whatcombe, Higher and Lower 212
Whistler, Laurence *106*
Whitchurch Canonicorum 28
Whitcombe 124
Whitcombe Church 124, *125*
White Horse pub, Stourpaine 162, *162*
White Lackington 134

279

White Mill, Sturminster Marshall 164, *164*
Whitefield 149
Wick 174
Wicken Stream (West Corfe River or Steeple Brook) 82, *84*
Wigbeth 227
Wimborne Minster 167, 222–223
Wimborne St Giles 218
River Win 96, 130, *130*
Winfrith 129
Winfrith Newburgh 131
Winfrith Nuclear Power Station 129
Winkton 236
River Winniford 30, *30*
Winspit Quarry 78, *78*
Winspit Valley Stream 77
Winterborne Came 124
Winterborne Clenston 212
Winterborne Farringdon (medieval village) 124
Winterborne Herringston 124
Winterborne Houghton 211
Winterborne Kingston 213
Winterborne Monkton 124
Winterborne Muston (Winterborne Turberville) 213
Winterborne St Martin 123
Winterborne Stickland 211
Winterborne Tomson 214
Winterborne Turberville (Winterborne Muston) 213
Winterborne Whitechurch 212
River Winterborne (Winterborne North) 210
Winterborne Zelston 215
Winterbourne Abbas 123
Winterbourne Steepleton 123
Winzer, Ann 135
Witchampton 221
Wolfeton House, Charminster 121
Wonston Brook 180
Woodbridge 188, 195
Woodlands 139, 225

Woodsford 105
Woodsford Castle 105, *105*
Woodville 194, 196
Wool 107
Woolcombe 10
Woolgarston 86, 91
Woolland 191
Woolsbridge 232
Wooth 35
Wootton Fitzpaine 25
Wootton Fitzpaine Stream 24
Wordsworth, William and Dorothy 26
Worth Matravers 76, *77*
Wraxall 111
Wraxall Brook 96, 110, *111*
River Wriggle 4, 8
Wych 37
River Wych (Corfe River) 82
Wyke 240, *240*
Wyndham, Hugh, judge 158
Wytch Farm oil field 74, *74*, 88
Wytch Heath 88

Y

River Yeo (Ivel) 4, *4*, 7
Yetminster 11
Yondover 41

My Notes

My Notes